D1285643

THE AUTONOMY THEME
IN THE *CHURCH DOGMATICS*:
KARL BARTH AND HIS CRITICS

THE AUTONOMY THEME
IN THE *CHURCH DOGMATICS*:
KARL BARTH AND HIS CRITICS

John Macken SJ

Lecturer in Theology at the
Milltown Institute of Theology and Philosophy, Dublin

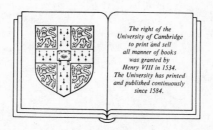

The right of the
University of Cambridge
to print and sell
all manner of books
was granted by
Henry VIII in 1534.
The University has printed
and published continuously
since 1584.

CAMBRIDGE UNIVERSITY PRESS

Cambridge
New York   Port Chester
Melbourne   Sydney

Published by the Press Syndicate of the University of Cambridge
The Pitt Building, Trumpington Street, Cambridge CB2 1RP
40 West 20th Street, New York, NY 10011, USA
10 Stamford Road, Oakleigh, Melbourne 3166, Australia

© Cambridge University Press 1990

First published 1990

Printed in Great Britain at the University Press, Cambridge

British Library cataloguing in publication data

Macken, John, 1943–
The autonomy theme in the *Church Dogmatics*: Karl
Barth and his critics.
1. Christian doctrine. Theories of Barth, Karl, 1886–1968.
I. Title
230′.092′4

Library of Congress cataloguing in publication data

Macken, John.
The autonomy theme in the *Church Dogmatics*: Karl Barth and his
critics / John Macken.
p.   cm.
Includes bibliographical references.
ISBN 0 521 34626 6
1. Autonomy (Philosophy) – Religious aspects – Christianity – History
of doctrines – 20th century. 2. Barth, Karl, 1886–1968. Kirchliche
Dogmatik. I. Title.
BT809.M33   1989
233′.5 – dc20   89–38037 CIP

ISBN 0 521 34626 6

BT
809
.M33
1990

GG

JESUIT - KRAUSS - McCORMICK - LIBRARY
1100 EAST 55th STREET
CHICAGO, ILLINOIS 60615

Contents

v

Preface

This book is a study of one of the leading themes of modern theological debate as it is treated in the *Church Dogmatics* of Karl Barth and of the criticisms made of that treatment. It is not intended exclusively for the Barth specialist. The problem of human autonomy before God echoes through the conflicts of Western theology since Augustine and Pelagius. It owes its formal philosophical expression to Kant and Fichte but it became a popular theme in modern atheism and has therefore been posed as an acute question to theology for the past two hundred years. In the introduction, which many readers may wish to postpone until they have sampled the rest of the book, I trace the way in which the autonomy theme was developed by Kant and Fichte and how it came to be posed as a key question to modern theologians.

Karl Barth faced, with the directness typical of him, not just the question of autonomy but the theological answers that Liberal theologians had tried to provide to it. His dissatisfaction with their answers led him to start a theological counter-revolution. Until recently this counter-revolution was thought to include a negative answer to the question of autonomy. But a closer examination of the *Church Dogmatics* reveals that Barth was anxious to offer a positive answer, one that he believed was better theology and therefore truer and more adequate than that of Liberal theologians. What it was and how adequate it may be is explored in chapter 1.

As one of the leading theologians of the century, Barth attracted an enormous body of criticism. Some of this secondary literature is of interest to the Barth specialist alone. But Barth's position has been so influential that wherever theological movement takes place, no evaluation can be complete without taking a bearing on the *Church Dogmatics*. The autonomy theme has played a major part in the theological debates of the past forty years since Bonhoeffer and the position of Barth has been one factor throughout the discussion. In chapter 2 I look at the evaluation of Barth's theology in that discussion. The concentration in this part on German Barth critics is due to their standing directly in the tradition of Kant and Fichte and to the relatively sharp focus which the autonomy theme receives in their work. A broader study would inevitably become more diffuse. The English-speaking world, when it poses the question of autonomy, does so in quite a different way and it interprets Barth too in response to other pressures, notably those exerted by English-speaking biblical fundamentalism and religious Liberalism.

That surely brings us to the third dimension of the book – my position as author and the set of questions and concerns from which I approach both the question of autonomy and the *Church Dogmatics* of Karl Barth. As a Roman Catholic interpreter of Barth, I have placed myself within the tradition of Barth's many Roman Catholic admirers and interpreters. The ontological concerns of Roman Catholic theology have accompanied me throughout. No doubt the autonomy theme can be approached from many other sides, but I believe no treatment would be complete unless it faced the ontological question. What does Barth say about the foundations of human autonomy? Are our being and our acts genuinely ours or are we merely passive instruments of the divine pleasure and insubstantial reflections of the divine activity? I was encouraged to see this traditional Roman Catholic question being taken up and echoed by many of Barth's Protestant critics in recent years in Germany. Their concern came precisely from their exploration of the autonomy theme in his writings and marks an encouraging ecumenical convergence.

This book grew out of one of those Roman Catholic doctoral dissertations in which the preferred Protestant partner in dialogue turned out to be Barth. To Professor Walter Kasper of Tübingen, who guided my research and who generously gave both of his enthusiasm and of his wisdom, I owe a great debt of gratitude. I wish to thank also Professor G. W. Hunold, who read the manuscript, Professors Trutz Rendtorff and Stephen Sykes for their encouragement, Professors W. Pannenberg and E. Jüngel for their ready availability and Professor John Thompson of Belfast for valuable help in the final editing. Professor Jüngel and Dr Hans-Anton Drewes kindly gave me access to the complete bibliography of secondary literature on Barth at Tübingen. The Society of Jesus generously set me aside for many years for the work and many others gave me practical help and support, among whom I would like to mention Fathers Patrick Riordan, J. Randall Sachs and Donal Neary, Mrs Nora Davitt and Ms Ruth Bray, the priests and people of Kiebingen and Bühl, the Berchmanskolleg community in Munich, and very specially my parents, Matt and Eleanor.

In the final stages of re-editing, I was painfully aware that the issue of exclusive or sexist language, which had not been raised on this side of the Atlantic when I began work in Germany, is now acute. I made some attempts to revise the book but was soon aware that rewriting on the scale necessary was not possible for me in the time available. I can only present it now with an apology and a promise to make amends if possible at some future date.

Introduction

THE HISTORY OF THE TERM 'AUTONOMY'

Autonomy[1] is a political and legal category first introduced into
ethical discussion by Kant. In the ancient Greek world, the term was
generally used for the rights of city-states to govern themselves, pass
their own laws, mint their own coinage, and the like, even if they were
externally dependent on a mother-city or other outside power. It was
not, therefore, the same as the modern concept of sovereignty, which
characterises a supreme authority, and whose external relationships are
governed by international law, the principle of which is that of coor-
dination rather than subordination. The term 'autonomy' was occasionally used in the Roman world but dropped out of use in the Middle
Ages, even though in the Middle Ages the practice of autonomy, in the
sense of the devolution of power and the grant of inalienable rights and
privileges to cities, corporations and minor statelets, went beyond
anything known either in the Roman Empire or in the absolute monarchies and centralised nation-states of modern times. Indeed the
emergence of absolute monarchies and centralised nation-states corresponded with the suppression of the autonomous rights and
privileges inherited from the Middle Ages.

The term 'autonomy' was also used for certain legal rights in German jurisprudence from the sixteenth century. Originally, it was
employed in the context of the religious conflicts and signified a certain
freedom of religion recognised in the political and juridical sphere. It
occurs first in a negative sense in the *clausula Autonomia*, which
distinguished between the person of an ecclesiastical prince converting

1

to Protestantism and the rights and possessions belonging to his office to which he had no further claim. It appears most predominantly in a famous pamphlet, *Autonomia*, written in support of the Catholic claim on such ecclesiastical offices and possessions. Here 'autonomy' is the coverall term of abuse for the opposing position, being understood not merely in a juridical but in a politico-theological sense as anarchy, a claim to arbitrary choice in religious matters.

Arbitrary choice was not, however, the position of the Protestant side, as might be understood from the rather sketchy account of the matter by Konrad Hilpert. Martin Heckel makes it perfectly clear that *neither* Protestants *nor* Catholics in sixteenth-century Germany were interested in a religiously indifferent jurisprudence nor in any other form of religious neutrality. Instead they each felt compelled to interpret the existing laws, based as they were in the medieval unity of religion and politics, in the sense of their own theological convictions. Protestant jurists urged the right (and duty) of reformation, Catholics the duty (and right) of orthodoxy. The consequence was one-sided confessional jurisprudence, and the inevitable conflicts were only provisionally resolved by the cultivation of a deliberate ambiguity in the law of the Holy Roman Empire. This was the fundamental reason why the Peace of Augsburg (1555) failed. It was only the Thirty Years War that brought both sides to admit a distinction between faith and jurisprudence.

The development of the concept of autonomy in a positive sense begins only after the Peace of Westphalia (1648), when the absolute necessity of religious peace led to the exclusion of the disputed religious authorities from the foundations of jurisprudence.[2] By 1648 Protestant theorists had come to agreement in principle with the natural-law theory worked out by their Catholic opponents such as Vitoria, Suarez and Bellarmine. Natural law offered an alternative to the theocratic principle and also formed the base for the work of Hugo Grotius. The experience of the benefits of religious peace on the basis of natural law led not only to the spread of the idea of tolerance but to the eighteenth-century interest in natural reason and the deism characteristic of the Enlightenment.

With time the word 'autonomy' came to be used for the right of individual citizens or corporations to run their own affairs within the limits of the larger framework set by the law, a sense which it still bears in modern jurisprudence even if it plays no great part in current legal controversy. The word is also used by some jurists for the principle of self-determination in the constitutional law of modern democracies.

Here, however, we are dealing with the post-Kantian era, when the original political and juridical use of the word had long been outweighed by its use in philosophy, first with Kant, in ethics, and later in a broader, less clearly defined but far more emotive sense.

Summary

'Autonomy' first appears as a political and legal term in ancient Greece, where it was used of certain rights enjoyed by city-states even when they were dependent on a mother-city or an outside power. It reappears in German jurisprudence after the Reformation, first in a negative sense in the Catholic polemic against the Reformation, as implying anarchy. As both Protestant and Catholic jurists turned to natural law to solve the problem posed by their inability to found consensus on an explicitly Christian basis, 'autonomy' is used in a positive sense and with time is used of the right of individuals or corporations to run their own affairs within the limits of the larger framework set by the law.

KANT AND THE TERM 'AUTONOMY'

'Autonomy' is one of the three conceptual models employed by Kant in his presentation of the basic principle of morality – the categorical imperative. After the first formulation of the categorical imperative[3] Kant offers three other formulations, the first in terms of a universal law of nature, the second in terms of an end in itself and the third in terms of autonomy.[4] Autonomy is the most adequate expression of the principle of morality because it expresses its unconditioned character.[5] Thus Kant devotes a major section of his *Grundlegung zur Metaphysik der Sitten* to the presentation of the autonomy of the will as the supreme principle of morality. It begins with a definition and with a restatement of the categorical imperative:

Autonomy of the will is that property of it by which it is a law to itself independently of any property of objects of volition. Hence the principle of autonomy is: Never choose except in such a way that the maxims of the choice are comprehended in the same volition as a universal law.[6]

Heteronomy is the opposite of autonomy; it means that the will does not establish its own law, but allows some object or other to usurp this law-giving function, either through material inclination or rational ideas.[7] In view of the subsequent history of the concept, it is essential to emphasise that for Kant 'autonomy' means acceptance, excogitation and application by the ethical subject of a universal and necessary law of reason. He does not spare the use of such terms as 'obedience', 'commandments', 'necessity', and 'absolute validity' to express the unconditional claim of this law on the ethical subject. Kant's emphasis in the use of 'heteronomy' is placed on countering the philosophy of eudaemonism or that of utilitarianism, which made happiness the basis of morality. Material inclination, goals and purposes peculiar to the individual, and external motivations such as reward and punishment, are all heteronomous.[8] The derivation of morality from the perfect will of God in theology rests for Kant either on the 'concept of the divine will . . . made up of the attributes of desire for glory and dominion combined with the awful conceptions of might and vengeance'[9] and as such may be reduced to the heteronomy of reward and punishment, or it rests on the idea of God's perfection. In the latter case, since we can have no intuition (Anschauung) of the divine perfection, we are compelled to construct the idea on the basis of our own concepts, in which case it falls together with the ontological idea of perfection, an idea which we can form only with the help of the concept of morality. We cannot therefore derive morality from the idea of perfection without constructing a vicious circle. By means of this argument, Kant reduces all possible principles of morality either to autonomous rational construction or to material inclination; all heteronomy is related to our sensual being and coincides with self-love.[10]

Kant subjects the moral instruction contained in biblical Revelation to the same dichotomy: either it coincides with a rationally self-evident or autonomous morality, in which Kant sees true Christianity to consist, or it is a human falsification of divine Revelation and as such heteronomous 'pseudo-service' (Afterdienst).[11]

Autonomy and self-determination

Autonomy, for Kant, is the idea of a self-appropriated universal rational law, and the very opposite of arbitrary self-determination. Like many of his contemporaries, he had inherited from Stoic philosophy the ideal of autarchy, that is of rational self-sufficiency and independence on the part of the free individual. However, he reinterpreted the ideal of aut*archy* as auto*nomy*, in which the rational law-giving function of each individual should ensure the harmony of the freedom of each one with the freedom of every other individual. The rational law governing all alike is to be recognised by all as the condition under which alone freedom is possible.[12] This model not only formed Kant's political ideal, but is the key to his presentation of the pure principle of morality. This means that the universality of reason and the uniformity of the human subject in respect of rationality is presupposed by Kant. Indeed it is a constant theme of his that his moral philosophy (as opposed to his critique of pure reason) could be understood and accepted by everyone, not just by the professional philosopher.[13] It is not an elitist but an egalitarian philosophy. The political ideal which Kant brings into relationship with his moral philosophy is not the sovereignty of the independent state, but the autonomy of the free citizen within the state. The political and legal antecedents of the term 'autonomy' retain a constitutive role in Kant's conception: the overall framework of law, the independent law-giving function and the need for a rationally articulated inter-relationship with other political, legal, or, in this case, moral subjects.[14] The word 'autonomy' possesses the constructive force of a newly formed theoretical model and sets up a creative interrelationship between the political, legal and moral spheres.

Autonomy and freedom

Although moral autonomy is the excogitation and application of a rational law, the rationality in question is that of the pure practical reason. While postulated on the model of a universal law of nature and possessing the criteria of universality and necessity, it does not consist in the insight into the causal necessity of events characteristic of the theoretical or speculative reason but in the insight into the laws of moral necessity.[15] Kant is convinced that the understanding (Verstand) is compelled to operate under a principle of universal natural causality, in which every event is empirically determined. Only in this way can phenomena (Erscheinungen) constitute nature and yield objects of experience. On the other hand, if the subject is considered not as an empirically accessible phenomenon but as an intelligible noumenon it is possible to consider him as independent of the chain of causality, whose validity is confined to the world of phenomena, and to conceive of his being himself the origin of his action. Freedom, for the theoretical reason, means the ability to be the origin of something whose causality does not fall under another cause according to the laws of nature. It is a transcendental idea belonging to reason (Vernunft) rather than to understanding (Verstand) and cannot be an object of experience, since experience is possible only according to the principles governing the understanding.[16]

Kant's strategy here is a double one, as Gerhard Krüger remarks. In order to show that freedom is not impossible he must present the intelligible world and the divine intelligence as a possibility, problematically so to speak. But in order to show that freedom cannot be demonstrated he must present the experience of human nature and its limitation to empirical knowledge dogmatically.[17] To demonstrate freedom would be to destroy its unconditional character. Were it an object of empirical observation it would be subsumed under the laws of natural determinism and so contradicted.

Freedom and morality

The starting-point for the question of freedom is the absolute demand of the moral law. The claim of the moral law is the reason why freedom becomes known, because it makes it necessary for man to affirm his freedom. He judges that he is able to do something because he is aware that he must do it; he thus recognises in himself the freedom which he would not have known without the moral law. Freedom is not arrived at on the basis of observation; it must be postulated as a necessary presupposition of the moral law, as the reason why it exists. It is therefore given correlative to the moral law, not as an inherent natural quality but as an unconditional demand on man. It is not the same as spontaneity and it is not something in man's control like the objects of natural science which man's ability to think places at his disposal. Rather, man's spontaneity is claimed unconditionally by the moral law. This unconditional claim is not a limitation, much less a contradiction of autonomy, but is for Kant the essence of autonomy. It is the obedient use of man's spontaneity that makes this unconditional demand understandable and practicable. The law is both given *to* man and given *by* man. Only thus can he become a member of an intelligible world.[18]

Morality and knowledge

We have seen that for Kant the critique of knowledge is essential for the conception of freedom. Kant's demonstration of the finite nature of theoretical reason and the limitation of theoretical knowledge to the phenomenal world is the necessary presupposition for the primacy of his moral philosophy, the primacy of practical reason. For it is practical reason, with its immediate apprehension of an absolute imperative that alone can serve as a foundation for the postulate of freedom and in consequence for the postulates of the existence of God and of the immortality of the soul. Thus, while speculative metaphysics itself is rejected, the 'fundamental interests' of human reason – freedom, God and immortality, which are metaphysical in nature – can be affirmed. This takes place only by means of a revolution in metaphysical perspective: instead of ethics being based in metaphysics or theology, theology and metaphysics are based in ethics.[19]

With that, the modern problem of subjectivity took a new turn. Descartes had sought for objective certainty by starting from its diametrical opposite – radical subjectivity and methodical doubt. From this point he argued his way on the basis of analytical and synthetic reasoning, *more geometrico*, followed in this constructive method by the rationalists of the seventeenth and eighteenth centuries. Kant set strict limits to the scope of such theoretical reasoning: he confronted reason with its own finitude. Instead he sought certainty in the undeniable rational implications of ethical experience. Ethics thus took over the primacy at the heart of reality, even to becoming the basis of legitimation for religion and the arbiter of its truth. This means that autonomy, the free acceptance, excogitation and application of an un-conditioned moral law, became the paradigm of reality. In this unity of subjectivity and objectivity it became the model on which theoretical reason itself must pursue its activities. Ethics had become the norm for knowledge, not the reverse.

Kant's famous definition of enlightenment is consequently an ethical one:

Enlightenment is man's release from his self-incurred tutelage (selbstverschuldeten Unmuendigkeit). Tutelage is man's inability to make use of his understanding without direction from another. Self-incurred is this tutelage when its cause lies not in lack of reason but in lack of resolution and courage to use it without direction from another. *Sapere aude!* 'Have courage to use your own reason' – that is the motto of enlighten-ment.[20]

'Cowardice and inertia' are the causes of people remaining un-enlightened, continues Kant: they remain unenlightened because they want to.

The 'Autonomy of Reason'?

Here, Kant was only bringing to fulfilment a process that had been under way at least since Descartes: the transfer of attention from the body of knowledge to the quest for knowledge, from intellectual posses-sion to intellectual activity, from the static to the dynamic, from the hoarding of knowledge to the consumption and harnessing of knowledge. As an activity, theoretical reasoning falls under the moral imperative, and its unhindered progress becomes a moral right and duty, as Kant proclaims. To decree a limit to the pursuit of knowledge (that is Kant's judgement on legally imposed ecclesiastical confessions) would be a crime against human nature, whose primary vocation (Bestimmung) consists in this pursuit.[21] As a method, which it is a moral duty to follow, intellectual inquiry is morally obliged to question every previous standpoint.

Thus it is only logical that Kant, towards the end of his life, in unpublished papers, began to apply the term 'autonomy' to the theoretical reason as well as the practical, to the system of ideas which is the condition of the possibility of experience:

All philosophy is (1) autognosis (2) autonomy. Science and wisdom.

Transcendental philosophy is the idea of the system of ideas through which the totality of possible experience in the subject conceives itself a priori as united in one totality by means of a synthetic principle: not proceeding as an encyclopaedia (for that would be an empirical aggregate) but as autonomy.

Transcendental philosophy is the reason (autonomy) constituting itself as an absolute totality of ideas, which precedes all experience a priori, but also grounds the possibility of experience. It is not merely that logical exercise of the reason that has regard only to the formal aspect of knowledge, but reason as its own author. Mathematics as an instrument also belongs to philosophy.[22]

It could indeed appear that Kant is here tapping his way forward towards an Idealism in which the totality of thought and experience is posited by an absolute subject. Idealist historiography attempts to portray Kant as a mere link in a historical process in which the factual sequence of popular or influential philosophic systems is determined by an immanent and irreversible logic. Ernst Feil justly protests against the misinterpretation of Kant's concept of autonomy perpetrated by this influential school. Dealing with the *Opus Posthumum*, Feil quite rightly insists that even here Kant carefully holds to his own distinction between the world of ideas and that of experience. It is always a question of that activity of the pure reason that precedes experience and grounds the possibility of experience. Feil's insistence on this point is totally justified by Kant's public disavowal of Fichte's *Wissenschaftslehre*, published in 1799, in which Kant insisted that pure philosophy (Wissenschaftslehre) is mere logic which does not extend to the material element of knowledge and therefore not to knowledge of real objects. And Kant held to real objects: his criticism of Fichte's philosophy was that Fichte was no longer interested in judging the object but merely in the judging subject, and this was sufficient for Kant to declare that he would have no part in it.[23]

Conclusion: Kant and autonomy

Kant's philosophy was not an inevitable stage in a unilinear development. Instead his work, with its logical distinction and balance of
opposing elements, has proved to be a primer to which subsequent
philosophers have regularly needed to return to clarify their thought.
It pointed certainly in the direction of Idealism, but only at the sacrifice
of the objective intention which had caused Kant to hold consistently
to the distinction between pure reason and knowledge informed by
experience, even when his chief attention was given to the systematic
explication of pure reason *insofar* as it precedes experience. Kant's
work pointed also in the direction of positivism, an impulse which was
not, however, taken up until after the collapse of Idealism in the
Neokantian philosophy of natural science. But a pure positivism would
have neglected the other side of Kant – his moral philosophy and the
postulates of the practical reason, which Neokantianism did not do.

The same holds true of Kant's idea of autonomy. The popular interpretation simply assimilates Kant to the post-Fichtean notions (in
themselves a misrepresentation of Fichte) of autonomy as absolute self-
determination. But this falsification imposes a caricature of the idea of
autonomy itself. Kant's idea of autonomy is not absolute self-
determination, but self-determination according to the rational and
moral being which is given to man and which contains in itself the
rational and moral law. The subsequent reception of the autonomy
theme, especially the theological, would quite rightly have many objections to raise against the conclusions that Kant drew from this
principle, inspired as these were by the overoptimistic rationalism of
the eighteenth century. But it did no service to Kant nor to its own
interests by adopting a caricature of his idea of autonomy inspired by
a very different school of thought. The genuine dialogue with Kant's
position was therefore postponed.

Summary

Kant used the term 'autonomy' in an applied sense, of the role of the
rational individual in accepting, excogitating and applying the universal and necessary moral law. It is opposed to heteronomous ethics, by

which Kant means eudaemonism or utilitarianism, in which the individual follows material inclination, goals and purposes peculiar to himself, or external motivations such as reward and punishment. Autonomous obedience to universal, rational moral law turns the Stoic ideal of self-sufficiency into the political ideal of the free citizen within the state, whose rational and moral relationship with everybody else ensures the harmony of each person's freedom with the freedom of all.

The necessity of obedience to rational moral law is the reason why freedom must be postulated by the reason even in the face of the determinism that is, according to Kant, the only assumption under which the empirical understanding can operate. Ethics, as obedience to the unconditional and universal claim of the law of reason is therefore the very essence of autonomy for Kant. The foundation for theology and metaphysics is also to be found in the undeniable rational implications of the ethical imperative. Therefore, for Kant, autonomy in the sense of the free acceptance, excogitation and application of a universal moral law became the paradigm of reality and the model on which the theoretical reason itself must pursue its activities. Kant's definition of enlightenment is therefore an ethical one. Enlightenment becomes a moral right and duty. In Kant's final jottings, 'autonomy' is used of the activity of the pure reason itself, although Kant held to the principle of objectivity as well as subjectivity and thus rejected Fichte's Idealist principle of absolute subjectivity.

FICHTE: THE *ICH* AS FIRST PRINCIPLE OF PHILOSOPHY

Kant's philosophy of autonomy expressed itself characteristically in pairs of mutually opposing and complementary principles: the theoretical and the practical; within the theoretical, the rational concept (Begriff) and the empirical intuition (Anschauung); within the practical, the objective, universal law of reason and the subjective principle of acceptance, excogitation and application on the part of the individual. Fichte, in his first programmatic work, *Ueber den Begriff der Wissenschaftslehre oder der sogenannten Philosophie* (1794), takes as his aim the elimination of this dualism. Philosophy is a science; science is systematic in form. Every science must have a first principle under which all its propositions can be subsumed; it can only have one first principle, otherwise it would not be one but a number of sciences.[24]

The one principle on which Fichte believed it possible to construct a systematic philosophy was that of reflective self-consciousness; the reflection of the subject on itself constituted the *Ich*, the Ego. The Ego posits itself; it looks for no explanation or ground outside itself, since otherwise it could not function as the first principle of philosophy. It is as the absolute subject that it posits itself. Everything outside itself, the Non-Ego, is also posited by the Ego. Fichte had thus eliminated the Kantian dualism in theoretical knowledge, by eliminating the thing considered in itself[25] and absorbing the empirical intuition into the spontaneous and creative intuition of the Ego.

Dieter Henrich, in a brief but epoch-making study of Fichte's thought, has shown that the theoretical question, how the self-positing subject might properly be conceived and grounded, remained to the end of Fichte's life the guiding principle of development in his thought.[26]

Fichte's principle of unity in philosophy demanded not only that the gap between concept and intuition be bridged, between the subject and the object as a thing considered in itself, but also that the isolation of theoretical from practical reason be overcome. In a very revealing passage in his *Erste Einleitung in die Wissenschaftslehre* he poses the difficulty of choosing between the two polar opposites in the Kantian philosophy of freedom – the principle of determinism in nature and the principle of freedom implicit in moral experience. Fichte suggests that there may be no compelling reason why one must choose either determinism, which he calls dogmatism, or Idealism. Yet choose one must, for the two systems are incompatible. The choice is that of a first ultimate proposition on which one's philosophy rests, a proposition which must be self-evident and non-derivative. The starting-point cannot lie therefore in discursive reasoning but prior to it, in the sphere of freedom. Discursive reasoning argues deductively on the basis of such a first principle, but it cannot ground a non-derivative proposition. The first principle is therefore a free act and Fichte does not hesitate to call it arbitrary choice. This choice must have some basis, however, and Fichte finds it in inclination and interest. The interest that freedom will follow is an ethical one, as Fichte makes clear, and freedom will dictate the choice of Idealism. The Idealist is characterised by moral wholesomeness, by independence and by an original belief in himself.[27]

The 'dogmatist' on the other hand is described in terms of ethical debasement:

What sort of philosophy one chooses depends, therefore, on what sort of man one is . . . A person indolent by nature or dulled and distorted by mental servitude, learned luxury, and vanity will never raise himself to the level of idealism.[28]

The self-positing subject and the autonomy theme

For Kant, the limitation of the theoretical reason had cleared the ground for the primacy of the practical reason. For Fichte, the principle of unity compelled the foundation of reason as a whole on one systematic principle. The choice of this principle is placed prior to discursive reasoning. It takes place in what in Kantian terms was called the practical reason – in the ethical sphere. But the ethical sphere is for Fichte the sphere in which the self-positing subject becomes aware of his freedom, a freedom in which he constitutes reality rather than passively accepts it, which grounds all knowledge and all belief because knowledge and belief is a product of the spontaneous and creative reason of the self-positing subject. The absolute and universal moral law to which the Kantian subject was to render unconditioned obedience must be thought of not merely as excogitated and applied but also as freely posited by the absolute subject and therefore as within the power of this subject rather than above it.

In his *System der Sittenlehre* Fichte thus expands Kant's concept of autonomy and offers a threefold definition. The first element in this definition is the reflective act, in which the free intelligence freely subjects itself to the law. The second consists in the absolute independence, in which the will is determined solely by itself according to the law and not according to any source of determination outside itself. The influence of such a source is here called heteronomy. The third element in this definition concerns the origin of subjection to the law. This can arise solely through the absolutely free reflection of the Ego on itself in its true essence, that is in its independence.[29] Fichte's expansion of Kant's definition of autonomy is thus intended to emphasise at all points the absolute self-determination of the ethical subject.

The self-positing subject and heteronomy

For Kant, heteronomy meant the substitution of material interests (including those of reward and punishment) for the rational insight that accepted, excogitated and applied the universal moral law. Fichte's principle of unity and the consequent elimination of dualism demand that he ask whether one's drive as a natural being and one's inclination as a pure spirit are two different drives. As we might expect, his answer is in the negative. He postulates that both come from one original drive (Urtrieb). Nonetheless, despite the fundamental unity, the basic drive manifests itself under two aspects: I can think of myself as object and then it appears as natural desire. I can think of myself as subject and then it appears as a purely spiritual drive, namely the law of independence (Selbständigkeit). The spiritual drive, that of the reflecting subject, obtains the primacy over the drive of nature, which is the object of reflection. Reflection raises itself above nature and encompasses it and therefore the reflecting subject is higher than nature; its drive is directed at absolute self-activation and is consequently opposed to all pleasure (Genuß), which is a mere passive surrender to nature.[30]

Here the Kantian principle of practical reason has been transformed into a subjective drive – the spiritual drive – and the goal of practical reason – the moral law – has been transformed into absolute self-determination for activity. The Kantian idea of heteronomy – determination of the will by material interests – is transformed into that of passive surrender to nature. At this point Fichte unites both natural and spiritual drives in a dialectic. Both together constitute the one Ego and each surrenders something of itself in their necessary combination. The higher, spiritual drive surrenders its purity, namely its non-determination through an object; the lower, natural drive surrenders its goal of satisfaction; the result is objective activity. But freedom remains the first principle and strives continually towards the unattainable goal of absolute independence of nature. Therefore the goal of ethics is to indicate how mankind can approach this final unattainable goal.[31]

For Kant, the fulfilment of the moral law must be possible and this affirmation had been the grounds for affirming the reality of freedom. For Fichte, freedom is the unquestionable first principle and its realisation in the concrete is only possible to a degree. Not every material determination can be called heteronomy, for material determination can be posited by the Ego and this material determination is opposed by Fichte to determination from outside ourselves, which he calls heteronomy.[32] But it is clear that abandonment of the drive to pure activity, with its unattainable goal of absolute self-determination, in order to enjoy the material objectifications already determined by the Ego would also be a surrender to heteronomy.

Self-determination and intersubjectivity

It would be a mistake to see in Fichte's principle of absolute self-determination a radical individualism. The contrary is in fact the case. Absolute self-determination is an ideal which it is man's ethical task to strive after but which he cannot attain. His progress in striving after it is, however, the common task of the human community. Fichte held indeed that the Ego could only posit itself as an individual. But the notion of the individual and of his free activity implied a limitation and this limitation implied the notion of other activity on the part of other agents. The very possibility of my becoming aware of my freedom in the first place depends on an impulse from without that summons me to activity. Such an impulse cannot come from the object constituted by my activity. It implies the existence of at least one other rational being that summons me to activity but yet leaves me entirely free for self-determination. The primary condition for self-consciousness is therefore the existence of a real rational being outside myself. In this sense human beings are dependent on one another in a free community of rational discourse.[33] Ethical progress towards the ideal of absolute self-determination takes place in ethical interaction within this community. If one falls short, the other seeks to raise him to the ideal. In this process the morally better man, Fichte declares, will always win and so society brings about the perfection of the human species.[34]

Thus Fichte's concept of individuality or personality is a rational one, conditioned by intersubjectivity, and this intersubjective aspect is won from the notion of self-determination itself. The individual Ego is bound up in a superindividual unity whose goal is moral progress towards absolute self-determination. Within this unity is implied a limitation of the drive towards independence on the part of the individual, namely insofar as this drive itself is originally conditioned by the freedom of the other. There results an absolute prohibition of anything that would destroy the freedom of the other.[35]

The self-positing subject, individuality and the divine

The conflict implied in radical individualism is resolved by Fichte in a devaluation of the empirical individual in favour of a higher unity. The Ego (Ichheit) and individuality are two quite different concepts, he declares. To the charge of sublime individualism levelled against his philosophy, Fichte replied that the problem with his critics is not that they did not possess the concept of the pure Ego in its rationality and spirituality but that the weakness of their character caused them to identify the Ego with their individual persons and make the latter the final goal of their activity. They regarded their individual person as the only genuine substance and held reason to be a mere accident. In his philosophy the opposite was the case. Reason is the only subsistent reality and individuality is a mere accident; reason is the goal, personality the means; personality is only one particular way of expressing reason and must continually lose itself in the universal form of reason: 'Reason alone is eternal, in our view, while individuality must constantly decay. Anyone who does not first accommodate his will to this order of things will also never obtain a true understanding of the Science of Knowledge.'[36]

Therefore, in his later philosophy, Fichte turned his attention to the ground of the free subject of all experience beyond the limitations of the conscious subject that knows himself as subject and object. He adopted other expressions such as 'Life' rather than the 'Ego' of his earlier period or spoke of 'the absolute' in terms which he had previously applied to the 'Ego'. His unceasing quest for a theory that would articulate the ground of the absolute subject led him to a form of theism: the self is a divine manifestation. Not that Fichte went so far as to affirm God's existence in the traditional sense, as the knowledge of a reality distinct from man and the world. We can only speak of a Fichtean affirmation of a mysterious and inconceivable ground of self-consciousness. He spoke only of 'the divine', not of God. Fichte radicalised Kant's identification of the intrinsic rationality of the moral law with the rationality of the moral law as willed by God and so identified 'the divine' with 'the absolute'. This was understood as the dynamic life of which man, especially in his moral activity, is a manifestation. Man or the human race is a manifestation of the divine life. The line of division between finite and infinite passes through the inner core of man not outside him; insofar as he is a purely rational being he participates in the absolute form of pure reason which is the divine or God. Thus Fichte could speak of the divinely inspired man or pen the lapidary phrase:

'What the divine man does, is divine.'[37]

The reception of Fichte's philosophy

The reception of Fichte's philosophy led in two quite different directions. On the one hand the path which he himself followed in intellectual consequence, as Dieter Henrich has shown, led to the development of German Idealism, prompted by the questions that Fichte himself was unable to solve, such as the ground of freedom, the identity of the absolute subject and the relation of the finite and the infinite. On the other hand, as Henrich admits, Fichte's contemporaries saw in him the philosopher of the new freedom that emerged in the French Revolution:

The fundamental idea on which Fichte's *Wissenschaftslehre* of 1794 is based is the statement: the Ego simply posits itself. With that Fichte had given extreme expression to the sentiment of freedom. His contemporaries understood it as the justification of the ideals of the French Revolution, as expressing the decision to subject the world to the conditions demanded by reason, as the Jacobin principle of tolerating nothing that was not one's own work. The liberation of humanity and the triumph of theory appeared to have become a single event.

It is true that Fichte's life was inspired by such experiences and also that his thought emerged from them. To grasp freedom was the motive that made him a philosopher.[38]

It is therefore not surprising that many, down to the present day, who could not or would not follow the speculations of the later Fichte, with his depreciation of individuality and his pantheist mysticism, made their own selection from his ideas in order to affirm the comparatively simple (and ultimately destructive) concepts of freedom, absolute self-determination and ethical progress that they found in his earlier philosophy.

Fichte had in any case transformed the autonomy theme. Without making extensive use of the term itself, he had tied its usage to the questions of the absolute subject of all experience, absolute freedom and unlimited self-determination. The German Idealists after Fichte set themselves the task of reconciling autonomy, now understood as absolute self-determination, with the factual heteronomy with which the empirical and historical subject is confronted. Both Hegel and Schelling understood Christianity as the condition which alone made the historical realisation of autonomy possible.[39]

Summary

Fichte aimed to eliminate the Kantian dualism of subject and object. Philosophy must be based on one principle only. The ethical dignity of the subject demanded the choice of freedom over determinism, of subjectivity over objectivity. Therefore Fichte's one principle was reflective self-consciousness in which the subject posits itself and all else in a free act. The ethical sphere, like all else, is freely constituted by the self-positing subject. The goal of practical reason is absolute self-determination for activity and this is what Fichte means by autonomy. Heteronomy is passive surrender to nature or determination by anything outside the Ego. The realisation of absolute self-determination in the concrete may be limited, but the role of ethics is to point us towards this unattainable goal.

Fichte did not hold to a radical individualism. He developed instead a philosophy of intersubjectivity. My awareness of freedom comes from the encounter with rational beings outside myself. Ethical progress implies a free community of rational discourse in which the empirical individual yields to the demands of a higher unity. Individuality is a mere manifestation of the divine or of the absolute within humanity. In his later years, Fichte turned his attention more and more to the

inexpressible divine ground of ethical subjectivity and away from concern with the empirical individual. Fichte's later philosophy thus
developed the notion of absolute subjectivity along the lines of German
Idealism. But there were many who were inspired by Fichte's early
philosophy to think simply in terms of radical freedom, absolute self-
determination and inevitable ethical progress. In each case, Fichte had
transformed the autonomy theme beyond recognition.

AUTONOMY OPPOSED TO THEISM?

The anti-Hegelian reaction of the 1840s understood Christianity to be
opposed to the historical realisation of autonomy in the sense of self-
determination.[40] Feuerbach, who claimed to reject theism and atheism
alike, understood theology to be a misguided anthropology in which
man projected his own essential characteristics on to a deity. Yet Feuerbach did not affirm these characteristics of the empirical subject but of
humanity in general. He took a stand against individualism and proclaimed as his chief philosophical principle the unity of man with his
fellow-man. From the abolition of the alienation implicit in theology,
Feuerbach expected a reconciliation of man not only with his fellow-
man but with himself, including his body, and with the world of
nature. He was, however, opposed to autonomy in the sense of absolute
self-determination.[41] While Feuerbach sought to transform religion
and theology into an affirmation of humanity, Marx built on Feuerbach's criticism of religion an argument for the active destruction of
religion as a condition for affirming the subjectivity of man. Man's
work alone was to be understood as the generative principle in the
world:

A *being* only considers himself independent when he stands on his own feet;
and he only stands on his own feet when he owes his *existence* to himself.
A man who lives by the grace of another regards himself as a dependent
being. But I live completely by the grace of another if I owe him not
only the maintenance of my life but if he has, moreover, *created* my *life*
– if he is the *source* of my life. When it is not of my own creation, my
life has necessarily a source of this kind outside of it. The *Creation* is therefore an idea very difficult to dislodge from popular consciousness.
But since for the socialist man the *entire so-called history of the world* is

nothing but the creation of man through human labor, nothing but the emergence of nature for man, so he has the visible, irrefutable proof of his *birth* through himself, of the *process of his creation.*[42]

Here the Fichtean theme of the absolute self-determining subject is applied to man the subject in opposition to the divine subject that is independent of and superior to man in biblical Revelation. The autonomy theme thus became a leading motif in atheism in the form of a Promethean self-assertion of man. Man's autonomy is understood in the sense of an absolute autarchy which logically excludes the possibility of theism, which is presented as absolute heteronomy and the negation of man. In this autarchy every external point of reference is either eliminated or subordinated to man, and the original sense of the word 'autonomy' with its implication of a larger frame of reference has been lost. It was Nietzsche rather than Marx who drew the full implications of this idea in a consequent nihilism. It is this conception, which should properly be called autarchy rather than autonomy, that is in dispute between modern atheism and modern theology.[43]

A related use of the autonomy theme is that of the replacement of theology, with its affirmation of a divine subject, by natural science, with its subject man. This was the thesis of Auguste Comte, whose positivist philosophy had begun to appear in the 1830s. The identification of autonomy, in the sense of man's self-determination, with the advance of science led to the theory of a growing autonomy of man that coincided with his increasing mastery of nature. The idea of absolute self-determination, which as Fichte had seen was a goal to which empirical man could only approximate in an unending ethical striving, was thus merged with that of the unending process of scientific discovery with its distant goal of absolute power over nature, including the nature of man himself. Philosophers of history reached back into the past in order to substantiate this correlation between autonomy, in the sense of man's growing self-determination, and scientific progress. They combined the Renaissance, the Reformation, the Enlightenment and the Industrial Revolution in a historical scheme in which man progressively liberated himself from the absolute heteronomy which, by contrast, ruled in the priest-ridden Middle Ages. Thus Dilthey, in his *Weltanschauung und Analyse des Menschen seit Renaissance und Reformation,* presented the 'autonomy of reason' as the leitmotiv of modern historical development, an autonomy consistent with a joyful affirmation of life and the world against the Christian denial of life.[44] The affirmation of a growing self-determination of man due to his advance in scientific knowledge does not itself imply atheism, however, nor do the many other uses of the term in modern scientific discussion.

Autonomy is frequently used in modern science of a functional independence within a larger framework or environment, for example the autonomy of the organism in biology, of the individual person or the social unit in sociology, of the stages of development of the child in psychology and education.[45] Here the original political and legal metaphor is retained. There is therefore no one clearly defined concept of 'autonomy' to which the theologian can appeal if he wishes to draw a balance of current thinking on the question in order to judge its use in theological discussion.[46] The preoccupation of theologians with the controversy with modern atheism tended to lead them to adopt a concept of autarchy under the title of autonomy and thus to concede to their opponents much of the ground at issue.

Summary

Fichte's pantheist mysticism was limited in its appeal. His effect on the notion of autonomy was to change the emphasis from the observance of a universal moral law of reason to the absolute self-determination of an absolute subject. Both Hegel and Schelling believed that this idea was embodied in Christianity. Feuerbach rejected both belief in God and the notion of absolute self-determination in favour of a philosophy in which the unity of the human race overcame alienation. Marx understood man's work alone to be the generative principle of humanity, opposing it to belief in God. Thus the autonomy theme became a persistent strand in modern atheism: man the subject must be affirmed in opposition to the divine subject that is independent of and superior to man. Here autonomy is understood as autarchy: man is self-sufficient and any point of reference superior to man is excluded. But the autonomy theme has a broader usage. It could be identified with man's scientific progress and mastery of nature or with the functional independence of the biological or social unit. The theologian should beware of adopting the atheist definition of autonomy as autarchy and thus conceding much of the ground at issue.

1

Autonomy in the *Church Dogmatics*

THE BACKGROUND: BARTH'S REACTION AGAINST
LIBERAL THEOLOGY

In the nineteenth century the reception of the term 'autonomy' in Protestant theology was largely positive, often unquestioned. It was made
possible by the identification between the Enlightenment and essential
Christianity which had already formed Kant's religious ideas and led
to Hegel's mediation between the Reformation and the spirit of the
French Revolution. Reformation Christianity was presented by Hegel
as the historical condition under which the subsequent realisation of
autonomy alone was possible. Schleiermacher's theology was opposed
to Hegel's, but his foundation of theology on the intuition and feeling
of absolute dependence on God and his mediation between faith, ethics
and cultural values included an affirmation of autonomy. Schleiermacher presented the Church as the centre and motivating power for
the self-realisation of man in his essential freedom. He was even to
some extent sympathetic to the claim of the romantic or Idealist subject
to sovereign, unrestrained freedom.

However, the identification of the essence of Protestantism with the
absolute autonomy of the self-determining subject in popular Idealism
met with opposition. The dissolution of traditional Christian doctrines
by the left-wing Hegelians, including Feuerbach and David Friedrich
Strauß, discredited this identification as did Kierkegaard's insistence
on the radical finitude of the individual subject. There took place a
revival of interest in positive theological foundations and in the

authority of the Bible, manifested in both popular religious revivalism and in traditional Protestant Orthodoxy. This trend had its counterpart in political conservatism. Indeed the theological reception of autonomy in the nineteenth century runs parallel with the political acceptance of the ideas of the French Revolution and of liberal democracy. The authoritarian, anti-revolutionary movement in favour of the monarchist Restoration appealed for legitimation to the authoritative element in the Protestant tradition. The ecclesiastical and theological extremes in German Protestantism reflected the political divisions of the day, and liberal and conservative parties in ecclesiastical politics enjoyed a rise and fall in fortunes in striking parallel with those of their secular counterparts.[1]

While the appeal to the Idealist notion of absolute autonomy had become a source of controversy, the appeal to the Kantian notion of autonomy remained generally attractive. The great Liberal theologians of the latter half of the century adopted Kant's foundation of theology on ethics with enthusiasm. The Neokantian distinction between the realm of fact and the realm of value left room for the affirmation of an independent ethical-religious sphere. The Neokantian thesis of the autonomy of the various sciences in the sense of their functional independence of one another allowed for the assertion of the scientific status of ethics and of theology despite the growing importance of the positivist and determinist conception of science. The school of Albert Ritschl, with its distinguished exponent Adolf von Harnack, dominated German Protestantism in the years leading up to the First World War. The Liberal theology, as its name indicated, also had its political counterpart. The new awareness of national unity following on the reunification of Germany under Protestant leadership fused with the Protestant cultural heritage into *Kulturprotestantismus*, in which Kant could be celebrated as 'the philosopher of Protestantism'[2] and Harnack could accept the invitation to write the speech for Kaiser Wilhelm on the declaration of the First World War.

Barth grew up with the trends and tendencies of nineteenth-century German Protestantism. His father was a lecturer in a biblically oriented theological seminary in Basel and later retained, as professor in Bern, his positive theological and biblical orientation, although without fanaticism. To his father's distress Barth launched himself into the world of Liberal theology and remained an enthusiastic follower of this school until the support of almost all his admired teachers for the

First World War made him think afresh. His close friend Eduard Thurneysen, who shared this conversion, wrote of Barth's sense of the failure of theology, the Church and society in general at the time of the First World War as the occasion for the reorientation of Barth's theology.[3]

Barth, as he later confessed, was at first motivated more by a critical and polemic reaction to the theology of the previous century than by a clear perception of the alternative. The reaction began with Schleiermacher and included everything that followed him in theology.[4] Barth's dissatisfaction therefore extended to the entire history of theology since the Enlightenment. He evidently felt the need to go back behind this entire development and start anew as is clear from his renewed preoccupation with Kant. He was not, however, satisfied with the results of his Kant studies and did not take up Thurneysen's suggestion of studying Hegel, but returned to what he called relearning the ABC of theology – to exegesis.[5] And what Barth found in and through the two editions of his Commentary on Romans was the theme of the divinity of God conceived precisely in opposition to the self-assertion of man: this, he wrote later, was the 'rock of bronze' which he struck, the divinity of God and God's divinity. That meant God's independence and uniqueness not only in opposition to nature but also (against Idealism) in opposition to the intellectual and spiritual world (dem geistigen Kosmos). It meant affirming his unique existence, power and initiative above all in his relations with men. It meant the polemical assertion of the claims of the divine subject in opposition to a theology that had reduced itself in the wake of Idealism to a concern with the subjectivity of man, a theology that was religionist and therefore anthropocentric.[6] It demanded a theocentric theology so logical and radical that it not merely put in question but absolutely and in principle rejected every expression of the religious self-consciousness or the reflective reason in theology. Every theological statement must be derived 'from above', from the Word of God.

Barth's prophetic call to the judgement pronounced on man by the Word of God and his proclamation of the crisis in which every human institution was in consequence placed read as a judgement on the proud *Kulturprotestantismus* of the preceding era and on the Liberal theology that had built and served it. Others added their voices to that of Barth: Eduard Thurneysen, Friedrich Gogarten, Emil Brunner, Rudolf Bultmann. The attempt of the 'German Christians' to revive the identification between Protestantism and nationalism in favour of the National Socialist regime cemented the claim of the 'dialectical theologians' to represent the conscience of German Protestantism and ensured that their theology had a lasting effect.

Nonetheless the dialectical theologians themselves divided on the question as to how theology should take account of the humanity to which the Word of God was addressed and which was in some sense prior to and distinct from Revelation. Thus Barth and Brunner disputed the question of nature and grace and Barth also rejected Bultmann's adoption of existentialist philosophy as a basis for understanding the Word of God.[7]

Barth's development during these years consisted in the refinement and ever more consistent application of his principle of Revelation: the primacy of the divine subject. His study of the epistemological question reached its peak with his book on Anselm, *Fides quaerens intellectum*, followed shortly afterwards by the revised edition of the Prolegomena to the *Church Dogmatics*. We do not here attempt a historical and genetic account of Barth's development during these years. This is not merely because the enormous mass of material now available on Barth's early theological schooling, his years as a young Liberal theologian, his socio-political engagement, the transition to his break with Liberal theology in the two editions of his Commentary on Romans and the subsequent development and gradual modification of the radical antithesis between God and man there adopted would further extend an already over-extended chapter; it is also because the *Church Dogmatics* genuinely represents a new beginning in which Barth now rigorously excluded 'anything that might appear to find for theology a foundation, support, or justification in philosophical existentialism'. He thereby began anew with the application of his principle of Revelation, but no longer in the polemic style of his earlier dialectic period. Instead the intention was now more positive and constructive: dialectic had given way to analogy.[8]

AUTONOMY, THEONOMY AND HETERONOMY IN THE PROLEGOMENA

Human autonomy and the Word of God

Barth adopts the term 'autonomy' in the Prolegomena to the *Church Dogmatics* to explain and sum up the relation between dogmatics and Revelation.[9] It has here the function of elucidating a central *theologoumenon*, namely the Protestant Scripture principle. The explanation takes the form of three interrelated concepts: theonomy, autonomy and heteronomy. The primacy in the triad belongs to theonomy. By 'theonomy' Barth means that it is Revelation as the Word of God (to which the Scripture bears witness) that is the norm to which dogmatics must conform.[10]

Autonomy and heteronomy are understood as subordinate, concrete and relative expressions of the principle of theonomy. Theonomy is not an elusive and empty abstraction, but in the human sphere it takes on a definite, concrete and relative form or rather two complementary forms, one objective – heteronomy – and the other subjective – autonomy. Barth, who attaches great importance to the order in which things are said in the *Church Dogmatics* because it establishes the relative priority of the different elements in his argument, chooses to give the first place to heteronomy but not before making a brief anticipation of his treatment of autonomy:

But again we have to bear in mind that the theonomy established, recognised and effectual in the human sphere is not in any sense an empty abstraction, which cannot be grasped in practice, or can be grasped only arbitrarily or accidentally. On the contrary, where it is established, recognised and accepted, it has a definite, relative form. Therefore in the sphere of the human thinking and speaking of the teaching Church, it is not the direct and simple counterpart of an autonomy of man. In our final section we shall certainly have to think about a human autonomy in dogmatics which is the correlative of theonomy. This will correspond to the doctrine of freedom in the Church, in which we attempted to understand the Evangelical Scripture principle on its subjective side, but only secondarily, when we had first tried to understand it on its objective side, in the doctrine of authority in the Church. It is not, then, our business to speak of autonomy in dogmatics until we have first made it clear that the theonomy of dogmatics has as its primary counterpart a hetero-nomy.[11]

Barth gives heteronomy therefore the priority over autonomy in his understanding of the relation between dogmatics and Revelation. The concept has, however, a limited function: it serves to define the Protes-tant Scripture principle in its objective aspect. It is localised: it belongs to the sphere of the human thinking and speaking of the teaching Church and defines the form of authority proper to this Church. It is no 'absolute heteronomy' but is merely the concrete form taken by theonomy. Its law is no other than God's law − theo-nomy − but in relative and only penultimate form. It is no second authority set up alongside that of the Word of God: we look through and beyond all that is here called authority to the sole and exclusive authority of the Word of God. As Barth notes, this subordinate function corresponds to his doctrine of authority in the Church, a relative, direct and formal authority which is founded upon, but also conditioned and limited by, the final authority of the Word of God.[12]

CONTRAST WITH TILLICH

Structurally the interrelationship between theonomy, autonomy and heteronomy adopted by Barth in the Prolegomena parallels that developed some years earlier by Tillich. Tillich correlated theonomy as *Gottesgesetzlichkeit* with autonomy as *Selbstgesetzlichkeit* and heteronomy as *fremdes Gesetz*.[13] The difference between Barth and Tillich lies in their starting-points. Tillich affirmed with Barth that Liberal theology had been a failure and that the judgement proclaimed in the Word of God placed man in a crisis. But he thought that the Word of God was not an appropriate starting-point from which to address modern man. For modern man the Bible represents heteronomy: it 'bore the seal of the Grand Inquisitor'. Tillich wished to mediate between the claims of modern culture and the new theology of the Word of God. Credibility could only be attained by going the route of a philosophy of culture in which theological content could be revealed in the achievements and crises of autonomous culture itself.[14] Tillich adopts the Kantian definition of autonomy: the obedience of the rational individual to the law of reason that he finds within himself. This autonomy is operative in the history of culture; there it functions as a dynamic principle that tends towards rationalisation and becomes alienated from the other element that Tillich sees as essential to reason – 'depth', transcendence. Theonomy represents the goal of a process in which autonomy becomes aware of and responsive to its transcendental ground.

For Tillich the modern era is characterised by the development of autonomy in the late Middle Ages and a corresponding reaction in which the Church closed itself against autonomy in heteronomy. Autonomy, which is described mainly in positive terms, thus includes negative traits. Heteronomy, which is basically a negative element, also contains a positive aspect in that the 'depth' of reason finds expression in cultic and mystic forms which Tillich characterises as heteronomous. When autonomy has lost its depth and content in rationalism heteronomy brings the neglected elements to expression. It thus plays a role in the re-establishment of theonomy, which is the successful but always fragmentary reconciliation of autonomy with its transcendent depth. Theonomy is, however, also presented as a dark, mysterious, subpersonal depth that belongs together with autonomy – the principle of form and structure – to an ultimate metaphysical polarity in being itself.[15]

Thus for both Tillich and Barth heteronomy plays a subordinate instrumental role in the mediation of theonomy and autonomy; for Tillich and, as we shall see, for Barth the principal elements are theonomy and autonomy. For both Tillich and Barth heteronomy takes one concrete shape in Church authority. Tillich portrays its role primarily in negative terms: it reacts against a false cultural development and itself requires a further negation before a healthy relationship is re-established. For Barth it is a positive role even if it remains relative, conditioned and limited. Tillich's speculations correlate metaphysical principles with epochs in the history of culture. Barth understands theonomy and autonomy in terms of two subjects – God and the individual human being – that confront one another in the clear light of a historical encounter: Revelation in Jesus Christ.

THE SPECIFIC FORMS OF HETERONOMY

Theonomy – the one demand of obedience to the Word of God – issues in three concrete demands and takes three specific heteronomous forms: that of a biblical, of a confessional and of an ecclesiastical attitude.[16] The biblical attitude is, however, described in *subjective* terms: it is the attitude of the human beings who are the biblical witnesses (Zeugen) rather than being defined in terms of the (written) biblical witness (Zeugnis):

> But as from the absolute authority of Holy Scripture as the Word of God there results the relative authority of the biblical Canon, so from the absolute requirement of the obedience of faith to the prophetic and apostolic witness there results the relative requirement of a basic mode of thinking and speaking which corresponds with this obedience of faith. This is what we have to describe and understand as the biblicism or biblical attitude of dogmatics.
>
> We call it 'biblical' because it has its prototype and exemplar in the attitude of the biblical witnesses themselves, because it consists in the regard for and imitation of this prototype, that is, in the institution of a kinship between the outlook, approach and method of the biblical writers and those of the Church preacher and therefore of the dogmatician.[17]

This description of the biblical attitude is reinforced by Barth's distinction between dogmatics and exegesis. Dogmatics is not limited simply to reproducing and explaining the text of the Bible. It will always have the biblical text in view but itself consists rather in a concern with Church proclamation, which also applies Scripture and is in that sense itself *productive*: 'not merely by reproducing and explaining it, but also by applying and thus in some measure producing it'. Barth frees dogmatics from the need to provide proof-texts for its assertions in the sense of having to base them on definite biblical passages or refer them to specific biblical contexts. While insisting that it must remain 'responsible' to the biblical text, he claims the freedom for dogmatics to take up questions and concerns that cannot be answered directly by reference to specific biblical phrases or contexts of thought. Heteronomy means here that dogmatics cannot claim 'to be an autonomous branch of Church theology in independence of the witness of Scripture', that is cannot claim to draw on other sources of its own, but only from Scripture, though it is not tied to the letter of the biblical text.[18]

It is no accident that Barth places the Canon and text of Scripture under the heading of the confessional attitude of dogmatics, and describes the biblical attitude in terms of the outlook (Geistesverfassung) of the biblical witnesses. Barth rejects all narrow 'biblicism' and especially the doctrine of the literal inspiration of Scripture.[19] The Protestant principle of Scripture is identified with the Word of God as revealed in the witness of the biblical *authors*, though it is not identical with this, and their witness is expressed in, but is again not identical with, the letter of Scripture and with the Confessions of the Church.

In describing the confessional attitude demanded of dogmatics, Barth also begins with a *subjective* description: the utterance of the Word of God in its concrete objectivity is also conditioned through the voice of the 'Fathers' who established and moulded the Church. However, the attention to the witnesses runs here parallel to a somewhat greater emphasis on witness as given in *objective* texts – dogma, doctrinal decisions, the Canon and the text of the Bible, the history that moulded the Church and the Confession which obtains in it.[20] While this Confession is relative and determinate in its status, it is exclusive in its authority. The dogmatician does not operate within an area of free choice characterised by subjective right and good conscience.[21] He must confine himself to the essential and necessary witness of faith. For the dogmatician to take up an independent standpoint outside or above the individual Church Confessions is, suggests Barth, an expression of the theology of the Enlightenment. Expressing 'in all probability' subordination to a general philosophy of religion (Barth drops the name of Schleiermacher here), such a stance means the end of Church dogmatics. Barth here confesses the faith of the Reformed Church in the conviction that it is the only valid and universal expression of the faith of the universal Church, and as such corresponds to the objective norm of dogmatics.[22]

To the Fathers and the Confessions, however, the dogmatician is not absolutely bound; he is only bound until 'we are forced to understand it [our ecclesiastical stance] differently as a result of further enlightenment by the same principle [obedience to the Word of God]'.[23] The theology of the Fathers and the Confessions serves only as a pattern. The aim of dogmatics is not the restoration of their theology; it must be used 'as a pattern only in proper [and independent] subordination to the Word of God attested in Scripture'.[24]

The ecclesial attitude demanded of dogmatics means that it has to listen to the teaching Church of today. But in stating this Barth is merely describing his relationship as 'solidarity' with the Church in its contemporary situation. The dogmatician is confronted with 'the babel of voices in the teaching Church' and must himself listen through the confusion for the essential function of the Church – her priestly prayer on behalf of men which is the presupposition for her prophetic teaching towards men. The ecclesial attitude means that the dogmatician sees his function in solidarity with the proclamation of the Word of God in the Church today not in academic isolation nor from the standpoint of a past century nor in mere subservience to the spirit of the age.[25]

It is thus a personal and subjective commitment to the essential function of the Church (which the dogmatician must himself grasp) in the factual situation of the Church today.

The three heteronomous demands with which the principle of theonomy confronts dogmatics represent therefore no absolute heteronomy but very relative and only partially concrete demands. They confront dogmatics with the three concrete forms of the Word of God outlined in *KD* I/1, no. 4. But each of these forms is only relevant insofar as it leads to a subjective grasp of the Word of God that manifests itself in and through them without being identical with them. What the dogmatician adopts is not in the last resort an external code or canon, whether Bible, Creed or teaching authority in the Church, but an internal attitude which accepts these outward things insofar as he himself judges to be manifest in them the Word of God that lies above and beyond heteronomy or autonomy.

AUTONOMY UNDER THE WORD OF GOD

Barth treated heteronomy, under the heading 'Dogmatics as a Function of the Hearing Church', as the norm to which dogmatics is subject. As the method followed by dogmatics, Barth takes up the question of autonomy under the heading 'Dogmatics as a Function of the Teaching Church'.[26] Autonomy is the second concrete and relative form taken by theonomy and represents the *subjective* possibility of pure doctrine. It can be understood only in correspondence and correlation with heteronomy – both together denote the necessary obedience of Church proclamation and dogmatics to the Word of God: 'Both the autonomy and heteronomy of dogmatics describe as from below, and from the point of view of man himself, what from above and from the point of view of God is to be described as theonomy.'[27] The core of Barth's doctrine of autonomy lies in the assertion that obedience would not be real if it were not exercised in freedom. Obedience if it is real implies both an alien law and that this same law is also its own law.[28]

Obedience, then, implies the fully free decision of the human subject of dogmatics, a free decision in which theonomy finds its concrete and relative form, because in this decision the human subject is tied to the work and action of God that takes place in the Word of God. It is not by chance that Barth takes a further step not just behind Scripture to the Word of God to which it bears witness, but behind the Word of God to the work and action of God. Dogmatics may not try to present the content of the Word of God by an objective description and analysis. In doing so it would miss the essential character of the content of the Word of God as 'a conversation, a process, a military action, an act of sovereignty'.[29] Dogmatics must therefore break through to the level of subjectivity behind the Word of God, to its character as conversation or dialogue with another subject, to the act of sovereignty of the God who demands obedience. This breakthrough cannot be achieved on the level of heteronomy, in terms of an objective law. Only in the fully free decision of the human subject can dogmatics participate in the conversation, process, military action and act of sovereignty, in the work and action of God. This takes place by 'allowing ourselves to be drawn into the sphere of our effective operation' and by 'adopting it as the way of our own thinking and speaking'. It has the character of a personal encounter with God, 'so that from both points of view we have to do with an encounter between God and man as between persons.'[30] It is precisely this subjective and interpersonal act of obedience that Barth calls 'autonomy'.

An arbitrary decision on the part of the autonomous subject is therefore excluded by the character of obedience, but this does not mean that we are dealing with an established dogmatic content. On the contrary, whether a particular decision reflects autonomy or not depends on the gift of grace and of the Holy Spirit for which man can only pray. The absolute obedience due to the Word of God becomes a concrete and relative demand addressed to the individual autonomous subject. For him it represents 'the necessary and only possible decision', in which he must respond to a demand which is not made of him from outside, but 'which the human subject must address to *himself* in full and free obedience to the Word of God, which he alone can address to himself'.[31]

The consequence which Barth draws here is that the decision made, necessary and absolute though it be for the individual concerned, cannot have the character of a demand for obedience for other individuals. It can only be represented to others as the decision which this individual has made, as a challenge, suggestion or *consilium*. Barth does not exclude the possibility that such a decision about the demand of the Word of God here and now might become for others too the necessary and only possible decision, with the force of a binding command: 'What this means is that it has pleased God to ratify our decision as the right one, and to use it to declare his will to others.'[32] But no matter how much support such a decision may attract, even if it attain the formal character of a decision of the community, it cannot attain the status of a command (much less a commandment). It can only be understood as a free decision 'which as such can only challenge others to make similar free decisions'.[33] It is impossible for any human being to press his own understanding of the divine law upon others as though it were identical with the divine law itself. The choice of dogmatic method is thus left to the free decision of the individual dogmatic theologian, which does not mean that he is free to make an arbitrary choice, but that he must decide in entire inward obedience,[34] in autonomy under the Word of God.

Barth's account of autonomy as the method to be followed by dogmatics would therefore appear to give the dogmatic theologian – the subject that conceives and constructs a theological reception of the Word of God – a relatively free hand. This impression is reinforced by the relativisation of the heteronomous element, its sublimation into the internal attitude which the theologian adopts to the Word of God that remains above and beyond its concrete forms. Barth claims, however, to block the activity of the theologian at its most decisive and sensitive point. Obedience to the Word of God imposes methodical restrictions, the chief of which is the sacrifice of dogmatic system.

SUMMARY

In the Prolegomena to the *Church Dogmatics* 'autonomy' belongs with 'heteronomy' and 'theonomy' to a triad that was used by Barth to explain the Protestant Scripture principle. Theonomy – God's rule in

Revelation – takes two concrete forms, heteronomy and autonomy. Barth takes heteronomy first. It represents the objective side of the Scripture principle, the givenness of the Word of God in Scripture. But this heteronomy is relative, not absolute, and Barth dissolves its objectivity in subjective terms. The three concrete forms of heteronomy are described as (subjective) attitudes: biblical, confessional and ecclesial. In regard to the biblical attitude, Barth does not hold to the literal inspiration of Scripture but only to the witness the biblical authors give to the Word of God that remains above and beyond the text. Church Confession is the objective norm of dogma, but the confessional attitude does not treat it as an absolute bond but as a pattern to be followed as long as the Word of God does not indicate something else. The ecclesial attitude demands solidarity with the contemporary Church, but this is a matter of looking beyond the babel of voices to the essential priestly prayer and prophetic teaching concealed behind it. The only function of heteronomy is to lead to autonomy, the subjective possibility of grasping the Word of God.

Autonomy is the method of dogmatics, namely the free exercise of obedience to the Word of God. It must be free because the essential character of the Word of God is dialogue, personal encounter with another subject, namely the God who claims obedience. The result must be that we adopt the work and action of God as the way of our own thinking and speaking. Autonomy is not, then, an arbitrary exercise, but it is objective only in the Holy Spirit and in grace. It possesses final authority only for the individual personally addressed. For others it remains a suggestion or indication which God may perhaps confirm as authoritative for them too. No one can press his understanding of the divine command on others. It must be grasped only in entire inward obedience to the command of God.

Dogmatic system versus the Word of God

BARTH DISALLOWS DOGMATIC SYSTEM: MAN AS SUBJECT

By 'system' Barth understands 'a structure of principles and their consequences, founded on the presupposition of a basic view of things (einer Grundanschauung), constructed with the help of various sources of knowledge and axioms, and self-contained and complete in itself.'

The development of such a system presupposes, as Barth immediately adds, the formulation of a priori first principles and it is in their analysis that the development of the system must consist.[35] It is, as we shall see, no accident that Barth here juxtaposes a general formulation of system with the much more stringent formula of an analytic and deductive system that Fichte proposed as a correlative to the self-positing activity of the absolute subject.

Barth's objection to system is that first principles or a *Grund-anschauung* will inevitably take the place of the Word of God as the basic determinant of theology. The human subject – the dogmatic theologian in question – is then occupied with constructing a system and is 'relieved of the duty of obedience in other respects'. That would be the end of both freedom and obedience, and therefore of autonomy in Barth's sense. Not only the strict analytic system but many other widely accepted methods of 'systematic' theology are rejected by Barth, such as the quest for the 'essence of Christianity' or the identification of fundamental articles of faith.[36] What might otherwise be supposed to be the field in which the dogmatic theologian demonstrates his skill and exercises his individuality is thus placed outside the pale of legitimate theological freedom.

Despite his rejection of dogmatic system, Barth admits that dogmatic method must inevitably aim at definiteness and coherence (Be-stimmtheit und Zusammenhang) in its presentation, with the consequence that 'something like a system' will assert itself more or less spontaneously. Barth insists that such a systematic presentation, if it is to be acceptable, must remain not only provisional but incomplete. What Barth most energetically rejects is not the order and coherence of the system as such, but the principle behind it, which in the last resort can be traced back to the subject behind the system, to the human 'will to system' (Wille zum System).[37] The choice of dogmatic method cannot serve the purpose of enabling the dogmatic theologian to survey and control his object. This object stands outside and above all human viewpoints. It is not something which is under our control, but which exercises control over us. The autonomy of dogmatics consists in its free submission to the sovereignty of the Word of God alone. The Word of God is not object but subject; Barth thus returns to the category of a personal encounter, to an intersubjective act of obedience.

Barth's insistence on the personal leads him to resort to the categories of actualism. The truth of the Word of God is the truth of the work and action of God taking place in it. This cannot be 'condensed and summarised' in an idea or principle. Instead it must be 'concrete', by which Barth understands here a temporally restricted validity: 'in relation to what is at any given time the most recent stage of the process or action or sovereign act of which it is the occurrence'. Dogmatics may report on this event, but such a report may not be confused with the object of dogmatics, which is that sovereign event that impels both dogmatics and the teaching Church and is the basis of their dynamic. This event is the work of God and not the result of the human 'will to system'. The consequence is the elusiveness of the Word of God, which is 'not any kind of truth that can be controlled' but 'something which exercises control of us'.[38]

Barth does not conceal the fact that this anti-systematic restriction is a methodical choice on the part of the human subject of dogmatics. He speaks of the 'unceasing and ready vigilance that the object is able to speak for itself'. In support of this intention Barth resorts afresh to the rhetoric of dialectical theology. The human 'will to system' is treated as a quest for security from the demands of the Word of God. Apart from the one presupposition – that the Word of God will speak for itself – the dogmatic theologian must methodically exclude all other presuppositions.[39]

Barth knows how to present a thoroughly modern argument for this denial of the systematic activity of the theologian, namely in terms of the rhetoric of the Enlightenment, in the theme of openness for the truth and in that of unhindered progression in the discovery of truth:

But this means that from the human point of view the position which in a system is occupied by the fundamental principle of interpretation can only remain basically open in Church dogmatics, like the opening in the centre of a wheel. It cannot be occupied even hypothetically or provisionally by any *a priori* decisions. It is ready to receive those decisions with which the object will urgently confront human thinking and speaking. It is ready for new insights which no former store of knowledge can really confront on equal terms or finally withstand. Essentially dogmatic method consists in this openness to receive new truth, and only in this.[40]

The rejection of the system, like the rejection of permanently valid articles of faith in the Church, is primarily intended to allow free scope

to the action of the Word of God; secondarily it is presented as a liberation for the Church and for dogmatics: 'The establishment of specific,
irrevocable, fundamental articles will block the way to freedom both
for itself [dogmatics] and for the Church. It will also block the onward
course of the Word of God within the Church.'[41] Barth's rhetoric of
liberation (we shall have to return again to the question of what sort
of liberating intention lies behind it) presents system as a restriction,
within which death from suffocation threatens.[42] However, this
rhetoric is here employed not, as in the Enlightenment, to urge the
claims and the competence of the human subject but to restrict its
activity and establish its limits.

BARTH ACCEPTS 'SOMETHING LIKE A SYSTEM':
GOD AS SUBJECT

Barth's rejection of the 'will to system' in dogmatics is based on the
belief that the object of dogmatics − the Word of God − is the action
of a sovereign subject distinct from man. Barth believes that the working of this subject will of itself yield the same benefits as might be
claimed for the construction of a system on the part of the dogmatic
theologian:

[Dogmatics'] concern must essentially be not to be anxious, not to try to concern itself overmuch, especially in the form of a well-meant but prematurely
intended occupation of that open position by a basic principle or view which
first has to be purified. Dogmatic method consists essentially in the expectation
that there will eventually be this purification and the consequent emergence of
the essence of Christianity; that no harm will be done to anything true and
right which we might think we know, and announce and accept, as a basic principle for dogmatic work; that it will be revealed and confirmed as true and right
if only it does not try to prove itself prematurely, if only it is not too precipitate-
ly laid as a foundation, if only it is left to the confirmatory control of the object,
if only it is not too soon withdrawn from the crucible in which it must be
purified and refined by the effect of this object.[43]

Far from being a rejection of system as such, therefore, Barth's position
is based on a change of subject. A system may be expected to assert
itself − but as the work of the divine subject rather than as that of the
human subject. The human subject must guard against his own 'will

to system', his tendency to anticipate the working of the Word of God, by adopting a deliberately anti-systematic strategy. Thus he can leave the centre of constructive activity open and pave the way for the affirmation that the resulting system is not due to his activity but to that of the Word of God. We have seen how sparing Barth is with such an affirmation: autonomy under the Word of God means that the individual may and must operate in the conviction that what he affirms may and must be the Word of God, but that this conviction has for others only the status of a challenge or suggestion inviting them to inquire for themselves what the Word of God is saying to them. Nonetheless both dogmatics and the teaching Church must actually believe that what they say, they say not of themselves, but because they have heard it from the Word of God.[44]

Barth thus affirms that if the dogmatic theologian practises autonomy – obedience to the Word of God as he hears it – if he holds to the Word of God attested in Scripture as his material principle (Barth coins the rather unexpected phrase 'materiale Autonomie'),[45] 'something like a system' may emerge. He speaks in rather paradoxical terms but without apparent irony of such a systematisation as a 'sin forgiven':

In this work – it cannot be otherwise in view of its object – we have to do with the question of truth. It is, therefore, inevitable that as a whole and in detail the aim must be definiteness and coherence, and it is to be hoped that the definiteness and sequence of the truth will actually be disclosed. But this being the case, is it not also inevitable that 'something like a system' will assert itself more or less spontaneously in dogmatic work? Why, then, should a 'system' be so utterly abhorrent? If it asserts itself spontaneously in this way, can it not be forgiven? And if so, why should we be frightened away by a law forbidding systems? May it not be that a 'system' which asserts itself spontaneously (not as a system, but as a striving for definiteness and coherence) signifies obedience and is therefore a shadow of the truth? It may well be so. But even in this case the danger is still there. The fact that unauthorised systematisation may be forgiven does not mean that the tendency to systematisation is authorised. Nor does the fact that even in the fatal form of an intrinsically unauthorised systematisation true obedience may finally be demonstrated and a shadow of the truth disclosed.[46]

That Barth himself took liberal advantage of the reluctant permission to systematise implied in the formula 'a sin forgiven' is self-evident. The *Church Dogmatics* has been universally admired for its systematic consistency and ambitious architectonic construction. Barth cannot even be declared unequivocally innocent of the playful development of form for form's sake.[47] Eberhard Jüngel's characterisation of Barth's theology as 'pointedly opposed to system' is indeed true, and his insistence that 'what is systematic in this theology is its power constantly to correct the process of dogmatic thinking in view of the subject matter' reflects Barth's own intention.[48] What is implied in this statement is, of course, that Barth also takes responsibility for the process of thinking itself and for its development.

The question is thus transferred to the way in which Barth actually carries out his intention. What strategies does he adopt in order to ensure that the systematic elements in his theology correspond to the Word of God rather than to constructions of his own? How can we distinguish the latter from the former? The point of greatest difficulty is the need for an objective description of the human assimilation of the Word of God in human words and forms and their attribution to the subject man. That would complement Barth's subjective description of autonomy and his only partially objective description (heteronomy) of the work of other subjects – the biblical authors, the Fathers and the Confessions, and the teaching Church of today. There is one aspect of this problem which, as Henri Bouillard pointed out, Barth never tackled directly. It is the classical question of the analogical use of language. Instead Barth turned back to the question of which subject is the origin of appropriate language about God. Ways of speaking that originate with the subject God can be said to correspond to Revelation; not so those that originate with the subject man.[49] It is the same here with the question of system: Barth is compelled to find a strategy that enables him to claim that the systematic unity in his theology originates not with himself but with the subject God.

BARTH'S ANTI-SYSTEMATIC STRATEGY:
THE CLASSICAL TOPOLOGY

The framework of Barth's *Church Dogmatics* is limited to a simple scheme based on the classical *loci theologici* – God, Creation, Reconciliation and Redemption – that Barth adopts with anti-systematic intent:

The *Loci* of the older orthodoxy were in fact basic dogmatic tenets which did not pretend to proceed from a higher unity than that of the Word of God itself, or to express any higher syntheses than arise out of the Word of God, or to be rooted and held together in any higher system than that of the Word of God.[50]

Barth follows this statement with a demonstration that the impossibility of reducing all of the four *loci* to a system based on any one of them still obtains. The Word of God alone can provide the basis (Begründung) of knowledge and also the coherence (Zusammenhang) of the lines drawn from these four points. The activity of the human subject, in the sense of his intention to undertake anything of his own at this point, must be stilled. The fundamental unity in dogmatics can only consist in the unity of God himself:

The aim of initiating the unity of dogmatics is one which never has been and never will be accomplished [without] one of the four given points throw[ing] the other three more or less into the shade, thus doing violence to the real content of the Word of God, not least in the particular point emphasised. If we keep these points separate and distinct and allow the lines that are to be drawn from them to retain their independence of each other, we are in no sense guilty of any arbitrary dismemberment of the one Word of God. That this [the Word of God] is one in the *actus purissimus* of its actualisation by God, which is identical with the *actus purissimus* of the existence of the Trinity, is a truth which Church proclamation and dogmatics recognise when they renounce the attempt to usurp a kind of transcendent vantage point in the existence of God Himself. It is in this way, in differentiation, that the Word and the existence of God are revealed to us, that God grounds the knowledge of Himself, even the knowledge of Himself in His unity. This distinction and independence of the four *Loci* arises from the fact of the self-revelation of the one and triune God.[51]

That man is incapable of realising this unity, that his attempts to do so always lead to contradictions, is not, according to Barth, due to the necessary limitations of human knowledge. Just as the transcendental unity of human knowledge may not be employed as an argument in favour of a theological system, its rejection cannot be based on the necessary limits of man's perception and conceptual powers. Just as in the case of man the questioner, so here in the case of man the synthesiser man's activity is restricted because Barth allows of only one originating subject, God, in relation to whom the activity of man the subject is one of receptivity in personal encounter.[52]

Barth's insistence on God the subject could nonetheless give the impression that he wishes to articulate the whole of dogmatics in terms of the freedom and sovereignty of an absolute divine subject, and to reduce the other theological *loci* – Creation, Reconciliation, Redemption – to functions of this fundamental truth. He admits that this could provide a compelling system and that the divinity of God is indeed the primary truth in the biblical message. But he rejects the proposal. The concept of God is not given to us as a key to a metaphysics of God which would enable us to read off his action in Revelation as a necessary or contingent series of consequences. The doctrine of God is given to us only in and with the knowledge of his action. It cannot be reduced to a mere premise of that action but neither can it become a systematic principle set above Creation, Reconciliation and Redemption. It must be taught together with and alongside of them.[53] Similarly the doctrine of the Trinity could be taken as the systematic principle on which dogmatics is to be constructed, but here the same objection is valid: the knowledge of the Trinity is given only in and through the various *loci* of Revelation. We cannot construct our own image of God 'according to the measure of what we men call unity' but must orientate ourselves by the fact of Revelation: 'It is in this way, in differentiation, that the word and the existence of God are revealed to us, that God grounds the knowledge of Himself, even the knowledge of Himself in His unity.'[54]

God the subject is thus specified in his Revelation, a revelation that on the one side limits the constructive activity of the reflecting human subject and on the other specifies the divine subject whom he has to do with, whom he encounters.

The autonomy of dogmatic thought, so Barth concludes the treatment of this question, is not primary but only secondary autonomy; it is only a function of theonomy. Man is employed as God's instrument against his own tendency. We are left to confess that 'in God's judgement we are exposed as liars, and that we shall think and speak the truth always against our own selves'. Here Barth momentarily drops the theological construction with which he had explained the interrelationship of the divine and the human subject so far. Autonomy is now no longer the concrete and relative form of theonomy – the primary

autonomous subject is God himself: 'The autonomy of dogmatic thinking
. . . implies (like its heteronomy . . .) the autonomy of the Holy Spirit.'[55]

SUMMARY

Autonomy does not give the dogmatic theologian an entirely free hand.
His will to obey the Word of God must be shown in his letting go control of the object and abandoning the human compulsion to control
material by imposing a system. He must accept that the object of theology
lies outside and above all human viewpoints and is a sovereign event,
the work of God. It is revealed only in the here and now and its particular manifestation may have a temporally restricted validity. The one
presupposition for the dogmatic theologian is that the Word of God will
speak for itself. Barth presents this traditional Reformation principle
with the rhetorical flourish of the Enlightenment: openness to the truth.
The appeal to enlightenment is now urged against the claims of the
human subject to dominate the process of inquiry. Dogmatics must not
try to anticipate the work of God, who will himself reveal what is the
essence of Christianity.

Barth demands an anti-systematic strategy on the part of the theologian.
Definiteness and coherence are legitimate aims and as a result 'something
like a system' may spontaneously occur. But striving for system and the
tendency to system must be rejected. Everything turns on the question
of which subject – God or man – is the originator of language about
God. The anti-systematic strategy that Barth adopts is a deliberate differentiation of doctrine. It must be explicated under several headings,
none of which can be reduced to any of the others. Barth uses the classical
loci – God, Creation, Reconciliation and Redemption. None, not even
the doctrine of God, can form the basis of a systematic unity, for God
is known only in his action, in differentiation. In one place Barth then
changes his vocabulary, speaking of a primary autonomy predicated of
God as opposed to the secondary autonomy of dogmatic thought.

AUTONOMY IN THE DOCTRINE OF ELECTION

Man as subject: Jesus Christ

In the doctrine of Election, Barth employs the term 'autonomy' to
articulate the freedom of man before God. God acts in his election as a

free subject, in unconditioned sovereignty, and his election is prior to any choice that man could make. But he freely chooses man and wills not to be without him.[56] The act of election does not exhaust itself in God's activity but in it there begins the encounter between God and man. Over against himself, God creates man. His election affirms man's existence, summons and awakens faith and in faith encounters a human decision:

Such is God's activity in predestination in so far as He is its Subject. But it is not the whole of this activity. In it there begins the history, encounter and decision between Himself and man. For the fulfilment of the election involves the affirmation of the existence of elected man and its counterpart in man's election, in which God's election evokes and awakens faith, and meets and answers that faith as human decision. The electing God creates for Himself as such man over against Himself. And this means that for his part man can and actually does elect God, thus attesting and activating himself as elected man. He can and actually does accept the self-giving of God in its twofold sense, and on the basis of this self-giving he has his true life. There is, then, a simple but comprehensive autonomy of the creature which is constituted originally by the act of eternal divine election and which has in this act its ultimate reality.[57]

God's election of man is mirrored in man's corresponding election of God, a human act in which man possesses and exercises his own life and his own power of decision. Characteristically, Barth immediately qualifies his affirmation with several sentences emphasising the priority, freedom and sovereignty of God in the election: 'as the One who elects God has absolute precedence over the One who is elected' . . . 'All that man can and will do is to pray, to follow and to obey'.[58] Nonetheless, without competing with or taking from God's sovereignty in the slightest, Barth wishes to affirm at this point the autonomy of man.

This autonomy is characterised as the 'autonomy of the creature', that is as an autonomy consistent with man having been put into existence by God. However, we are not dealing here with Creation in general nor with man in general. The scope of the statement is defined by the theological theme most characteristic of the *Church Dogmatics*: the man elected by God and autonomous before him is Jesus Christ.[59] Precisely because of the identity between God and Christ Barth can here omit the third term of the triad in which he had defined the relationship between the Word of God and the dogmatic theologian. Here there is no mention of heteronomy. Instead God's action and man's response – theonomy and autonomy – dovetail in a problem-free correspondence (Entsprechung). In Jesus Christ there is no need to maintain a diastasis between God and man:

The honour of the Son of Man adopted to union with the Son of God can and will consist only in promoting the honour of His heavenly Father. Only as the Son of Man is adopted into this union can He receive, receive His own task, receive the co-operation in suffering which is laid upon Him, receive finally the attestation from above and His own exaltation and glorification. 'Not my will, but thine, be done.' And this certainly means theonomy, the lordship of God at every point.[60]

The treatment of the prayer of Jesus in Gethsemane in the course of the *Church Dogmatics* confirms that Barth does not allow a heteronomy between Jesus and the divine will. In the section devoted to Gethsemane in *KD* IV/1, Barth distinguishes what Jesus wishes from what he wills: 'for, according to the sense of the texts, we cannot speak of any intention which was opposed to that of God and which he then renounces'. Barth's emphasis here, as in almost all of the places in which he uses the text, is on the outcome of the prayer: 'a radiant Yes'. It is here that Jesus' decision is made and here that his freedom is exercised – in prayer! The only suggestion of heteronomy, a suggestion that God's will at this point remains external to Jesus and has the character of a demand from without, occurs in the phrase: 'he does not cease to allow that God is in the right, even against Himself'. But even here Barth knows how to turn the apparent counterargument into an argument in his favour: 'This prayer is, as it were, a remarkable historical complement to the eternal decision taken in God Himself, one which was not taken easily, but with great difficulty.' The suggestion of heteronomy is read back into God himself and what Jesus experiences is now a confirmation of his perfect identity with God and God's will: 'And, of course, the question of the Crucified: Had God forsaken him? (Mk 15:34), points even more strongly in the same direction'![61] Ulrich Hedinger draws a particularly striking contrast with Tillich: Barth could never incorporate the freedom of Jesus into the phenomenon of human freedom, as Tillich did in the case of Jesus' temptations. Barth's whole ductus demands that freedom be understood not in terms of the human phenomenon but only in terms of Christ and his obedience. The difficulty with Barth's concept will arise, as we shall see, when he tries to approach the human phenomenon of freedom in its necessary distinction from the freedom of Christ.[62]

In affirming the autonomy of man in these terms while maintaining the sovereignty of God, Barth feels the need to repudiate the charge of a divine egoism in God's relationship with man: 'Yet we must not emphasise any less strongly that the motive for this establishment of the kingdom is not in any sense an autocratic self-seeking, but a love which directs itself outwards, a self-giving to the creature.' God seeks himself and reveals himself in all his actions and their goodness consists in that, but in doing so he really gives himself and this giving means a genuine independence on the part of the creature: 'But He wills and fulfils and reveals Himself not only in Himself but in giving Himself, in willing and recognising the distinct reality of the creature, granting and conceding to it an individual and autonomous (selbständig) place side by side with Himself.'[63]

The identity and independence (Barth no longer uses the term 'autonomy' here, which occurs in the English translation) can only be granted by God. Any other would be demonic, an independence that Barth describes in paradoxical terms as evil, something not given by God but eternally denied by him:

Naturally the individuality and autonomy are only of such a kind as His own goodness can concede and grant. God could not be God if He willed and permitted any other individuality or autonomy side by side with His own. An independent individuality or autonomy could be only devilish in character. It could belong only to evil. Evil as such does not and cannot receive any individuality or autonomy from God.[64]

Here Barth returns to the term 'obedience' among others (confirmation, glorification) in contrast to rivalry with God or mere subjection to his will like that of a puppet or a slave:

To the creature God determined, therefore, to give an individuality and autonomy, not that these gifts should be possessed outside Him, let alone against Him, but for Him, and within His kingdom, not in rivalry with His sovereignty but for its confirming and glorifying. But the sovereignty which was to be confirmed and glorified was the sovereignty of His love, which did not will to exercise mechanical force, to move the immobile from without, to rule over puppets or slaves, but willed rather to triumph in faithful servants and friends, not in their overthrow, but in their obedience, in their own free decision for him.[65]

Barth appeals to Jesus' words and actions, to his unheard-of claims, as evidence of a freedom coexisting with, or rather consisting in, obedience. Barth can affirm Jesus as a free subject not in spite of, but precisely because of, his being moved by God:

The perfection of God's giving of Himself to man in the person of Jesus Christ consists in the fact that far from merely playing with man, far from merely moving or using him, far from merely dealing with him as an object, this self-giving sets man up as a subject, awakens him to genuine individuality and autonomy, frees him, makes him a king, so that in his rule the kingly rule of God Himself attains form and revelation.[66]

Here competition is ruled out; theonomy and autonomy combine in perfect harmony: 'How can there be any possible rivalry here? ... How can there be any question of a conflict between theonomy and autonomy?'[67] Precisely because of his recognition of God's precedence, in his 'responsibility' as Barth characterises it, Jesus Christ is himself a sovereign independent being (Wesen) in the realm of creation.[68]

The characteristic attitude of the autonomous creature, Jesus Christ, is no longer characterised simply as obedience but as prayer. The autonomous man is Jesus Christ in his prayer. Prayer is the activity in which the human being may stake the only claim he is entitled to make, but in staking it he can nonetheless be called a ruler:

God's eternal will is the act of prayer (in which confidence in self gives way before confidence in God). This act is the birth of a genuine human self-awareness, in which knowledge and action can and must be attempted; in which there drops away all fear of what is above or beside or below man, of what might assault or threaten him; in which man becomes heir to a legitimate and necessary and therefore an effective and triumphant claim; in which man may rule in that he is willing to serve.[69]

Summary

A wealth of theological themes transforms and develops Barth's treatment of autonomy in the doctrine of Election. Autonomy is affirmed in Barth's insistence on the independence of the creature in its own existence and individuality, its own decision, choice, action and knowledge. At the same time its link with God receives a double specification. It owes its entire existence, including its freedom and independence, to the divine initiative, an initiative in the form of a free decision, motivated by love, which excludes any other basis of existence for the creature. It exercises its existence, independence and freedom in accepting and affirming the choice made first by God, in responding to it in an obedience which corresponds to God's initiative in which alone its freedom can consist. Any other possibility is unreal. The reality of this creaturely autonomy and its perfect correspondence to God's rule, to theonomy, can be affirmed in Jesus Christ, whose identity with God excludes the possibility of an element of heteronomy in their relationship. The exclusive divine initiative motivated by love, Christology as the core of anthropology, the rejection of any understanding of human existence apart from Christ, and the notion of correspondence (Entsprechung) between God's action and man's response, themes which dominate in the further development of the *Church Dogmatics*, are all incorporated here in the 'autonomy of the creature'.

THE DOCTRINE OF CREATION: AGAINST RIVAL CONCEPTS OF AUTONOMY

Man without God: Fichte as a warning example

Barth reckons with concepts of man's identity and independence that are not identical with the obedient autonomy that corresponds to God's initiative. In writing of this alternative to his concept of autonomy, Barth generally does not use the term 'autonomy' but rather equivalent terms: 'Eigenheit und Selbständigkeit',[70] 'menschliches Selbstvertrauen',[71] 'Eigengesetzlichkeit . . . Selbstbehauptung',[72] 'eigenmächtiges . . . Denken',[73] 'Mündigkeit'.[74] In this tendency to avoid the term 'autonomy' in a negative sense there is a parallel with Fichte's tendency to prefer other terms to 'autonomy' such as 'Selbstbestimmung', 'Selbständigkeit', or 'Selbsttätigkeit'. Barth does in fact in this context discuss and dismiss Fichte's anthropology.

Barth understands Fichte as a warning example, a *Gegenbeispiel* to his own anthropology, an example in which the impossibility of a non-theological understanding of man and his freedom may be demonstrated. Barth is not unsympathetic to Fichte's point of view. He believes that Fichte's starting-point, the perception of man's ethical freedom as opposed to his determination by nature, represents a genuine human phenomenon.[75] However, on the claims made by Fichte for the significance of this phenomenon Barth registers a sceptical judgement.

It is Fichte's method of postulating his basic premises on the basis of practical reason on account of the impossibility of reaching a satisfactory solution on the basis of theoretical reason that offers Barth the ground for his attack. In view of Fichte's ability to argue for a complete determinism, Barth asks by what right the opposing voice of freedom can be heard. In view of Fichte's affirmation of the circular character of knowledge and consciousness, image and reality in which the Ego is unable to define its own limits, Barth asks whether Fichte's Idealism is in fact consistent with the notion of a step into freedom. The step into freedom becomes a paradox: 'in spite of everything he trusts in the protest of his inner voice in a way which his naive self-knowledge forbids'.[76]

Barth concedes for the sake of argument that the step into freedom might be made. Barth's question is then how Fichte can at once affirm, with the step into freedom, that man can claim to posit the universe, to be superior to everything that is external to himself including death, and to regard this and all possible worlds to be his possession and at his disposal. Fichte presents an exemplary account of man's self-discovery as an ethical being. But in Barth's view he loses sight of this phenomenon in identifying the ethical subject with the stream of life or the one eternal life force. The ethical phenomenon of man is simply not identical with man in a sovereign unity with the totality that exists apart from him.[77]

Underlying the later Fichte's disregard for the phenomenon of human individuality in his attempt to conceive of an absolute subject is his failure from the earliest beginnings of his philosophy to face the question of the limitations of the empirical human subject:

It is obviously at this point that the weakness which from the very outset vitiated Fichte's view of man is avenged, viz., the lack of a limit, the fundamental lack of a counterpart, the absolute subjectivity to which his man was condemned from the very first.[78]

In suggesting a motive for this failure, Barth renews the charge of atheism against Fichte:

We have already said several times that Fichte had some reason for trying to work exclusively with this presupposed idea of the autarchy, the absolute subjectivity of man. The reason is quite simple. Fichte was determined to view man apart from God.[79]

Barth does not intend to contest the fact that Fichte philosophised at great length on the divine and disputed vehemently the charge of atheism. But the divine that Fichte affirms is not the God of Christianity, and Barth, employing the same argument which he uses against natural theology, identifies Fichte's divinity with man himself:

A Fichtean dialogue can only be an alternative form of monologue − a form which may occasionally be interesting and desirable because Fichtean man is both subject and object, both I and Thou, and because there are contexts in which this fact must be brought out. A God to whom man belongs as to another; a God who can act in relation to man and become his Saviour; a God who has His own glory in which the essential concern of man is to be seen; a God who reigns; a God in relation to whom man gains his freedom and whom he must serve in his freedom; a God who confronts and limits man and is thus his true determination, is for Fichte non-existent. Fichte's god is Fichte's man, and Fichte's man is Fichte's god.[80]

This is why Barth sees in Fichte a warning example and why, in relation to Fichte, he employs terms equivalent to 'autonomous' that possess for Barth the strongest negative overtones: 'autark', 'souverän', '[s]ein eigenes Geschöpf', 'absolut innerlich', 'prinzipielle Verschlossenheit', 'sich selbst verfügbar'.[81] Barth agrees with Fichte only insofar as both affirm the Kantian philosophy of practical reason in relation to the ethical phenomenon of man and both affirm the Kantian antinomies of the theoretical reason.

Barth's negative judgement on Fichte forms part of his presentation of the development of modern thought as a whole. The characteristic of modern man is his 'absolutism', by which Barth means his attempt to understand and control his own existence and only secondarily and incidentally and purely in corroboration of his own competence to refer to God.[82] This was 'the spirit of all European humanity as developed since the sixteenth century', the spirit of Descartes, Leibniz, Goethe, Kant, Fichte, Schelling, Hegel and Nietzsche. It was the logic of man alone, without God, ultimately without his fellow-man as Barth said of Nietzsche.[83] It was the spirit of natural theology, insofar as man ascribed to himself the capacity to know God without having recourse to God's own self-revelation. It included the attempt of German Idealism to understand Revelation as the culmination of natural knowledge, which was an education to Titanism. Man was punished for this Titanism by falling back into a vicious circle in which dogmatism alternated with scepticism in a dialectic of certainty and uncertainty. In the absence of the divine subject in relation to whom man can be defined and without whom he cannot know his own boundaries, man is compelled to project himself into the infinite and make an absolute of his own being.[84] But, as Karl-Gerhard Steck remarked, Barth did not lay the blame on the 'evil world' as did the Popes since the 1830s and the critics of modern culture. Unlike them, he did not expect natural man to behave any other way: this is his spontaneous tendency. Instead Barth places the blame exclusively on the theologians and the Church in their failure to maintain the distinctive claims of Revelation.[85] In a biting satire he attacked the theology of secularisation and demythologisation for its concessions to autonomous man.[86]

SUMMARY

Barth wrestles with other concepts of autonomy. Fichte is treated as a warning example. Fichte's affirmation of freedom was a mere postulate made in the face of scientific determinism. Yet once it was made, Fichte claimed to be one with the subject that posited the universe and superior to all that was external to himself. The Fichtean subject had no limit and no counterpart. Thus Fichte rejected the God of Christianity because he was other than man.

Modern man is a Fichtean absolutist who claims to be master of his own existence. German Idealism treated Revelation as the culmination of man's natural knowledge. It was an education to Titanism. Modern man no longer knows his own boundaries and in consequence is caught in a vicious circle of dogmatism and scepticism, of certainty and uncertainty. Barth does not waste time in blaming the world for this; instead he blames theology and the Church for failing to preach the full message of Revelation.

Existentialism and autonomous self-understanding

The recognition of a fundamental limitation of man's horizon in existentialist philosophy and of man's confrontation at that limit with the mystery of a transcendent other is, Barth concedes, a significant step beyond Fichte's Idealism and shows striking parallels to Christian theology, particularly that of Luther.[87] Barth pays particular attention here to Karl Jaspers. Jaspers appears in his philosophy to fulfil some of the conditions set by Barth for a knowledge of man: he affirms a limitation of man's horizon and at this horizon the discovery (in the limit-situations) of a transcendent other with which man is confronted. Barth rejects the interpretation, however, that sees in this philosophy the realisation of significant elements of the Christian tradition. Traces of this tradition are indeed visible in Jaspers's philosophy – it evidently grew up in the shadow of Christianity. It speaks of man's being as a dynamic movement based on openness, as an act in relation to an other-than-himself and in encounter with this other rather than as self-grounded. But its account of this 'other' is vague, a vagueness which the talk of 'limit-situations' cannot dispel.[88]

Jaspers's 'other' is not genuinely other, that is it is still a question, not an answer. It is indefinable and cannot be objectified. It could, suggests Barth with a play on the famous question of Descartes, just as well be an evil demon who deceives us as a gracious God. Jaspers assures us that it is 'the wholly other' but 'in this connexion he has nothing to offer except this solemn assertion'. In any case the primary referent here is man's subjectivity: 'we should remember that the problem of this transcendence is such that first and last we seek in it *ourselves* – the answer which it is the business of *our* existence to find'.[89] Man's questioning cries out for an answer and if this answer is not forthcoming in the form of a genuine 'other', then man is alone in the field, absolute and self-sufficient: 'we should again be understanding man in search of himself and therefore transcending himself as a self-contained and complete reality.[90]

The unconditional trust to which man is supposed to be called in the limit-situations betrays the same ambiguity. It presents itself according to Jaspers as the result of a decision, but a decision which might just as well go the other way and consist in the refusal to trust or to surrender oneself. Barth again asks if, in view of this ambiguity, this transcendence is genuine, and suggests that, along with the alternative of heroic self-surrender or Titanic refusal to trust, the human possibility of apathy, indifference and resignation must be seriously considered. Man is not confined to the alternative of being either religious or anti-religious: he can be religiously indifferent even in limit-situations.[91]

Furthermore, it is affirmed that man is capable of making this act of unconditional self-surrender, of absolute trust. But if this is so, argues Barth, man already carries this self-transcendence within himself. Transcendence does not need to come to man from without, strictly speaking it cannot do so. Man simply discovers in himself his own self-transcendence. For Barth this means that every step of this philosophy is thereby falsified: man's existence does not consist in a search; he does not exist in self-transcendence; he does not genuinely encounter the other.

There is here no real distinction between existence and transcendence; despite the original intention of existentialism we are dealing with a closed and comprehensive human reality beyond which there is nothing, certainly nothing like a God distinct from and superior to man and the world.[92]

It is notable that here again Barth, arguing back from Christian Revelation, makes axiomatic use of the distinction between God the subject and man the subject. God is genuinely other than man and his gracious self-revelation makes it possible for man to encounter what is genuinely other than himself, to respond to it and in the process to achieve self-definition, that is the awareness of his limits over against God and the world. This arguing back from Christian Revelation reveals the form of transcendence described by Jaspers in its character of immanence and subjectivity. The assertion of an encounter with a mysterious and transcendent other must be qualified by Jaspers with the observation that this 'other' remains beyond man's horizon. The sense of the encounter with the transcendent is thus concentrated in man's confrontation with his own limitations and the unlimited self-surrender which he may (or may not) exercise in the outcome of a struggle with himself. In the sense in which one might speak of autonomy in this context, it is not the autonomy of the absolute subject who posits the universe and is therefore superior to all its vicissitudes, but that of the existential subject who must rise above his limitations and his angst because he is left alone with them in an enigmatic universe. The existential subject is condemned to autarchy – self-sufficiency – as a fate which he cannot escape. It is not a question of his exercising autonomy or not within the context of a universe governed by laws or created by a gracious God. The die is already cast, not to choose is to choose and the only question is the quality of the inevitable choice.

THE 'AUTONOMOUS' PERSPECTIVE:
PHENOMENA AND REALITY

With some hesitation about this use of the term (the first use of 'autonom' in this context is placed in quotation marks) Barth defines his position in regard to man's self-understanding outside the context of theology:

In this sub-section we have spoken of man's attempt to understand himself when he is presumed to be able to do so in his own strength and by his own resources. The naturalistic, ethical and existential views of man are the most important stages on the way of this autonomous self-understanding.[93]

Barth's response to these anthropological perspectives is not simply 'no'. It is in fact a qualified 'yes'. It is 'yes' insofar as natural science, ethics and existentialism correctly describe certain human phenomena. It is 'no' insofar as these perspectives might claim to reveal more than these phenomena. From the purely human perspective man sees no more than these phenomena, which he interprets one way or another. But they cannot be seen in proper perspective until they are revealed in the light of the Word of God. Although Barth refuses to base his theology on anything outside Revelation, he sees in his analysis of these other anthropological perspectives a *confirmation* of the theological premise that the reality about man can be seen only in the light of Revelation.

We can only dispute from the outset the supposition that any understanding of real man can be attained at all by man's autonomous attempt at self-understanding in any of its phases. And in any case we have found this presupposition to be confirmed by the inner incompleteness and obscurity, the self-contradiction, of the portrait of man which has emerged at every stage of this path and in the total result.[94]

Everything which can be thought and said about man reads like a commentary on an unseen text which must first be read before the commentary makes sense. Within the proper context, that of divine Revelation, the human phenomena fit into place; they refer to a reality which does not become apparent on the path of autonomous human self-understanding; in the light of this reality they can be called symptoms of the reality of man, that is their relation to the reality is apparent. Outside of the knowledge of this reality the circle of man's autonomous self-understanding is not broken.[95]

What man sees within the 'autonomous perspective' can therefore be affirmed even though it is not properly understood outside of the context of Revelation. It is a 'relative' autonomy that can be affirmed, because it allows of another level of discourse:

Very generally, the difference consists in the fact that the sovereignty in which man claims to know himself is renounced, or rather that it is regarded as relative rather than absolute. Hence it is seen that, while the conclusions of autonomous human self-understanding are not necessarily false, but in their limits may well be accurate and important, they are all bracketed, and no decisive enlightenment about man is expected from within these brackets, but only from a source outside. This source is God. He, the Creator of man, knows who and what man is. For man is His creature, and therefore in the last resort known to Him alone. He must tell man who and what he really is if this is to be known to him.[96]

Here Barth binds the talk of 'autonomous' self-knowledge in natural science, ethics and existentialist philosophy into his own concept of autonomy. What can be affirmed is not sovereign or absolute autonomy, or autarchy, but a relative autonomy which stands in relationship to Revelation. Within the perspective of Revelation the autonomous human subject is enabled to perceive his limits. And this is the point at which phenomenon and reality are distinguished. Here autonomous man knows of the all-embracing reality which ontically and noetically grounds his being and his knowledge. He and his world are a reality distinct from God but created by him, and this relationship cannot be thought away because it is not peripheral to man but is constitutive of his reality.[97]

SUMMARY

Unlike Idealism, existentialism recognises the human limitations. Karl Jaspers's theme of openness and encounter with the other bears many resemblances to Christianity. But the 'other', in Barth's view, is vague, a question rather than an answer. Ultimately the existential other leaves man alone. The primary referent is still our human subjectivity. Man's self-transcendence in existentialism presupposes both his aloneness and self-sufficiency and his ability to make an act of unconditional trust. Ultimately he makes his own act of self-transcendence, which means for Barth that he does not genuinely encounter the other in the radical way that characterises Christian Revelation. The existential subject is condemned to self-sufficiency.

Barth does, however, give a qualified 'yes' to the self-understanding acquired by man through natural science, ethics and existentialism. There, phenomena or symptoms of human existence are correctly described. Once no claim is being made to a human sovereignty or self-sufficiency the findings of natural science or philosophy can be affirmed. But they are seen in their proper perspective only in the Revelation that comes from God. Here man is enabled to perceive his limits and see all else within the relationship of God to him that is constitutive of his reality.

Freedom, subjectivity, correspondence, the analogy of relation, the Christological foundation of anthropology

In his theological anthropology Barth develops several themes intimately related to the 'autonomy of the creature', without making further use of the *term* 'autonomy'. The development of his thought at these points is important for the understanding of his use of the term in the last published fragment of the *Church Dogmatics*, the doctrine of Baptism.

It is exclusively in terms of Revelation that Barth wishes to understand human freedom and subjectivity and with that the being of man himself. The concept of freedom is so comprehensive, he argues, that it forms the limit of what can be said of man. Freedom he describes as man's being in responsibility before God. This freedom is constituted and given by God, who alone is originally free. It constitutes the being of man and therefore real humanity. It is thus the decisive definition of man as subject. Man is first of all object, something posited in its own being by another, namely God. But in that very fact he is also subject because 'among all the objects posited by God it is the characteristic mode of this one to posit itself and therefore to be subject'. Man is the only creature whom God calls to free personal responsibility before him. This is his objective being. Man exists insofar as he decides for God. He is active, not static, not passive. Barth adopts the notion of man's being as act and as decision, as in Idealism and existentialism. But it is used exclusively of the act of his relationship to God and not apart from this: 'Man is, as he knows God; he is, as he decides for God.' The freedom that constitutes his being means the freedom actualised in the event of his knowledge of and obedience to God. It has no existence prior to or apart from this: 'The human subject is not a substance with certain qualities or functions. It is the self-moving and self-moved subject in responsibility before God, or it is not a subject at all.' Real man is his history as enacted before God; here he is free, a subject, himself – not otherwise.[98]

Thus although Barth otherwise rejects the notion of freedom of choice he can accept it here, but only insofar as a definite choice for God is made: 'It is certainly freedom of choice . . . it is the freedom of the right choice.' For freedom only exists insofar as it is exercised here. To choose this is to choose oneself in one's possibility, being and freedom. To choose otherwise would not be to choose freely; it would not be to posit oneself but to betray oneself. This freedom includes man's preservation from evil: 'potest non peccare, non potest peccare'. This choice is that which corresponds to the free choice made by God.[99]

We have seen how in the doctrine of Election Barth articulated the autonomy of the creature in terms of a problem-free correspondence

(Entsprechung) between the will of the Father and Jesus Christ in his humanity. Barth makes further use of this notion in articulating the relationship between Christology and anthropology. Jesus' being is totally for God and totally for his fellow-man. Here, even though Jesus lets his own being be determined by the need of another, alien being, there is again no shadow of heteronomy. Jesus cannot even be called selfless because in this way he is supremely himself. His existence is identical with his work. In his divinity he comes from and is directed to God and in his humanity he comes from and is directed to the cosmos. His humanity corresponds exactly to his divinity, mirroring and reflecting it. There results a similarity in which each is to be recognised in the other in a twofold determination of the one by the other. Yet both remain strictly distinct, in words that echo the council of Chalcedon: 'without admixture or change, and yet also without separation or limitation'.[100]

This formal parallelism involves an inner material connection between the divinity and the humanity of Christ. Jesus' being for his fellow human beings is not arbitrary. It is founded on the inner being of God, to whom being-in-relationship belongs as his nature. There is thus established a set or ladder of relationships between God and man: the inner relationships of the Trinity are mirrored in the relationship *ad extra* between God and the humanity of Christ and this in turn in the relationship between Christ and his fellow-men. The set of relationships can be continued: there is a further reflection in the relationship between man and his fellow-men.[101] Barth chooses this notion of correspondence and relationship as the one and only articulation of the analogy between God and man. It is an analogy of relation (analogia relationis). It is opposed to an analogy of being since the being of God cannot be compared with that of man (an argument which again shows that Barth believes that the analogy of being consisted in such a comparison). The comparison is between the relationships. It consists in the fact that the freedom in which God posits himself is the same freedom as that in which he is the Creator of man. The eternal love within the Trinity is the same love which is addressed by God to man.[102] The point of comparison is therefore not being but freedom and love which are clearly rooted in the subjectivity of God, which again shows itself to be one of the fundamental criteria for Barth's thinking.

The ladder of relationships leads downwards until it establishes criteria for the humanity of man. It also leads upwards from Revelation in Christ to the being of God himself. Barth argues that there is nothing arbitrary or accidental in the freedom of God for man, but that here God is true to himself. The mystery of God is not a riddle but is full of meaning and wisdom. The relationship with man is not alien but 'we might almost say appropriate and natural' to God. Yet Barth is careful to emphasise that the humanity of Jesus is not directly but only indirectly identical with God. It belongs to the creaturely world, to the outer sphere of the work of God. It is not an identity. Here the correspondence is that of a disparity: total sovereignty on God's part and total dependence on man's.[103]

In the humanity of Christ God repeats in a relationship *ad extra* a relationship proper to himself in his inner divine essence, in the Trinity. There he posits himself, is posited and is himself in both. He is the Lover, the Loved and the Love. The repetition of the inner divine essence in Jesus Christ is the true and original correspondence and similarity (Urentsprechung, Urähnlichkeit) between his divinity and humanity and the foundation for the ontological character of the being of Jesus for his fellow-men. Barth then argues, not without some awkwardness, that if Jesus' being is for his fellow-men there must again be correspondence between this being and the being of all men. At least God cannot have given them a nature that would be in contradiction to, or alien or even neutral in regard to Jesus Christ. They need not and cannot be identical with Jesus Christ but they are destined to become the covenant-partners of God in him. What they are in this relationship is not real in themselves but in him. This means – according to the axiomatic and exclusive argument characteristic of Barth – that no other picture of humanity can be used as a starting-point. Since (this is the implicit argument) there can be only one principle and one starting-point in any argument, the truth about man can be established only here. There can be only one constant and certain factor: in theological anthropology what man is is decided by the humanity of the man Jesus. The humanity of Jesus is the basic form of humanity and the criterion for all statements about human nature.[104]

The freedom and subjectivity of man is constituted in his being called to responsibility before God, in the act of his relationship to God, as we have seen. This statement is equivalent to saying that man's freedom and subjectivity is constituted in Jesus Christ, in whom alone man is related to God. It is also equivalent to the doctrine of Justification. Man does not attain his humanity, as in Idealism or existentialism, through an endless ethical effort based in a conflict between nature and freedom. The autonomy of the creature is the act of the subject that abandons the ethical Ego in order to find itself in the judgement of God alone. The basic act of subjectivity and of the practical reason is therefore prayer.[105] Barth not only tries to derive all significant statements about man (*real* man) in the anthropological field from Christology but also all ethical statements. In this he is only partially successful: the principle is illuminating but remains too formal. The concrete material determinations lean heavily on experiential and empirical observations; there results a phenomenology that Barth formally rejects but admits – even explicitly! – in practice.[106]

The ontological character of Barth's language about the reality of man in Jesus Christ, as opposed to a humanity that exists for itself apart from Christ, has given rise to the speculation that Barth affirms of the relationship between Christ and other men something akin to the hypostatic union between the humanity of Christ and his divinity. Just as it can be argued that the anhypostasis of the humanity of Christ and its enhypostasis in the Logos take nothing from the humanity but actualise it and set it free, so the foundation of man's being (Dasein) outside of himself and in Christ would make him truly human. It leads to no loss of identity but merely to the surrender of his autonomous egoistic being (Dasein) and thus to a true creaturely independence.[107] The precise meaning of and justification for such statements about Barth's anthropology is a matter of dispute, to which we return in chapter 2. What can be said here is that Barth derives no direct answer to the question about man from Christology nor does he allow of one derived from man's self-understanding. He first asks about the humanity of Christ and then talks about man as a consequence of and in analogy to Christology.[108] Barth consistently underplays the question about man's being as such in favour of a concentration on its meaning and goal in Christ just as he seeks to underplay nature in favour of grace.[109]

SUMMARY

Barth attaches a relative insignificance to anthropological statements made on scientific and philosophical grounds. The truly significant statements about man are to be made on a theological basis. Freedom is to be understood as responsibility before God and as such constitutes the being of man. The human being is first an object, posited by God, but the character of this object is in turn to posit itself and be a subject. Barth defines being as act and decision, just as in Idealism and existentialism, but for Barth the definition is true exclusively within the relationship with God. Man has no existence prior to or apart from this relationship. Freedom exists only insofar as a person decides for God.

Autonomy without heteronomy is a reality in the problem-free correspondence between Jesus' divinity and his humanity. This is one of a ladder of relationships that begins in the inner-trinitarian being of God, extending to God's outward relationship with the humanity of Christ, then to Christ's relationship with his fellow human beings, and to their relationship with one another. The point of comparison in all these correspondences is not being as such but the freedom and love that is rooted in the subjectivity of God. This ladder of relationships establishes criteria for the humanity of man. The being of Jesus has a constitutive ontological character for humanity. It constitutes the one truth about humanity from which all other statements must be derived. Human freedom and subjectivity are constituted exclusively in relationship to Christ, not on the basis of ethical effort, but on that of Justification. The human being must abandon his pretensions to an ethical Ego in order to find himself in the judgement of God alone. The basic act of human subjectivity is, then, prayer. Anthropology is not Christology as such, but is a consequence of and in analogy to Christology.

THE DOCTRINE OF RECONCILIATION: CORRESPONDENCE AND DISTINCTION BETWEEN GOD AND MAN

Correspondence and distinction between Christ and other men

The notion of correspondence and the formal parallelism which it allows is the structural principle on which Barth builds his doctrine of Reconciliation. To the humility of the Son of God corresponds the exaltation of the Son of Man, to the Lord as servant corresponds the servant as Lord. The unity of both aspects can function as a third term that allows the integration of traditional triplets into the scheme such as the threefold office of Christ or the theological virtues. There results a greater degree of systematisation in the doctrine of Reconciliation than in the other parts of the *Church Dogmatics*.[110] Correspondence allows not only the mutual determination and convergence of Christology and anthropology but also an antithetical parallelism in which polar opposites may reflect one another and thus establish and maintain radical distinctions.

In this way Barth sharply distinguishes the humanity of Jesus Christ from his divinity. The human nature of Christ is not divinised or invested wtih divine qualities. Following the Reformed tradition Barth rejects the Lutheran doctrine of the *communicatio idiomatum*, more specifically the subdivision of this doctrine, the *genus majestaticum*. The notion of a divinised human nature of Christ, deserving of our worship, leads, Barth argues, to German Idealism and the subsequent anthropocentric theology.[111] In order to bar the door to any form of divinisation of man Barth is compelled to place Christ's humanity below with man.

Barth prefers to explicate the determination of the human nature of Christ in terms of a *communicatio gratiarum*, 'the total and exclusive determination of the human nature of Jesus Christ by the grace of God', and asks why that should be too little.[112] This determination through grace corresponds to the obedience (humility) of the Son of God. The exaltation of the Son of Man means the realisation of an analogical human existence that corresponds to the obedience of the Son of God and therefore to Barth's idea of human autonomy. In this Jesus Christ proves himself to be the true man. Similarity and dissimilarity are here so combined that Barth's claim that the humanity of Christ represents the criterion for all humanity is reinforced rather than diminished:

But it does not alter the human essence that it becomes the recipient, the only and exclusive recipient [exclusively and utterly the recipient], of the electing grace of God. The likeness between the Son of Man, Jesus Christ, and us is not broken by the fact that He confronts us in this unlikeness. On the contrary, as the recipient of the electing grace of God, His human essence is proved by its exaltation to be the true essence of all men.

It is genuinely human in the deepest sense to live by the electing grace of God addressed to man. This is how Jesus Christ lives as the Son of Man. In this He is the Mediator between God and us men in the power of His identity with the Son of God and therefore in the power of His divinity . . . How can this fail to be the supreme thing that can be said of His human essence, and therefore that which also distinguishes Him from all other men?[113]

The differences between our human nature and that of Christ lie in the title, not just the degree, in which the same nature is determined by the divine grace:

He is totally unlike even the most saintly among us in the fact that His human essence alone is fully, because from the very outset, determined by the grace of God. This is the qualitatively different determination of His human essence, and of His alone as that of the One who as the Son of Man is also and primarily the Son of God. But he is like us in the fact that His human essence determined in this way is in fact the same as ours.[114]

Autonomy, profane humanity and the cosmos: the prophetic office of Christ

In the third part-volume of the doctrine of Reconciliation (*KD* IV/3) Barth explicates the prophetic office of Jesus Christ. He declares the existence of Jesus Christ the Reconciler to be the central point from which everything else must be understood: God (who reveals himself exclusively in Christ), man and the world.[115] This theme now drives Barth to explicate the universal scope of Reconciliation and to relate Christ to humanity outside the limits of the Christian community and to the cosmos, the world of Creation considered apart from man. He speaks of the unity of the order of Creation with the order of Reconciliation:

As Jesus Christ lives, God and man live in this conjunction. We do not have God here and man there; God is the God of man and man is the man of God. This is the epitome of the whole order of creation. This order, too, has its dignity, validity, power and persistence in the fact that Jesus Christ lives. But it has its content and fulness in the fact that the life lived by Jesus Christ is the life of grace, that it is the life of the Saviour. From the standpoint of this content and fulness, the one order of God is the order of reconciliation. As such it is more than the order of creation, since it is the free order of the mercy in which God is not content merely to be with man as in some sense his great Neighbour, but in which, even though man is a poor and bad neighbour who has forfeited rather than deserved it, He goes and comes to him, to take him to Himself in His own person, not merely as one who is conjoined with Him, but as one who is His faithful covenant-partner. Yet as the order of reconciliation it is also the confirmation and restoration of the order of creation. The eternal meaning and content of the order of creation are worked out in the one order of God in the fact that this order is also that of reconciliation. The unity of the two, the transcending and restoring of creation in reconciliation, or, as we might say, the unity of the form and content of the one order of God, is event and reality in the fact that Jesus lives.[116]

Evidently the explication of this one order of Reconciliation and Creation will once again throw up the question of the autonomy of man and the world in relation to God. Especially important in this connection is the discussion in *KD* IV/3 of the distinction between Jesus Christ as the Light of Life and the other lights which may be perceived in the world. This discussion is preceded by and linked with the treatment of words of divine Revelation that may be heard in the world outside of the Christian community, *extra muros ecclesiae*.[117] The keynote of Barth's exposition of both these questions is already given in the thesis which opens the chapter: 'Jesus Christ as attested to us in Holy Scripture is the one Word of God whom we must hear and whom we must trust and obey in life and in death.' It is a quotation of part of the first thesis of the Barmen Synod of 1934 in which Barth's rejection of all natural theology was adopted as their theological rationale by those who resisted the inroads of National Socialist ideology into the German Protestant Church.[118] Barth wishes to reaffirm this point of view and to allow of only one source of Revelation – Jesus Christ.[119]

True words *extra muros ecclesiae*

Barth distinguishes three forms of the Word of God. The primary and unique Word of God is Jesus Christ. But beside him other words may also be true (in the sense of Revelation) without being identical with him and without losing their entirely creaturely character and the human problematic that attaches to them. Barth places the Scriptures and the proclamation of the Church in this category, as a secondary form of the Word of God. A third form is then given with the possibility of similarly true words being spoken *extra muros ecclesiae*. The criteria which Barth sets for their being in this sense true ensure that they confirm rather than in any sense challenge the exclusive claim of Revelation in Jesus Christ:

To this question our first and general answer must be that in order to be true, and therefore to be words of genuine prophecy, such words must be in the closest material and substantial conformity and agreement with the one Word of God Himself and therefore with that of His one Prophet Jesus Christ. The truth proper to the one Word of God must dwell within them. Applied to such words, 'true' must imply that they say the same thing as the one Word of God, and are true for this reason.[120]

Although these true words are spoken *extra muros ecclesiae* the subject of their truth is distinct from the subject that happens to speak them. As human and creaturely words they cannot declare anything of their own or claim the truth to which they bear witness for themselves. They must be distinguished from the Word of God (in this they are placed on the same footing as the biblical text or the Confessions of the Church), 'accepting the fact that it alone is truth'.[121] They must place themselves in the same autonomy, that is obedience, as the Christian witness.

The difficulty here is, of course, that these words come by definition from outside the Christian sphere. How can they bear witness to its exclusive truth? Barth's explanation is to assert a cosmic dimension to the activity of Jesus Christ in giving prophetic witness to his Word. This cosmic dimension is based on the Resurrection, the Reconciliation of the world with God, and on the power of Christ over the entire cosmos and therefore on the power of his prophetic Word. Not just the Christian community but '*de jure* all men and all creation derive from His cross, from the reconciliation accomplished in Him, and are ordained to be the theatre of His glory and therefore the recipients and bearers of His Word'.[122]

Within this context Barth places even more emphasis than before on the subjectivity of Jesus Christ and less on autonomy in the sense of free and obedient receptivity for the Word of God. It is true that Barth ruled out a subjective intention of not corresponding to the Word of God in such 'true words': 'Neither objectively nor subjectively may they have any other intention than to correspond to it and thus to confirm it.'[123] But this restriction results from the axiomatic exclusion of every hint of a natural theology; that would be in contradiction of the Word of God.[124] The 'true words' do not, however, appear always to presuppose autonomy, for Barth states that they can occur even contrary to the knowledge and the will of those who speak them. He writes of the capacity of Christ to raise up from the stones children to Abraham, whether inside or outside the Church. Inside or outside the Church Christ healed the blind, deaf and dumb, including the prophets and apostles:

We may thus expect, and count upon it, that even among those who are outside this sphere [the Church] . . . He will use His capacity to make of men, quite apart from and even in face of their own knowledge or volition, something which they could never be of themselves, namely, His witnesses.[125]

In the very few examples given by Barth one can see the difficulty that on the one hand the explicit knowledge of the Word of God in Revelation cannot be presupposed and on the other every appearance of a natural theology must be avoided. Least problematic is the paradigm of the use of inert material, in itself bereft of the necessary power of expression, as a more or less fortuitous tool of the Word of God. Such 'words' are the earthly events and realities on which Jesus draws in the New Testament parables. But Barth also takes extra-biblical examples, including the sense of the mystery of God, the depth of man's need for redemption, the sobriety of scientific or practical inquiry after the facts, enthusiastic commitment in the cause of what is right, the ability to face death without fear, readiness to understand and forgive. Barth says that he could cite more concrete examples such as historical persons and events (just as Zwingli cited Hercules, Theseus, Socrates and Cicero) but does not wish to distract from the fundamental principles by citing examples that must inevitably be problematic and debatable.[126]

Two images illustrate the relationship between these other words and the truth of the Word of God which they express. One image is that of light-reflecting material. It throws back the light at a particular angle or in a particular refraction. It draws attention to the light but everything it reflects is drawn from that light and requires to be complemented by a knowledge that the light itself exists and is the source of the illumination. Another image is that of the centre and the periphery of the circle. These other true words have the dignity, insofar as they are witness to his one truth, of being segments of the circle. They can only do so insofar as they form exact segments of this circle and so correlate with its centre, differing therefore from the segments of other circles with other centres (from other theologies, especially natural theologies). They cannot express partial truths -- the one truth of Jesus Christ cannot be divided. Neither can they express it explicitly in its unity and totality. They therefore bear *explicit* witness to the truth under a particular aspect and *implicit* witness to the whole truth.[127]

It is clear that only those who know of the entire truth can correctly understand such words. It is the Christian community that has the privilege and the task of recognising, testing and making use of these words according to the criteria suggested by Barth: by their congruence with the Bible and the Confessions of the Church, by their fruits in the world and the service they render to the building-up of the Christian community.[128] It is the Christian community that has the primary task of speaking words that are true in the sense of Revelation in the world. That they can also be spoken *extra muros* is a mystery:

The clear task of speaking such true words, and the clear promise of the necessary freedom and power, are given to the Church and thus to ourselves. We have no knowledge of any similar tasks or promises given to representatives of secular history as such. Hence we cannot see or understand how a man may be, or come to be, in a position to speak true words in this qualified sense from the outer or inner spheres of secular darkness.[129]

That this should occur is something extraordinary and often bears witness to the failure of the community to utter such words itself in fulfilment of its mission.[130]

Autonomy and profane humanity: rebuttal of Bonhoeffer's thesis

Within this context, we find mention of the profane world. Christ summons extraordinary witnesses to his truth in the profane world as well. Because it is an instance of the Word of God this witness cannot itself be 'profane' but must be an instance of 'the strange interruption of the secularism [profane character] of life in the world'.[131] Barth distinguishes two kinds of profane world. A pure, virtually absolutely profane world exists where the Gospel is unknown, not only in parts of the world where Christianity has never penetrated or has been suppressed but also within the Christian world among nominal Christians. A mixed and relative profanity is found among Christians insofar as their lives are not penetrated by the Gospel but are more or less marked by a practical atheism.[132] In relation to the first form of profanity we find Barth taking up the Bonhoeffer theme of *Mündigkeit* (the world 'come of age' – this part of the *Church Dogmatics* dates from 1959 when the discussion of this theme was well under way) and in this connection the theme of 'autonomy' as understood in Promethean atheism:

(And there is consequently a whole human world that for one reason or another is or obstinately considers itself still or once again 'of age [mündig] in relation to the Word of God though scarcely in relation to all religion. And that means a human world that considers itself sovereign.)[133]

Interesting here is the rejection by Barth of Bonhoeffer's thesis in his *Letters and Papers from Prison*. Bonhoeffer had maintained that autonomy or 'coming-of-age' represented the concrete historical truth about man today, the entirely positive culmination of a process that began in the Middle Ages and had reached its climax in his time. Man's autonomy had developed so far that he was now able to dispense with religion, which was thus revealed to be a transitional phenomenon in the history of humanity, a sign of man's immaturity, of his not having yet been 'of age'. Bonhoeffer regards autonomy as an indication of the strength of man but does not believe that it need be directed against the Word and the claims of Christ, that it need be atheistic. He calls on the Church to find ways of speaking of God in the autonomous world, to claim the world 'come of age' for Christ just as the Old Testament expressed God's claim to the positive realities of earthly life.[134]

Barth may not differ from Bonhoeffer on the claims of Christ, but he contradicts his analysis of the human situation. He doubts whether the world that claims to be of age can be free of religion (schwerlich aller Religion) and has no hesitation in affirming in profane humanity an age-old tendency and desire to make itself independent of the Word of God and to claim for itself the sovereignty that is due to Christ alone. But in doing so it bears witness not to any sort of strength but to its weakness: 'While man may deny God, according to the Word of Reconciliation, God does not deny man.' Insofar as man does so he blinds himself to the truth about himself. Promethean atheism is an attempt to be godless, but is not a concrete possibility because it has no basis: the cross of Christ has already reconciled the world to God. There is therefore no profane realm that lies outside the universal power of Christ:

Nor does the fact that he [man] does not recognise the sovereignty of Jesus Christ, and if he did would perhaps rebel against it in his autonomy, result in its losing any of its validity even in relation to him. How can it be any less probable, or even impossible, that it should actually be exercised and demonstrated in relation to him too? No Prometheanism can be effectively maintained against Jesus Christ. As the One who suffered and conquered on the cross, He has destroyed it once and for all and in all its forms. But this means that in the world reconciled by God in Jesus Christ there is no secular sphere abandoned by Him or withdrawn from His control, even where from the human standpoint it seems to approximate most dangerously to the pure and absolute form of utter godlessness. If we say that there is, we are not thinking and speaking in the light of the resurrection of Jesus Christ.[135]

Summary

Correspondence, including correspondence between God and man, is the structural principle on which Barth builds his doctrine of Reconciliation. But correspondence means not only the mutual determination and convergence of Christology and anthropology but also an antithetical parallelism in which corresponding polar opposites maintain radical distinctions. Thus the distinction between Christ's divinity and his humanity is sharpened, a distinction that serves to maintain the Barthian distance between God and man.

In *KD* IV/3 Barth wishes to articulate the universal scope of Reconciliation and therefore to relate Christ to humanity outside the limits of the Christian community and to the cosmos. Inevitably the question of the autonomy of man and the world in relation to God is raised. In discussing the relationship between the light of Christ and the other lights that may be perceived in the world, Barth holds to his Christocentric principle: the one source of divine Revelation is Jesus Christ. Other words can be true insofar as they conform with this one Word.

When earthly creatures speak words that are true in the sense that Revelation is, they do not do so of themselves but only in virtue of the cosmic activity of Christ. Their speaking does not correspond to an autonomous, that is free and spontaneous, receptivity for the Word of God. These true words can, on the contrary, be spoken without the knowledge and will of those who speak them. Barth uses the images of light-reflecting material, which is not itself the source of any light, or of segments of a circle, where the centre rather than the circumference is decisive. Such words can, in fact, only be rightly understood by those who are at the centre of the circle, who are in possession of the whole truth in the form of explicit Christian Revelation.

Barth rejects Bonhoeffer's thesis that autonomy represents a progressive mastery by man of his world to such an extent that he is able to dispense with religion. Barth sees in the same phenomena rather a Promethean atheism, directed less against religion than against the demands of the Word of God. Mankind always tries to claim for itself the sovereignty due to God alone. But such a rebellion cannot succeed. There is no profane sphere outside the control of Jesus Christ.

NATURE AS DISTINCT FROM GRACE: THE LIGHTS OF THE WORLD

The Lights of the World — *theatrum gloriae dei*

Barth allowed for 'lights', 'words' and 'truths' that belong to the created world in itself. His thesis is 'that the creaturely world, the cosmos, the nature given to man in his sphere and the nature of this sphere, has also as such its own lights and truths and therefore its own speech and words'. He did not, however, state this thesis until he had hedged it well in with qualifications and restrictions in the spirit of the first Barmen thesis. These 'lights' and truths are not instances of the Light of Christ, the one Light of Life, nor are they in any sense Revelation, not even in the sense of being true words of Revelation *extra muros ecclesiae*.[136]

Just as there is no profane realm that is withdrawn from the cosmic influence of Christ, so these realities do not exist in abstraction from him nor do they ultimately make sense without him. Nonetheless, they are distinct and have a distinct subject:

First and last it [the statement of these realities] is possible, tenable, fruitful and helpful only in relation to Jesus Christ. It is included in what is to be said concerning Him. Yet in its immediate and most obvious content, in which its distinctiveness consists, it is not a statement concerning Him nor a further development nor description of the assertion that He is the only true light and Word of life. As a specific declaration . . . it refers to a very different subject. It has to do with lights, and in a qualified sense with words, truths and even 'revelations', but not with the self-revelations of God.[137]

In relating these words to the prophecy of Jesus Christ, Barth returns to his thesis in *KD* III/1, no. 41, of the *Church Dogmatics*: the created world is the external basis of the Covenant, just as the Covenant is the internal basis of Creation. The world is distinct from God but brought into existence by him, predestined in the eternal election of Jesus Christ to be the scene of his work, that is in the phrase of Calvin's that is the leitmotiv of this section on the lights of the world: to be the *theatrum gloriae Dei*. This reality – heaven and earth, time and space, being and knowledge – is posited by the Creator in view of Jesus Christ but distinct from him. It is the Creator's faithfulness, a key word in this discussion, which keeps it in existence and gives it its permanence. The concept of faithfulness reconciles the divine freedom with the permanence of Creation. This permanence is such that it is not cancelled nor changed by sin nor altered by Reconciliation; as the scene of the drama of man's sin and Christ's Reconciliation it remains unchanged.[138]

Hendrik Berkhof points out a very significant difference between Barth's and Calvin's use of the term *theatrum gloriae Dei*. For Calvin the created world in its awesome majesty is the living expression of the presence of God in nature and history, the theatre of God's glory.

Barth took up this expression but did not mean, as Calvin evidently did, that the world itself is the theatre in the sense of the drama, the self-manifesting action of God. Instead he regarded the world merely as the backdrop against which the real action takes place. For Barth the Lights of the World are the self-manifestation of the Creation; for Calvin they were the self-manifestation of God in Creation.[139]

Here there occurs one of those curious plays with formal principles in which Barth's concern to carry through the axiomatic use of his own categories leads to caricature. He wishes to reserve the category of history entirely for Revelation in Christ: 'we can speak of the being, activity and speech of Jesus Christ only in relation to specific events, only in the form of a narration of a history'. The created world, he admits, also contains events but these are, he claims, so similar that they are non-events: 'in it we have a sequence and repetition of the same events, or of events which are so similar that there can be no question of a decisive difference between one and another'.[140] He reserves as it were the Hebrew linear view of history for the divine drama and seeks to foist the Greek cyclic view on the world that is its frame. He is, however, not unaware of the suggestion of sophistry in his argument here and seeks to defend his position as a question of theological *priority*:

It is only in the form of the events in which this theatre or setting also exists, in the form of certain of these events, that against this background there take place reconciliation, the life of the Church and the awakening to faith and obedience. On a theological estimation the important thing in the existence of this theatre and setting is not the fact that histories are found in it too, but that, even when seen and understood as history, it is a sequence and repetition of the same or very similar events. The important thing is that in this field we have dominant lines, continuities and constants which characterise the whole. This theatre cannot be identified with the being, activity and speech of Jesus Christ, nor with its regular mediation in Scripture and the existence of the community, nor with the extraordinary forms of His presence and action. For if there are not lacking lines and continuities and constants in the life and work of Jesus Christ too, the theologically significant thing in this case is that along these lines we are dealing with history, with concrete events, not with the general feature which they share but the particularity with which they take place in this way here and now.[141]

The key phrase 'general features' (das Allgemeine) betrays the over-riding concern that impels Barth to caricature world history – his desire to exclude all possibility of a natural theology. This anti-historical theology of world history as distinct from Revelation effec-tively excludes the dominant theme of modern history: the idea of development and evolution which in the eighteenth century had encouraged the rise of natural theology and in the nineteenth had pro-vided the key argument for atheism as the natural consequence of the growing autonomy of man in the sense of autarchy.

Knowledge as distinct from Revelation

The general theme of 'lights', truths, 'words' and the possession by the cosmos of a language of its own leads naturally to the question of epistemology.[142] The world is both intelligible and intelligent. Barth is aware that this statement can only be made in regard to man: strictly speaking we can only affirm the intelligibility and intelligence of the world with regard to man's intelligence. Barth acknowledges the force of the argument, a key argument for holding to an absolute autonomy of man whether in a positivist, Idealist or existentialist sense. Barth argues that a radical Idealism goes beyond the limits set by our creation by God: it appears merely to draw the obvious conclusion set by one of these limitations, but in its absolute form it actually affirms more than we can claim to know:

We should be transgressing another of the frontiers set to its [the world's] being if we were to maintain that it existed merely *in intellectu*, and therefore, since we do not know of any other *intellectus*, only in that of man.[143]

Barth once again develops his argument in the direction of sophistry. He enters the caveat that we cannot assume that there does not exist somewhere in the created world an intelligence other than man's. We can only affirm with certainty that the world *also* exists in man's in-telligence, a quality which he terms 'esse etiam in intellectu'.[144] This relativisation of man's intelligence in relation to a *possible* other subject spills over into talk of man as the receptive party and the world as the active one in the process of knowledge: 'the world created by God does not merely exist but also speaks to one at least of His creatures, i.e. to man, giving itself to be perceived by him'.[145] Barth's answer to radical Idealism lies in the affirmation or postulation of other *subjects* rather than in a critical analysis of the epistemological problem and the claims of realism. The figure of speech in which sensation or activity is predicated of inanimate being, as in this passage of Barth's, is termed in classical rhetoric the pathetic fallacy. It should not be passed over lightly in the reading of this text for it represents a highly significant strategical move on Barth's part: a pre-emptive strike against the exclusive claims of the human intellect since the Enlightenment. The relationship between man and his world is again spoken of as a mutual relationship of subject and object: 'between this object which is also subject and this subject which is also object'.[146] To the world over against man Barth even grants the classical formula of the Protestant scripture principle: 'In respect of man . . . the world created by God is also . . . a text which may be read and understood, and at the same time its own reader and expositor'.[147]

Thus for Barth man's intelligence and its function must be relativised in relation to God, in relation to other possible intelligences and in relation to an active communicating power attributed to the cosmos itself.[148] The existence of the world cannot therefore be reduced either absolutely or in principle, methodical or existential, to man's knowledge but enjoys an independence and even a priority over against it.

Barth's chief interest lies in showing that the finality of the Word of God means 'the challenging and relativising of all created lights and words and truths'. He does not merely make the point by repeating the axiom of Revelation – that properly revealed knowledge must come from outside the created realm because it originates in the free action of God. He sets himself the apologetic task of showing the immanent limitations and the inherent problematic of human knowledge. It swings to and fro between the extremes of scepticism and dogmatism. It contains an apparent contradiction between the principles of explanatory law and of freedom. It can only lay claim to a conditional necessity and a conditional freedom. It consists in a series of hypotheses. As against all dogmatism, it can make no final statements, shed no eternal light, yield no primary or ultimate truth. It is provisional and has no claim to be absolute.[149]

The echo of Kantianism in these critical restrictions on the scope of human knowledge is no accident. Barth would wish of course to make his criticism of knowledge purely in the light of Revelation, without which man cannot perceive the relativity of his knowledge. But he claims that this is precisely the key to Kant's restrictions on human knowledge. When Kant wrote *Religion within the Limits of Pure Reason*, the limits in question were not those between pure reason and experiential, as in Kant's three critiques, but between Reason and Revelation. Revelation was therefore present to Kant as the limit or horizon of his thought. Kant allowed the possibility that the theologian might take up his task of proclaiming Revelation and disputed the competence of the philosopher to deny Revelation merely because it could not be affirmed by philosophical arguments. Barth concedes that these concessions of Kant might have been motivated by the wish to conform with the religious edicts of the Prussian government, but argues that to interpret Kant in this sense is to cast unjustified reflections on his character. Barth proposes three options for theology in relation to Kant. It could basically adopt his philosophy of religion, as did Ritschl and others; it could supplement it by asserting an immanent power of religious perception through feeling, as did Schleiermacher; or it could question the autarchy and competence of human reason in relation to the question of religion. This was his own option and he claimed that it was a justifiable interpretation of Kant.[150]

When Barth comes to enumerate and describe six characteristics of the lights or truths of the created world – existence (Dasein), rhythm, contrariety (Gegensätzlichkeit), laws, freedom and mystery[151] – he treats the immanent mystery of the cosmos as the indication of a limit which in no way implies the existence of anything beyond itself. The world merely indicates that its immanent points of reference are inadequate without being able to indicate that any other point of reference exists. The positive value of this silence of the world is that it clips the wings of would-be natural theologians. It means that the quest for speculative knowledge about the absolute is fruitless and teaches the world to be content with its limits. We can also spare ourselves the trouble (Sorge) of taking responsibility for our being (Dasein) – a clear rejection of existentialism. With his customary dialectical and rhetorical skill, Barth takes over the arguments of the humanists for his own cause. His position is *more* liberating for man. It is the rejection of natural theology and existentialism rather than that of Revelation that will set man free to devote himself to his task within the world. The ban on speculation in the name of Revelation will lead to a more rational and fruitful expenditure of human energy and creativity than is possible under atheism.[152]

Freedom as distinct from Revelation

Inner-worldly freedom is treated by Barth in striking parallelism to his treatment of inner-worldly knowledge. This freedom is sharply distinguished from God's freedom and from the freedom which is given as a grace to man by God. Barth plays down man's initiative even in regard to his own inner-worldly freedom in favour of a passivity. He portrays the cosmos as representing the first step towards freedom:

The existence of the created world . . . is also a summons and an invitation to the active ordering and shaping of things, and therefore to a step into freedom. Man at least exists as (indem) this call comes to him and he accepts it (ihn vernimmt).[153]

Before Barth proceeds to describe this freedom, he surrounds it with a host of restrictions:

He [man] does not accept only this call. Heard and accepted by him there is also the voice of existence as such, over the reality and substance of which he has no power or control; the voice of the rhythm of being which he cannot escape but which, whether with exultation or the deepest melancholy, he must accept willy-nilly; the voice of the cosmic contrariety which he may approve or bewail but which is given and within which he must therefore live his life; and the voice of natural and spiritual laws which he cannot set aside for all his awareness of their relativity, but can only recognise as valid and direct himself accordingly.[154]

Only now can he speak of man's inner-worldly freedom: 'But as the world gives itself to be known by him in all this objectivity, is he not claimed as one who knows, and therefore as an active subject?'[155] The use of the pathetic fallacy, of the world as subject, is not merely taken over from the section on knowledge, but in relation to freedom − again

as a pre-emptive strike against the modern philosophies of freedom –
it is carried to an extreme:

The encounter of the intelligible with the intelligent cosmos does not mean
only that the former declares and makes perceptible to the latter its being,
movement, order and forms. It means also that it awakens and stimulates it to
a spontaneous work of ordering and fashioning corresponding to the particular
way in which it, too, is the cosmos. As the intelligible cosmos exists wholly for
the intelligent, it desires and demands that in its own way and work the latter
should also exist for it. To put it dramatically, it yearns and cries out to be
humanised.[156]

The formal parallelism with man's listening to God's Word in Scripture, to autonomy as Barth had formulated it in the Prolegomena, is
not missing: Barth describes man's freedom as a listening to and an
obedience to the cosmos. Barth affirms freedom, but, like knowledge,
only within the limits of its problematisation and relativisation, not just
in relation to Revelation but also to the givenness of the world. Barth
has not a great deal otherwise to say about the positive value of this
inner-worldly element; he affirms it, but without once taking the
emphasis off its restrictions: 'It is freedom with this limit and commitment (Gebundenheit), so that it is not even remotely comparable, and
cannot be equated, with the freedom of God the Creator and Lord and
the freedom given by Him to man.'[157]

The relationship of the Lights of the World to Revelation and the unresolved problem of natural theology

Barth concludes his treatment of the Lights of the World that exist
beside and in distinction to the Word of God with a section on the relationship of the one to the other.[158] Two complementary and opposing
intentions make his task difficult: the continuing war on every form of
natural theology and the positive statement of the relationship in which
Revelation is said to integrate and restore the Lights of the World. The
negative statement has the first and the primary place; it rejects any
independence of these other words in relation to Revelation. The only
truth is Revelation in Christ and there is no other to compete with it.
Yet in making this statement Barth protests that he wishes to avoid
monism as well as dualism. He affirms a distinction which coincides

with the distinction between God and Creation. But the result is only a return to Barth's understanding of the phrase *theatrum gloriae Dei* in which the meaning of the world is exhausted in its being the empty stage on which the drama of Revelation takes place: 'The meaning of the being and existence of the world created by God is to be the fitting sphere and setting of the great acts in which God expresses and declares himself.'[159]

The positive statement is made under three headings, in each case an aspect not of the Lights of the World but of the Word of God: its categorical nature (Verbindlichkeit), its totality (i.e. it provides everything that man can desire) and its finality (it allows no argument).[160] But even in the positive statement the negative element is again given the primacy. The relationship is expressed in each case in a three-step form: first a statement about the Word of God, then another relativising the Lights of the World and showing their problematic, and only afterwards a third showing how they may be integrated and restored by the Word of God. The apologetic intention shows itself here in a heavy concentration on man: the first statement is concerned with the demand of the Word of God on man, the second with the inability of inner-worldly truths to say anything definitive to man, and the third with the positive relationship of these truths or words to the Word of God.

Nothing very concrete is said by Barth about the positive integration and restoration of the truths of the created world by the Word of God. After saying that these are mere forms and not content, that they are neutral truths and leave man cold, Barth says that they may be used or taken into service by the Word of God, which may hide its categorical demand in them.[161] When God speaks and only insofar as he speaks, he may enable them to harmonise with his Word so that their polyphony becomes a symphony.[162] In a parallel to the doctrine of Justification Barth says that they are clothed (überkleidet) with the glorious finality of God and so acquire final force and value and significance. They are allowed to reflect the Light of God (Revelation) and in this sense are taken into its service. But it preserves its absolute distinction from them.[163] Is the whole of Creation taken into this service? The predominant dogmatic statement does not affirm this: the lights of Creation *may* be taken into the service of the Word, but do not of themselves belong to it. The image of polyphony and symphony suggests that one might nourish the hope that all Creation *might* be taken into this service. The distinction between the internal and the external basis of the Covenant cannot, however, be removed, since the former is identical with God in his self-revelation and the latter cannot be that.

Is Creation taken into the service of the Word of God to such an extent that it is reduced to a mere function of the event of Revelation?[164] Once any possible source of knowledge for or about man is excluded, Barth is prepared to concede that a fuller and independent relationship between God and the world might exist. In dealing with the ethics of Creation in *KD* III/4, he says that we have no way of knowing whether God might not perhaps address his Word to other creatures in the cosmos: 'We dare not reject this possibility. But equally we dare not affirm it and base the understanding of our human life in this statement.' It might exist in a form hidden from us. We may give free rein to our imagination. But we must not claim that we have any knowledge or can find here a command valid *for us*.[165] The same tension is found in some passages where Barth admits the possibility of a natural theology while at the same time denying it any entrance to a serious discussion about God or man.[166]

Barth struggled with the problem of natural theology to the end of his life without reaching any satisfactory conclusion. In lectures published after his death that would have formed part of *KD* IV/4 had Barth been able to proceed with it, he makes another in a long line of course corrections. Moving now in the direction of Calvin's natural theology, Barth admits an objective knowledge of God in Creation. The principle is God's subjectivity: God makes himself known in nature. But to this objective knowledge corresponds a subjective blindness on man's part. Following Calvin, the principal statement here is man's blindness and guilt and the secondary statement is that man ought to know God and that his perverse behaviour bears witness that this is so. Barth is even prepared to admit occasional, irregular exceptions to this blindness provided that it is clear that man's subjective knowledge of God is not a datum on which one could count. It cannot be 'generalised and systematised and there is therefore no question of its serving as a basis for a natural theology'.[167] It has no value for the Christian theologian apart from its witness value against man. Nonetheless, as Berkhof remarks, this development is astounding. In

Calvin's theology this teaching was based in the doctrine of Creation and in the *gratia generalis*. Such a position would be contrary to Barth's radical Christocentrism. Yet this Christocentrism appears to be modified here by the admission of Calvin's double knowledge of God, the intention of which Barth (according to Berkhof) had always wanted adequately to integrate into his theology.[168] Had Barth lived to continue his work, renewed struggles and further qualifications might have been expected.

Summary

The lights and truths of the created world, considered in themselves and apart from their occasional service of witnessing to Christian Revelation, are also the object of specific reflection by Barth. He takes up a phrase of Calvin's (though not in the sense in which Calvin used it): the world and the lights in it are the 'theatre of God's glory', that is the empty stage on which the real action, entirely and exclusively the work of God, takes place. When they say anything it is to manifest themselves, never to manifest anything of God or his work. Barth even refuses the title of 'history' for earthly events, reserving it for the events of Christian Revelation.

Similarly Barth adopts various strategies in order to moderate the claim of the human intellect to self-sufficiency or autarchy, even in the sense of its being the only instrument of knowledge available to humanity. Human intelligence is relativised in relation to God, to other possible intelligences and to an active power of communication attributed to the cosmos itself. Barth makes use of the Kantian critique of human knowledge selectively in order to contrast human knowledge with Revelation, which comes from outside the created realm and originates in the free action of God. Of itself, the world indicates that its immanent points of reference are inadequate, without being able to offer any clue even as to the possibility of Revelation.

The freedom immanent in the world is treated in the same fashion as the knowledge immanent in the world. Barth sharply distinguishes it from the freedom given by grace and uses every argument to relativise its importance and its extent. It is not a spontaneous possession or product of the human being but is elicited from him by the cosmos.

Barth goes on to explain the way in which the lights and truths of the world are integrated and restored by the Word of God. In view of his absolute rejection of natural theology he can say no more than that the Word of God may make occasional use of them. Sometimes Barth appears to allow the possibility of a more direct relationship and in his last lectures even grants the possibility of an objective knowledge of God in Creation. But he does so on the condition that it is not perceived by sinful man and that the Christian theologian does not reckon with it. The rejection of natural theology remains his first concern here.

AUTONOMY AND BAPTISM: THE ETHICAL SUBJECT DISTINCT FROM GOD

The only published part of Barth's ethics of Reconciliation (*KD* IV/4) was the doctrine of Baptism. The first three parts of *KD* IV had dealt with God's work of Reconciliation; this volume was to deal with the human and Christian work that corresponded to it. Here Baptism and the Lord's Supper were to be understood in the ethical sense, as the foundation and the crown of the Christian life respectively. In between, the practical aspects of the Christian life would be presented with the Lord's Prayer as guide.[169] The radical distinction which Barth makes in the doctrine of Baptism between God as the primary commanding subject and the human ethical subject as the secondary obedient subject represents a development in his use of the autonomy theme. What Barth adopts is an axiomatic disjunction between God's act and man's: 'If . . . it is basically a divine action, how can it be understood and taken seriously as a human action?'[170] To this end he draws a radical distinction between Baptism with the Holy Spirit, which is the work of Jesus Christ alone, and baptism with water, which is entirely the work of man. In consequence, Barth is able to reject the sacramental understanding of baptism with water, arguing that it represents the conjuring away of the free man whom God liberates and summons to his own free and responsible action'.[171] His insistence on the ethical freedom in which baptism with water must be undertaken leads him to reject the practice of infant baptism.[172]

The primacy belongs to the divine subject. The first element is the change produced in man when God confronts him in a historical encounter. There he perceives the claim of God on him and thus becomes free to do what he did not and could not do before.[173] The human response is assent to the claim (Gott recht geben), an assent that is simultaneously decision and action and is expressed and confirmed in the performance of water baptism. There is no question of man's exercising a choice here. Water baptism is not necessary for salvation but it is commanded by God. God has refused and removed any alleged, false freedom to do otherwise and given the only genuine freedom as a free gift.[174]

Yet its character as made possible by grace does not remove the radical divine–human distinction which makes this an act of man only:

It is represented as a distinctly human action. That it is God's grace and gift to be awakened, summoned and empowered to do this, that man cannot start to justify God except in the freedom which is given him by God – that is one thing. What he does, however, when he starts to do this, the movement which he executes in conversion, is not superhuman or supernatural . . . Since it is effected in human knowledge, thought, resolve and will, it is, of course, 'only' human. It is not divine. It is human action which simply responds to divine action.[175]

It is of course its correspondence to grace which makes it human: Barth has not abandoned his Christological axiom. Its value lies in its correspondence to and confirmation of the divine initiative in Jesus Christ. But this is so without the need to postulate an immanent divine action within it. It remains human in the sense that it neither claims to contain the divine justification in itself nor to anticipate it, but is still exposed to the coming judgement.[176]

Thus, while the relationship of the two subjects must be affirmed, their action must be radically distinguished:

The act of God in this event is thus to be construed strictly as such, and the act of man in the same event is also to be construed strictly as such. Each of the elements both individually and also in correlation, and therefore the totality of the event, will be misunderstood if it is either separated from or, instead of being distinguished, mixed together or confused with the other.[177]

It is a question of 'the wholly different action of two inalienably distinct subjects', and this is the rule of all Christian ethics: 'without this unity of the two in their distinction, there could be no Christian ethics'.[178]

Barth's notion of correspondence is broad; it includes both parallel and polarity. The descending ladder of relationships, in which the higher determines and patterns the lower, implies a continual divine impulse running through all, including man's own subjective response to God and his relationship to his fellow-man. The mirror image, in which polar opposites reflect one another, suggests that the divine activity repeats itself in the human response, just as the image in a mirror appears to move closer as the primary moving subject approaches. Similar is von Balthasar's image of the hour-glass: the sand runs from above through the Christological constriction in the centre so that a corresponding movement occurs in which the sand rises from the bottom of the glass.[179] Barth wishes to affirm human freedom and therefore to assert more than a 'mere reflection' on man's side of the movement of God towards him. There can be no doubt of the seriousness of Barth's affirmation of human freedom in undertaking water baptism: it is so much the act of the human subject that it cannot be the act of God.[180]

Barth wishes to avoid both 'subjectivism from above' or Christomonism, in which Christ would be the only real subject and man purely passive, and 'subjectivism from below' or anthropomonism, in which man would be the only real subject and Christ's history a mere instrument or symbol of man's. The human subject is circumscribed by the sphere in which he operates – the material, temporal sphere to which water baptism belongs. This is also the sphere of the Church's activity.[181] The divine subject operates without mediation. The work of the Church and of the individual Christian is strictly a temporal correspondence on a lower plane to the divine action. The divine subject operates without restrictions and therefore not only on a higher plane but with complete freedom also on the lower plane, raising up witnesses and taking human and material elements into his service. The rejection of sacrament and also of supernatural transformation of man's activity or of synergism is not a restriction on the divine subject but on the human. It is the rejection of any pre-existing and definable human nature or potential that might be presupposed as the object of divine aid and of the corresponding notion of grace as a mere accident or quality of a pre-existing human nature. The human subject, however much his distinction from the divine subject may be urged, is defined in terms of correspondence with divine grace or not at all. Barth's argument becomes therefore a circular one insofar as the subject which is distinct from God is defined in terms of his correspondence with God. The distinction of the free human subject from the divine is itself a function of its more perfect, because free and willing, correspondence with God.

In *KD* IV/1 Barth had already pointed to man's duty to shape his existence in a way parallel to Christ's. Yet this did not mean that the essential moments in the existence of Christ (mortificatio, vivificatio) had already taken place in man or are real in him. Instead they had taken place outside him and for him in Christ. The result is that man is a new subject, but only inchoatively. He is no longer fully his old self (bei sich selbst) but his new existence lies still in the future. Now he is more or less an analogy, a likeness in unlikeness, a modest image (Gleichnis) of the being and activity of Jesus Christ. The result is that man is free to think his *few* thoughts, say his *few* words and do his *few* works in peace.[182] The human sphere is thus modest, limited, finite and yet undefined; it is nothing in itself. It exists only insofar as it can be used and at the same time be seen to be problematic and relative in the light of the Word of God. The latter preserves its radical distinction from every material and defined element.

In *KD* IV/4 two slight changes of emphasis occur. Firstly, the efficacy in man of the action of the divine subject outside and for him receives greater attention. Thus in treating of Baptism with the Holy Spirit, Barth stresses repeatedly how real is the internal transformation brought about by the Holy Spirit. It does not remain external but 'becomes internal to him [man]'. 'He is in truth a man who has been changed.' 'It is not just his enlightenment from without, but a lighting up from within.'[183] This new emphasis is the fruit of Barth's exposition of union with Christ in *KD* IV/3 which he describes as a union that includes a distinction of subjects, each of which, however, lives and exists eccentrically, that is in and with the existence of the other.[184] This new emphasis allows the greater distinction between the divine and the human subject in the sense that the proper action of the human subject can now be said to be inspired by grace. Indeed Barth goes so far as to say that the human subject may himself put grace into effect: 'Die Möglichkeit Gottes besteht darin, einen Menschen . . . seiner Gnade nicht nur passiv, sondern aktiv, als Einen, der sie selbst ins Werk setzen darf, will und kann, teilhaftig werden zu lassen.'[185]

The second change in emphasis in Barth's treatment of Baptism is the increased influence of the distinction between the divine and the human, the transcendent and the immanent, the finite and the infinite, which is characteristic of the tradition of Calvin and Zwingli and ultimately has its roots in a spiritualising philosophy. It concentrates on knowledge as the point of mediation between God and man.[186] The result is that certain elements in man's nature, especially knowledge and freedom, are enthusiastically affirmed but in one definite relationship and in one particular context. The movement of the Christian life is from acknowledgement to recognition to confession of the Word of God (anerkennen, erkennen, bekennen); the mission of the Christian consists in witnessing to this knowledge before the world.[187]

Konrad Stock points out that precisely because of the centrality of the Word of God for Barth reason (and rationality) play an important and positive part in his theology. Reason plays the decisive part in the perception of the Word as opposed to a religious faculty of perception of an irrational or prerational character as postulated, for example, by Rudolf Otto. As against Cartesian dualism, Barth regards reason as the essence of man and uses the term for the totality of the human faculties. It includes above all the ability for self-determination.[188] This ability is presupposed in Barth's account of autonomy–obedience. Man comes to himself precisely in his reason. The sacrifice of the intellect, Barth declares, could only be a work of man not of grace and is in any case unachievable. The work of the Holy Spirit does not mean that man takes leave of his wits but 'that he finally comes to himself, to rationality'. This rationality is of course exclusively that of reason enlightened and taken over by grace, as the continuation shows: 'to rationality, to perception of what he was in the counsel of God fulfilled at Golgotha'. In this sense Barth continues: 'there is no more intimate friend of sound human understanding than the Holy Spirit'.[189]

This argument enables Barth, at the end of his *Church Dogmatics*, to maintain his own articulation of the autonomy theme and to claim for himself the rhetoric associated with it:

What the free God in His omnipotence wills and fashions in Jesus Christ in the work of the Holy Ghost is the free man who determines himself [according to his] pre-determination by God, [yielding in freedom] the obedience of his heart and conscience and will and [of his] independent action. Here man is taken seriously, and finds that he is taken seriously, as the creature which is different from God, which is for all its dependence autonomous before Him, which is of age. Here he is empowered for his own act, and invited, commanded and encouraged to perform it.[190]

Just as he had emphatically rejected this language when it had been spoken of man outside the proclamation of the Church, and equally firmly when it had been presented by Bonhoeffer as a challenge to that proclamation from the world, so he is prepared to baptise it now that it has found a place in the service of that proclamation. This 'Light of the World', the affirmation of man as a being who is self-determining, of age, distinct from God, and independent, has been taken into the *ministerium Verbi Divini*, the service of the Word of God, and it is exclusively in this context that Barth is capable of affirming it. There is no call to make little of Barth's achievement in doing so, coming as it does out of decades of struggle in which the affirmation of human and creaturely reality gradually won ground without contradicting the absolute claim of the divine subject. At the same time, one cannot say that the affirmation of creaturely reality in Barth is now straight-forward and free of problems and that all the difficulties urged against him at this point have been cleared up.

Thus there is one discomforting parallel with Bonhoeffer in Barth's passionate affirmation of man's autonomy. Like Bonhoeffer's, it is clearly defined only in its negative aspect in an inner-theological controversy. The force of Bonhoeffer's affirmation of man's autonomy is the extension of man's growing competence to the religious sphere, so that man no longer needs the 'God of the gaps', the God of religion. Consequently he rejects both Liberal theology and the existentialist element in dialectical theology because both appealed explicitly or implicitly to religion. Positively Bonhoeffer had only a few hints to offer − non-religious language, religionless Christianity − which later interpreters rather arbitrarily employed in programmes of their own. Similarly the main force of Barth's affirmation of man's autonomy is directed in page after page against the powerful witness of Scripture and Tradition to an understanding of Baptism that is sacramental, not merely ethical. The positive aspect of his affirmation of autonomy need not be underestimated but it amounts to a new variation on the classical Calvinist and Zwinglian theology of the Word. It consists in a subsumption of Christian life under the categories of knowledge and of correspondence to and witness to divine Revelation. There can be no doubt of Barth's intention to subsume the whole of the Christian life, including the Christian's life and activity in the world, under these categories and to affirm them there. In this sense one can gladly and generously repeat von Balthasar's affirmation of Barth's openness to life and joy in the world.[191] The question is whether these formal word-categories are of themselves adequate to the task. As we shall see, most current Barth interpretation starts from the perception that they are not.

Summary

KD IV/4 was to deal with the human and Christian work that corresponds to God's work of reconciliation. Here the Eucharist and Baptism were to be presented in an ethical interpretation, but only the section on Baptism appeared. *KD* IV/4 builds on Barth's doctrine of union with Christ, developed in *KD* IV/3. This is a union of subjects each of which exists eccentrically, that is in and with the existence of the other. But Barth retains a radical distinction between the divine and the human subject. This distinction allows him to affirm the proper action of the human subject and this proper action can now be said to be inspired by grace. The internal transformation brought about in the human being by grace can now be said to be real. But the radical distinction between God as the divine commanding subject and the obedient human ethical subject is extended to an axiomatic disjunction between the action of the one and the action of the other. Any action must be clearly attributed either to one or the other: synergism is ruled out. Barth therefore introduces a radical distinction between Baptism with the Holy Spirit and baptism with water and rejects the notion of sacrament entirely. God's grace summons and empowers the human subject to act but the result is the wholly different action of two inalienably distinct subjects.

This means that human action and man's autonomy are given a distinction and a solidity new in Barth's thought. More than a mere reflection of the movement of God towards man, man's ethical response is so much the act of the human subject that it cannot at the same time be an act of God. Therefore Christ is not the only real subject and Barth explicitly rejects a 'subjectivism from above' or Christomonism. But there is no mediation of God's activity, simply a reflection of or correspondence to it. The rejection of sacrament is not a restriction on the divine subject but on the human. The distinction of the human subject from the divine is on the one hand a function of its more perfect, because free and willing, correspondence with God's action, but on the other hand the human sphere is modest, limited, finite yet undefined. It is still nothing in itself. It exists, but still only insofar as it can be used and at the same time problematised and relativised by the Word of God. The Word of God preserves its radical distinction from every material and defined element.

This new scheme allows Barth a more enthusiastic and one must say strategic use of the term 'autonomy' and the rhetoric associated with it. As a strategy, it is directed against the notion of sacrament. Instead there is a restrictive theology of the Word, employing formal word-categories and conceived exclusively in terms of knowledge and rationality as the only point of mediation between God and man. Reflecting the spiritualising philosophy of the Renaissance, this position not only contradicts the witness of Scripture and of Christian tradition to sacrament but is also inadequate to express the whole of the Christian life, including the Christian's life and activity in the world.

2

The autonomy theme in Barth criticism since 1950

BARTH CRITICISM BEFORE 1968: A NEGATIVE
BALANCE – WOLFHART PANNENBERG

After 1945 the dialectical theologians, notably Barth and Bultmann, dominated German Protestant theology. Barth's theology of the Word of God had proved its strength and integrity in its opposition to the ecclesiastical policy of the National Socialists and enjoyed a particularly high prestige. Yet even among those who had grown up with the theology of the Word of God and who were associated with Barth in that struggle its lack of mediation with experienced reality and with the intellectual problematic of the modern mind proved a difficulty. Even so close an admirer of Barth as Dietrich Bonhoeffer had come to the conclusion that Barth represented an unhelpful 'positivism of Revelation'. Barth's theology had had the merit of opposing anthropocentric theology but the meaning of Creation, Incarnation, the Cross and Resurrection for the world without religion came too short. The relationship to the modern world (in which Bonhoeffer saw the growth of man's autonomy) was too negative.[1] The younger generation of theologians that came after 1945 experienced this difficulty with acuteness as they took part in the great debates on hermeneutics and on secularisation.

An alternative to the theology of the Word of God was sought by a circle of young academics that met in Heidelberg in the 1950s and whose theoretical programme *Revelation as History* was jointly published in 1960.[2] The most detailed and systematic elaboration of that programme was that of Wolfhart Pannenberg. Pannenberg studied for two semesters under Barth at Basel in 1950–1. He was deeply influenced

by Barth but parted with him on the question of rational argumentation and of the significance of philosophy and the other sciences for
theology. Philosophical studies (with Nicolai Hartmann in Göttingen
in 1948–9, with Karl Jaspers in Basel in 1950–1 and with Karl Löwith
in Heidelberg after 1951), the exposition of the Old Testament
theology of history by Gerhard von Rad, and an interest in Hegel and
in modern anthropology, influenced the formation of his thought.
Pannenberg followed Barth's insistence on the sovereignty of God, the
uniqueness of Revelation and the universal significance of theology. He
disagreed, however, with Barth's opposition between Revelation and
natural knowledge and insisted in consequence on the theological integration of the other sciences, especially of philosophy.[3] Inevitably
this involved quite a different understanding on Pannenberg's part of
those points also on which he had agreed with Barth.[4]

Pannenberg's criticism of Barth

Pannenberg's criticism of Barth is of special interest for the interpretation of the autonomy theme in Barth's theology because it represents
the most comprehensive attempt to develop an alternative to that
theology and did so precisely in the name of critical reason and of an
attention to the reality of world history. The accusation of a 'positivism
of Revelation' is easily made but, as Pannenberg's Heidelberg col-
league Dietrich Rössler pointed out, to refute the appeal to the authority of the biblical and ecclesiastical tradition it is necessary to rework
the entire historical–critical debate.[5] It is also necessary to construct a
viable theological alternative. Pannenberg set out to do both. His
criticisms of Barth are therefore not only illuminating in themselves,
but his constructive effort can be read as a justification or a qualifica-
tion of that criticism.

Pannenberg's first published works are devoted to the interpretation
and criticism of Barth. His first was a response to von Balthasar's book
on Barth and was published in 1953 at a time when Pannenberg was
working on his doctoral dissertation on Duns Scotus.[6] Here Pannenberg not only tried to underline the differences between Barth's
analogy of faith and von Balthasar's suggestion of an analogy of being
implicit in that analogy of faith but rejected the notion of analogy

entirely. Consequently he rejected Barth's analogy of faith and with it the systematic structure of the *Church Dogmatics*. Pannenberg's rejection of analogy was based on the Scotist argument that analogy always included a univocal element, so that there was in fact no middle way between univocal and equivocal statements. In doing so he underestimated the force of the negative moment in the scholastic doctrine of analogy. The rejection of analogy was actively pressed by Pannenberg in the first decade of his academic career, after which the topic was allowed to rest.[7]

The extension of the argument to the entire theology of the Word of God, including its admission of the special status of the Bible, marked Pannenberg's third published work. Pannenberg first urged Jaspers's principle of transcendence and his criticism of every claim to the objectification of transcendence, including that of Christian doctrines such as the divinity of Christ. This criticism ran partly parallel and partly counter to the thrust of Barth's theology. Pannenberg simultaneously urged a countercriticism of Jaspers that coincided with Barth's criticism of Jaspers in *KD* III/2. The openness of the philosopher for transcendence remains limited, according to Pannenberg and Barth, because it remains *his* transcendence. The philosophical subject remains sovereign (eigenmächtig) and in control and can assert himself against the transcendent.[8]

Here we meet what was to be characteristic of Pannenberg's method: the mediation and mutual modification of philosophy and theology. On the one hand such categorical assertions as theology makes are relativised by the philosophical critique of every claim to objectify the transcendent. On the other hand the immanent standpoint of modern philosophy, centred as it is on the active human subject, is relativised by the broken objectivity of Revelation, which continually brushes aside the immanent forms to which the subject clings, supplanting them in new acts of transcendent Revelation. This process of ever-new Revelation is revealed in the prophetic criticism, in the newness of Revelation in Christ as opposed to current Jewish expectations, but especially in the Death and Resurrection of Jesus, which leaves nothing objective to grasp at. Transcendence is therefore incarnate in Christ, freeing man from every objectification.[9] The proclamation of the Gospel in God's name makes an unconditional claim. But this claim is not exclusive, since it cannot make any claim to an objective content. Where it did so it would be a 'servant of the Antichrist'.

Where Barth had seen the assertion of an analogy of being as 'the invention of Antichrist', Pannenberg rejects all analogy insofar as it backs any claim to possess an objective knowledge of Revelation. An exclusive claim for any particular objectification of the transcendent implies, in Pannenberg's view, the destruction of freedom and is the means by which men win power over the souls of others. The Word of God can only be proclaimed where objectivity is surrendered to the possibility of historical transformation. Christians are therefore compelled to seek 'total communication with all men and with every truth'; in common with all men they await the future Revelation of the one God at the end of time.[10]

The insistence on the sovereignty of God and the uniqueness of Revelation leads Pannenberg therefore in a direction opposed to the position of Barth. The consequence he draws is the rejection of the privileged authority of the Bible. Pannenberg traced the original appeal to authority on the part of Christian faith to the classical tradition of rhetoric. For Augustine the appeal to authority was a matter of persuading and convincing. *Auctoritas* was a matter of believing something on the word of another which one may later be expected to understand for oneself. For the ancients, only historical events had strictly speaking to be taken on the word of another; there understanding could not remove the need for faith. The modern era brought, unawares, a shift in the nature of the Christian appeal to authority. The Bible was now read as a human book with a human history. The historical-critical method made history into a domain of scientific examination and reconstruction. The traditional appeal to historical authority was perceived as superfluous and unreasonable, especially when the authority no longer promised to point the way to understanding but claimed to be beyond the reach of understanding. Such an appeal to authority must be blind and therefore arbitrary. It cannot be the understanding of faith that was intended by the Reformers, for whom the authority of the Bible was self-evident. To try to re-establish the authority of the Bible through an act of trust today is to propose quite a different concept of Christian faith to theirs. Christianity after the Enlightenment was faced with the choice either of justifying itself rationally without the appeal to authority or of abandoning the appeal to reason in favour of an authority that must now be judged arbitrary and subjective. Barth had opted for the arbitrary and the subjective.[11]

SUMMARY

Pannenberg's chief and insistent criticism of Barth is that Barth's appeal to the Word of God excludes any form of legitimation: the theologian has no proof to offer himself and others that he is not being merely fanciful, but hears and accepts God's Word. Barth's appeal to faith with no justification outside itself must be regarded as irrational. It is not the alternative to subjectivism that Barth claimed it to be but the furthest extreme of subjectivism made into a theological position.[12] Pannenberg argued instead for a mutual mediation of philosophy and theology based on rational argumentation.

Reason and religion

RATIONAL ARGUMENTATION

Against Barth, Pannenberg holds that rational argumentation has always been at least implicit in the Christian tradition since the early Christian presentation of the faith as the 'true philosophy'. It must be extended by the use of the historical–critical method to establish the truth of historical events.[13] The resurrection of Jesus can claim to be a historical event.[14] The authority of the Church, based in a unique access to information about historical events, must yield to the authority of scientific inquiry. All traditional authorities, including that of the Bible, must be regarded as a product of human understanding and human faith. Christianity must leave aside its heritage of uniformity based on authority and present itself in non-positive, non-authoritarian form.[15]

Pannenberg accuses Barth of having confused the probative and the heuristic elements in theology and thus of having destroyed the assertive character of theological statements, their claim to objective truth. The theologian's faith is characterised as private and subjective. Christianity must be treated as problematic, no matter how much the theologian may subjectively be convinced of its superiority. The Christian faith of the theologian may help him to form questions and conjectures which prove productive for his investigation, but it may also deprive him of an impartial appreciation of his object and even of his own tradition. A personal religious conviction cannot be used as the basis for an argument for which intersubjective validity is simultaneously claimed. Pannenberg equates personal conviction with personal religious affiliation to a religious tradition or community. Hence he rejects confessional theology, 'in which everything has already been decided on the basis of a particular standpoint of faith, a standpoint which has not been the object of open discussion'. Such a theology serves only to rationalise prejudices and can therefore lay no claim to intellectual seriousness and scientific legitimacy.[16]

Openness, impartial appreciation of the object, freedom from prejudice – this language carries the moral pathos of the appeal to reason characteristic of the Enlightenment and its heritage. It is opposed to the dogmatic approach, to the 'dogmatic prejudice which might interfere with the unprejudiced evaluation of phenomena'.[17] In applying these criteria to theology, Pannenberg hopes to come a long way in reconciling theology with the demand for autonomy of the reason.

Pannenberg's position means that the place of theology is not, as Barth claimed, within the Church. The probative context for theology is to be found in the pluralism of modern society, in its public institutions of learning and in the demands of a fair dialogue with other religions. This requires that theology must treat its own assertions as hypotheses that are subject to an appropriate examination and whose truth is not already established.[18]

A THEOLOGICAL REVISION OF THE PHILOSOPHY OF REASON: BRINGING BACK THE RELIGIOUS THEMATIC

We have seen in the last section how Pannenberg demands that religious assertions be submitted to the demands of rationality. However, it would be a serious misunderstanding of Pannenberg's intention and of his work to neglect the other side of his programme for a reconciliation between reason and faith. He demands a corresponding openness of rationality and of the academic establishment to the religious thematic, an openness that has not been characteristic of the proponents of the autonomy of the reason. Pannenberg demands, in fact, a major critical revision of the philosophy of reason in the light of the religious thematic:

If, however, theology admits the necessity of rational accountability for the Christian faith, the problem we found formulated by Hume immediately arises: Is not modern reason so fashioned that it leaves absolutely no room for Christian faith other than a subjectivity which lacks any intersubjective binding force? Is not any attempt at a rational accounting of the Christian faith foredoomed to vain compromises?

The recent history of theology provides an abundance of material for such a pessimistic conjecture. However, instead of taking an inventory of the theological compromises that have been made with 'the' modern reason and its understanding of the world, I want instead to ask whether there really is such a thing as 'the' reason, which is so monolithic in form that theology can only be dashed to pieces against it. Are there really compelling reasons to concede to Hume and his positivistic followers the pathos of speaking in the name of 'the' reason absolutely? Is it necesssary to acknowledge as the *non plus ultra* of historical reason a certain kind of historical positivism that allows the uniqueness of events to be lost on the basis of a postulated homogeneity of all events? Theology could still have the task of inspecting more minutely such sorts of absolute claims put forth in the name of reason. Only in this way will it be possible to obtain a critical concept of reason and knowledge that will for the first time make it possible to give a rational account of the truth of the Christian message and thereby would itself already be a step on the way to such an account.[19]

In his work *Theology and the Philosophy of Science*, Pannenberg carried out this programme. The immediate problem lay in the claim of natural science to sole validity as the source of knowledge or rather in the attempt of logical positivism to impose an ideal of scientific procedure which it claimed (falsely as Pannenberg showed) to derive from the natural sciences. This unitary concept of science contrasts and conflicts with the approach of the philosophical or human sciences (Geisteswissenschaften), which concern themselves with meaning. Pannenberg's purpose is to establish the essential unity of the human and natural sciences so that the study of meaning cannot be the reserve of the human sciences and cannot justify a theoretical opposition between human and natural sciences. In this way he hopes to reverse the process in which the individual sciences were divorced from the universal quest for meaning and the question of meaning was banished to the realm of subjectivity.[20]

Pannenberg finds a common structure underlying both natural and human or philosophical sciences – that of system. The concept of system is that of the ordering of parts into a whole. In historical explanation the system is provided by the ordered series of events and in natural science by the theoretical framework of explanatory paradigms or hypothetical laws.[21] The claim of natural science to base its findings on empirical observation is countered by means of the demonstration that scientific theories do not take the form of isolated hypotheses but consist in a complex system of theoretical constructions. It is this elaborate paradigm that determines what observations are considered relevant. The testing which the scientist undertakes applies at bottom not to a single hypothesis but to the whole system of, for example, physics that represents the general consensus among scientists at a particular time.[22] The criteria of predictability or falsifiability applied to general laws are countered by the claim that reality consists of singular events in history, so that even verified laws of natural science need not have eternal validity, and by the demand that the treatment of singular events in history should also be recognised as a valid object of science. But the verification of singular events in history is also not a question of observation but results from taking the balance of a great deal of evidence. For observation, prediction and falsification as criteria for scientific truth, Pannenberg substitutes the more general term 'critical examination'. The principal criterion in the testing of scientific hypotheses, whether they deal with natural science or history, is the ability to draw together and explain the available evidence. Science is the construction and appropriate testing of hypotheses that are as complex and comprehensive as possible.[23]

Such a broad definition of science can be extended without difficulty to philosophy and theology. The particular sciences gain precision by concerning themselves explicitly with a limited area of subject-matter. Their implications, however, embrace the totality of reality. Philosophy is concerned with a process of unrestricted reflection which challenges immediate assumptions, continually subjects its findings to renewed questioning and therefore raises explicitly the question of the totality of meaning that encompasses all particular knowledge and experience. In doing so, however, philosophy also proceeds by hypothesis. It can operate only by *systematically* describing the totality of meaning, and its advances are always made by means of total revisions in which each philosophical system is put in question by the next. No philosophical system is, however, more than an anticipation of the totality of meaning, which is not as such available for examination. The incompleteness of human experience and the openness of the world process itself mean that the totality of both human experience and the world process is accessible only in an anticipation of the final truth that can only be reached with the end of history. Philosophy thus leads inevitably to the religious question since the meaning of reality as a whole is the explicit theme of the religions, and conversely every treatment of reality as a whole can be called religious.[24]

Nonetheless, and here his distance from Barth is at its greatest, Pannenberg credits science with the ability to establish and judge the truth of religions. The chief function of theology is to formulate the claims and assertions of the religions in terms of hypotheses about reality as a whole. These hypotheses must then be tested, firstly for their consonance with the religious traditions that they claim to interpret, and then by the criteria that apply to philosophical statements. The criteria test philosophical hypotheses for their consonance with reality as a whole by confronting them with the findings of the various particular sciences and with the different areas of human experience, including prescientific experience. Philosophy must and can address itself to the task of systematising the different areas of experience and must do so with sufficient clarity that the significance of the various areas of knowledge and experience can be assigned. The claim is a large one and it is therefore no surprise that Pannenberg conjures up in this context the ghost of Hegel and of German Idealism. Idealism was the classic attempt to build such a synthesis; in its own way, Pannenberg claims, modern critical theory had attempted something similar.[25]

Pannenberg, however, feels himself obliged to take far more serious account of the limitations of human knowledge than Hegel did. It follows that the difficulty of building the synthesis of all human experience presents him with a peculiar problem in making a final judgement in philosophical and theological questions. Only the synthesis of all reality could adequately test the truth of philosophical and theological assertions. Are they therefore unverifiable? He meets the challenge by interposing a distinction between verification and final verification. Even here he can appeal to the parallel with natural science: there too it can be difficult to establish that final verification has been reached. It is necessary to satisfy oneself with criteria that will make possible at least a provisional decision, even if assent cannot be compelled by force of logic. Those hypotheses should be adopted that 'give the complex of meaning of all reality a more subtle and more convincing interpretation than others'.[26] Pannenberg warns against any claim of theology to more than this provisional and relative truth.[27]

Thus in one respect Pannenberg's and Barth's conceptions meet: in the estimation of human knowledge as provisional and relative. Here man ought to be aware of and accept his place. But whereas Barth *contrasted* divine Revelation with this provisional human knowledge, Pannenberg locates Revelation precisely in that knowledge. It is only in and within the creative, tentative process of human knowing that God reveals himself. Once one accepts that Pannenberg really intends to affirm God's revelatory activity in tentative human knowledge, there emerges another parallel with Barth. As in Barth's 'autonomy of the creature', Pannenberg locates man's true autonomy as well as his union with God in his acceptance, active as well as passive, of the mode in which God reveals himself. For Pannenberg, the important point is that man distinguishes himself from God, realises and accepts that he is not God. This self-distinction (Selbstunterscheidung) from God runs parallel to the self-distinction of Jesus of Nazareth from God. It was precisely in this self-distinction that Jesus was united to the Father. The same self-distinction unites the persons of the Trinity in their interdependence: each realises that he is not God in himself alone but only in conjunction with the others.[28] But whereas for Barth it was man's confrontation with the event of Revelation in Christ that implied and effected his self-distinction from God, for Pannenberg it is man's realisation that he is noetically and ontologically dependent on the eschatological future. Pannenberg even holds a metaphysics of futurity in which the being of each existent is constituted only in the final future, in its eschatological *Wesenszukunft*.[29] And whereas for Barth man must abandon his own intellectual quest and with it all concern with religious philosophy in order to throw himself on the event of Revelation in Christ, for Pannenberg man's concern with his quest for knowledge and meaning must lead him to recognise the universal importance of the religious thematic. In his subsequent attempts to grasp and affirm the meaning of reality an indirect revelation takes place.

SUMMARY

The key to Pannenberg's criticism of Barth is the universality of the religious thematic. A common structure underlies all the sciences:

system or the integration of parts into a whole. A common structure underlies scientific verification: the ability to draw together and explain the available evidence. Philosophy attempts to account for the totality of meaning. But the incompleteness of human experience and the openness of the world process mean that the totality is not available here and now. Philosophy thus leads inevitably to the religious question in which the meaning of reality as a whole is asked and answered. But religious answers do not lead to the kind of absolute knowledge that Barth claimed for the Word of God in Scripture. They attain only a provisional and relative knowledge and it is only there and in that indirect way that God is revealed.

True and false autonomy

TRUE AUTONOMY: THE REFORMATION AND THE ENLIGHTENMENT

The replacement of the paternalism of traditional authorities by the primacy of rational argumentation is the basis for the positive use of the term 'autonomy' by Pannenberg. In this he sees the major achievement of the Enlightenment. Against Hans Blumenberg, Pannenberg maintains that the modern reaction was not directed against a theological absolutism of grace but against an ecclesiastical authority which had, in the late Middle Ages, given up the rational justification of its claims and so placed itself beyond reason. Thus he can admit that the history of modern science was to a large extent an emancipation from theological presuppositions and at the same time claim that the demand for rationality was the genuine Christian tradition, that the roots of the drive to natural science were Christian and that Christianity had provided the basis of freedom on which the edifice of science could be erected.[30]

Pannenberg identifies the essence of this emancipation with the Reformation. He admits that Protestantism clung just as much as Catholicism to a traditional authority, in the case of Protestantism that of Scripture, and that Protestantism did not concede freedom of religion within the State until after the Wars of Religion. Nonetheless, he shows that Protestantism could legitimate the *tendency* towards emancipation from traditional authority by insisting on the immediacy of the Christian layman to God, an immediacy that, as he interprets it, required no more than a transitory spiritual mediation. His participation in the absolute truth of God freed the individual from every irrevocable bondage to human authority. This emancipation did not take place at the Reformation but it was its historical consequence, as Pannenberg affirms with Hegel, that the individual was affirmed by the Enlightenment to be his own law-giver, to be autonomous.[31] In a lecture on the Reformation delivered in the year of revolution, 1968, Pannenberg was especially generous in the use of the term 'autonomy'. The modern questioning of the authority of the Word of God is said to be a consequence of 'the autonomy of man' and the religious questions in general are said to have come under the aegis of human autonomy. The link with the Reformation is made clearer in the phrases 'free, autonomous judgement' and 'personal autonomy'. Elsewhere the same expressions are qualified by a rejection of 'radical autonomy' which raises individual subjective decision above universal reason.[32]

THE FALSE AUTONOMY OF THE SELF-POSITING SUBJECT

Pannenberg distinguishes between a true and a false autonomy. The term 'autonomy' is in fact not frequent in his writings nor does he make use of it as one of the key terms of his own thought.[33] In general he gives it a hostile reception:

When the highest value is no longer universal reason, but individual decision, radical autonomy has been often considered the peak of existential freedom. In a Christian perspective it can be the darkesst alienation from authentic existence, from one's own destiny and identity.[34]

Pannenberg sharply criticises the claim of radical autonomy to represent the authentic philosophy of human freedom: 'The constitution of freedom (and so of the subject itself) becomes a problem only because it cannot be conceived of as the self-positing of the subject and so not simply as autonomy.'[35] The freedom attained by autonomy is an empty and formal freedom which is closely related to the formal political freedom that is realised in modern democracy.[36]

By the expression the 'autonomy of the State' Pannenberg understands the 'religious neutrality of the State' or the privatisation of religion. This he sees as a dangerous illusion because the authority of the State remains arbitrary except insofar as it ultimately rests on a religious legitimation. Pannenberg speaks positively of theocracy: the biblical God raises the claim of theocracy, which need not be confused with clericalism. At the same time, he criticises the autonomy of economic development. Marx's theory of economic development reflects the autonomous development of the economic process that was made possible by the privatisation of religion. The exclusion of religion meant that the economic process got out of hand, so that modern society is still struggling with the consequences.[37]

The autonomy of the sciences falls under the same criticism as that of the State and of the economy. 'Autonomy' means that the sciences are emptied of meaning and become arbitrary in their application. Modern science places its findings at the free disposal of the human subject. This is the real reason why the particular sciences emancipated themselves from the question of universal meaning raised by philosophy. The question of meaning was to be left to those who made use of scientific knowledge as they set their own aims and created their own meaning. The autonomy of ethics, the historic core of the idea of autonomy in Kant's philosophy, is subject to the same criticism. The apparent independence of ethics in relation to the understanding of reality as a whole and in relation to social processes could only be maintained as long as the traditional ethical norms were taken for granted. The solution to the ethical problem can only lie in the religious thematic in which the philosophical question of universal meaning and the claim of the Christian tradition to represent the 'true philosophy' converge.[38]

Pannenberg's rejection of a false autonomy includes, like Barth's, the rejection of Fichte's account of subjectivity as well as the liberal philosophy of freedom. Pannenberg points to Dieter Henrich's study of Fichte to prove that Fichte himself saw that his theory of the self-positing subject was untenable. The Ego that posits itself and thereby brings its self-consciousness into being cannot be the same as the Ego that is posited, with the self-consciousness thus produced.[39] Pannenberg has more sympathy for Hegel's account of the subject, in which the subject is not limited by the other but is itself precisely in the other (im anderen bei sich selbst). However, even here, Pannenberg observes that the problem that faced Fichte remains unsolved: either the Hegelian subject posits or produces the other in which it finds itself, and the Fichtean problem of the non-identity of the productive subject with its product returns, or the Hegelian subject is distinct in origin from the other. In that case, either it remains in itself (bei sich selbst) in its relation to the other, without becoming identical with it, or it surrenders itself to the other, becomes itself something other and is no longer absolute. Pannenberg believes that Hegel remained imprisoned in the first alternative, in the vanity of romantic subjectivity in which everything is regarded by modern man as material for the exercise of unlimited freedom and every authority and order is experienced as a restriction on freedom. Hegel indeed saw the difficulty but instead of solving it he exacerbated it.

Pannenberg himself affirms the second alternative: the subject is not absolute but surrenders itself to the other and becomes in the process something other. The subject undergoes a process of change in history in which it receives its self from without. He develops his theory with the help of humanistic psychology: primal trust is said to be the basis on which the Ego is built. He argues that this basic trust grows beyond its first concretisation in the child's relationship with his mother until it becomes identical with the religious thematic.[40]

This historical–developmental account of the constitution of the subject is of first importance for Pannenberg's concept of freedom. Because the basic trust on which the identity of the individual is built is implicitly grounded in God, his peculiar worth as a person is not at the disposal of others. Because freedom is constituted in relation to the future rather than the past, to the process of change in history through which the subject receives its self, freedom can be affirmed and demanded irrespective of the presence or absence of concrete conditions within which freedom can be exercised. The task for the present is that of finding ways to ensure that every individual receives a maximum of opportunity for individual freedom, a freedom which is synonymous with individual immediacy to God.[41]

SUMMARY

Pannenberg affirms the autonomy theme insofar as it represents the revolt of rational argumentation against an authority that claims to be above reason. He follows the Enlightenment and Hegel in reading the Reformation as an affirmation of rational argumentation based in the immediacy of the individual to God. But his use of the term 'autonomy' is not frequent. He protests against its application to the State, to economics, to the sciences and to ethics because he believes that it is used to imply the privatisation of religion and the neglect of the question of universal meaning. He wishes instead to emphasise the universal relevance of religion and the claims of the Christian tradition.

Pannenberg holds that Fichte's theory of the self-positing subject is misleading. Instead he turns to humanistic psychology to show how the subject finds itself in surrendering to the other. Ultimately the other is God and through God alone the freedom and unique worth of the other can be affirmed without reservation.

Human freedom and the idea of God: criticism of Hegel and Barth

Freedom and religion are therefore, in Pannenberg's view, closely related. That has its consequences both for religion and for politics. Religion preserves the values of freedom and personality against the absolute claims of an authoritarian State and against radical individualism. This means that politics must recognise the importance of the religious thematic.[42] But it also means that religion must be such that it can embody the values of freedom. It must not stop with inner freedom, as Luther did, nor stop short of affirming a society based on freedom, as Calvin did, but must allow for a religious pluralism. Here Pannenberg identifies himself with that interpretation of Protestantism that understands it as the rejection of all authority that sets itself above the individual:

Only when the principle of the human mediation of God's rule by analogical representation lost its power in the minds of people, and instead the immediacy of each individual to God by faith was discovered, only then the rule of God was thought to exclude human mediation so that the independence of the individual from all human authority would correspond to his devotion to the rule of God alone.[43]

Here the parallel with Barth's theology is striking, especially with its rejection of human mediation in favour of the immediacy of the individual to God. But for Barth this immediacy and human freedom itself was defined axiomatically in terms of correspondence to the Word of God alone. For Pannenberg, this immediacy rests on the convergence of the religious thematic with the history of human personal, social and political freedom. This is so much the case that the latter can set criteria for the former – for religion and for the idea of God itself.

Thus Pannenberg takes up the challenge of modern atheism as a debate about the meaning and conditions of freedom. The question is whether man's freedom excludes the existence of a God or whether Hegel was correct in maintaining that the Christian God remains the condition for modern freedom. His response is to demand a total revision of the classical concept of God: the almighty, omniscient God who is perfect in himself before the creation of the world. Human freedom is the ability to transcend the given, to change it, and that means to transcend a God who belongs to the totality of the given. Here Pannenberg sees a justification for Sartre's sharp formulation of modern atheism as autonomy: 'Even if there were a God, it would change nothing.' The God who is conceived as a given cannot be God, the all-determining reality, since he cannot determine man's freedom.[44]

Is there an alternative? Pannenberg turns to his concept of reality as history, as a process whose development is incomplete. This implies that the very attempt to think of the totality of reality in terms of the definite unity of a system is false. The restriction must also be applied to the concept of God: it must even be seen to be blasphemy to think of God as a being that is simply there (als vorhandenes Seiendes) even if he is characterised as the already existent unifying unity of the world. In the Bible Pannenberg finds the idea of the Kingdom of God that is coming. Correspondingly, God may be thought of as the God whose dominion is in the process of coming, who can be identified with 'the power of the future'. Pannenberg is at pains to establish that it is the future that is real rather than the given. The future exerts an effective influence over the present – at least in the case of beings such as man that are oriented to the future – and is therefore 'real' (wirklich) without being given. Only such 'reality' can be reconciled with human freedom, with its realm of unrealised possibilities. It is only possible to reconcile the concept of God with freedom by thinking of him in terms of the reality of the future.[45]

The failure of previous theology, a failure that even Hegel did not overcome, was to think of freedom as either an outward characteristic or an outward expression of God, subsequent or subordinate to his absolute being, which had existed for itself from all eternity. Instead the being of God must be understood in terms of the absolute future of freedom, an absolute future that belongs to the essence of freedom because absolute freedom has no future outside itself and is therefore its own future. This absolute freedom of God shows itself to be creative in that it brings into existence a multiplicity of finite being. As freedom it is at the same time love and acquires a historical nature with determinate divine attributes at the same time as it makes itself the universal horizon that binds together the finite substances. What Hegel and classical theology failed to understand with regard to freedom – the freedom of God as well as of man – is its contingency (Zufälligkeit) in the sense of something that issues from the future, that cannot be derived from all that is already given, not even from that which the person who wills already is. On this element of the contingent depends the pluralism of the individual realisation of freedom. The Christian God can therefore be thought of as allowing a pluralism with regard to the freedom of man. Only the pure act of freedom conceived as a personal reality of a superhuman kind can form the basis of freedom among men. Even the abstract idea of freedom must take specific form and thus restrict the freedom of individuals. Human social organisation is still less capable of forming the basis of individual freedom, because here freedom is always limited.[46]

Pannenberg strongly criticises Barth's application of the category of person to God. This should only be used to express a liberative activity, manifest in the experience of the power of freedom over the givenness of the world. It must not be used to designate an anthropomorphic concept of God in the image of the modern romantic ideal of a subject in the possession of unlimited power.[47] In that case Fichte's criticism of the concept of God as personal would be justified, and this concept would bring a limitation with it that would contradict the transcendence of God. Pannenberg finds his criticisms confirmed when Barth insists on claiming the category of person for the one God, while he rejects it for the 'persons' of the Trinity. The unity of God can, according to Pannenberg, be thought of only as a trinity of persons, not as a concept, nor as a being (substance) nor even as an absolute subject. The warning is directed against Barth's emphasis on the claims and the sovereignty of God, as well as against Hegel's identification of the subject and concept of God.[48]

Pannenberg thus can speak of the personality of God only insofar as it contributes to the ideal of Christian freedom – 'individual autonomy'. Arguing from the non-givenness of the divine reality, precisely because it is personal, Pannenberg defines God's reality in terms of verbs rather than nouns, in terms of effect rather than its underlying cause. At this point the distance separating him from some aspects of Barth's thinking, namely from Barth's actualism, is not great. The divine being exists in its works, in the demonstration of its power; the revelation of the true nature of the divinity will simultaneously bring the final demonstration of its existence. But the future tense makes the far greater disagreement with Barth's theology evident. The divine being is in Pannenberg's view manifest only in a problematic way, in the universal history of religions. It is only in the history of religions, the history of man's understanding of the divine, that God comes to his Revelation.[49]

Finally we may note that the key to this concept of indirect revelation is the convergence between Pannenberg's reduction of the biblical witness to the insights and assertions of its human authors and his general epistemology, in which knowledge is a process based in creative spontaneity. The history of natural science, the history of philosophy, the history of religions, and the Christian tradition, are all subsumed under the same process – the formation of explanatory schemes whose function is to give an adequate account of the totality of phenomena. Immanent but also transcendent to this process of tradition and innovation is the action of the God of the future. It is especially manifest in the historical event of the Resurrection of Christ, which stimulated the human process of intellectual spontaneity, so that the New Testament came to be written. However, Barth's insistence on the exclusivity of Christian Revelation is rejected. Instead Pannenberg establishes a relative success on the part of Christianity in the task, common to all religions, of explaining the totality of reality. It had, namely, made history its theme.[50]

SUMMARY

Human freedom is intimately linked by Pannenberg with religion and with the concept of God. The State must take full account of the truth of religion if freedom is to be preserved. At the same time, religion must be such that it promotes freedom. In the argument from autonomy, modern atheism criticises religion for denying freedom.

Pannenberg takes this criticism seriously enough to demand a total revision of the traditional concept of God. God must be understood in terms of absolute freedom. The tradition allows for this new concept with the notion of the coming kingdom of God. God must now be understood as the power of the future rather than of the past. It is the future not the past that is real. The future allows for contingency rather than determinism and therefore corresponds to the pluralism necessary for the individual realisation of freedom. Only a God conceived of in terms of pure personal freedom can guarantee freedom. But this new concept of God must involve a trinity of persons. Barth's refusal to apply the category of 'person' to the persons of the Trinity is suspect and his restriction of its use to the divine unity is rejected. Barth is guilty of conceiving God in terms of the modern romantic ideal of a subject with unlimited power. Pannenberg would speak of the personality of God only insofar as it contributed to the growth of individual autonomy within the historical process.

Conclusion

A question can be addressed to Pannenberg from the Barthian perspective: Does the action, the subjectivity and the freedom of God as portrayed in the Scriptures reach adequate expression in this convergence between divine action, human spontaneity and world process? The question of the subjectivity of God being manifest in his action in the world had challenged Pannenberg since the emergence of the death-of-God theology. Previously his talk of God was characterised by the infinite difference between God and the world and by the rejection of analogy in favour of a doxology whose concepts became pure equivocation as they approached absolute truth. Now he began to speak of the activity of God in creation,[51] and in the history of Jesus Christ. Thus, in the postscript to the fifth edition of his Christology in 1976, he remarked that God's action in the history of Jesus Christ had not been overlooked in the original edition but admitted that it had not sufficiently been explicated as *God's* action, as the expression of the sovereignty of God and therefore of his divinity. He proposed to search for a solution in the direction of his ontology of the future. The ontology of the future was also Pannenberg's answer to the American process theologians. They urged that Pannenberg, working from the same principles of the totality of reality and the dynamism of history as they did, must also admit a mutual conditioning of God and world process. Pannenberg, in reply, argued that the metaphysics of Whitehead, the father of process philosophy, was bound to the past or present and was therefore determinate.[52] The idea of futurity was alone compatible with that of God's freedom and personality if determinacy were to be avoided.

It is, however, to be questioned whether the metaphysics of futurity, in which Pannenberg's interpretation of reality as ever-new history is driven to an extreme, can bear the weight placed on it. Where the theme is God's activity in relation to the world, the underlying programme tends to undermine protestations of God's freedom and sovereignty. A totality is conceived within which statements about God and the world converge. These statements are so ordered to one another that they could come to condition one another. God could be thought of as a function of the world or vice versa; his transcendence would be compromised, even though he is thought of as working backwards from the future.[53]

Pannenberg urges Hegel's idea of genuine infinity against Barth: that God cannot be thought of in mere opposition to the world but must in some way or other be thought of as embracing the world as well. Barth failed in this task because he refused to construct his idea of God through reflection on the factual and finite world of experience and of nature. Pannenberg works from the implications of the idea of God as the reality that determines all others, an idea which he tries to match by the totality of his conceptual framework.[54] This idea implies that in the process of history, once it has begun, the divinity of God is 'at stake'. The divinity of God not only requires to be demonstrated cognitively to man in view of the riddles that the world presents to the finite mind, but it is also ontologically at stake, that is God's very being, at least in relation to the world, is yet to be realised.

It seems that Pannenberg thinks of God as conditioning himself in relation to the world so that his own being in the Trinity is tied up with the outcome of the process. Thus the Resurrection is constitutive of God. God is God only through Creation and Redemption; he is no longer God primarily in himself and secondarily in history, as in the classical doctrine of the Trinity. Pannenberg understands the world as the sphere of God's self-realisation, even if he maintains, against Hegel's account of the absolute spirit, that God also possesses or would possess his independence and freedom apart from his self-realisation.[55] In contradicting Barth's attribution of personal subjectivity to the one God, he not only attributes personal subjectivity to each of the persons of the Trinity, but also appears to attribute to each a temporally distinct role in historical process that goes well beyond anything envisaged in the classical doctrine of attribution.[56] The rejection of analogy, at first an affirmation of equivocation, now threatens to lead to the opposite extreme – the dissolution of the classical distinction between God and the world.

Pannenberg's programme suffers from the absence of analogy. It exaggerates the convergence between concrete knowledge of present reality and religious assertions about ultimate reality that are not available for examination in the same way.[57] Similarly it exaggerates the convergence between the totality of meaning that we are able to grasp and reconstruct and the demand for universal meaning that we spontaneously raise but are unable to fulfil. Barth's argument against the rational optimism of the Enlightenment retains its force: there is a gap in reality as we experience it that we cannot bridge.[58] Pannenberg also seems artificially to separate the components of religious faith. On the one hand are explanatory schemes that are purely human constructions and are, if Pannenberg's rejection of analogy is maintained, equivocal in relation to the ultimate truth of which they claim to speak. On the other there is religious trust, for which the term faith is reserved, which is a commitment distinct from the intellectual affirmations on which it is based.[59]

The youthful reaction of Pannenberg and his contemporaries against the theology of the Word of God was similar to the reaction of Barth and his contemporaries against the ruling Liberal theology. It was one-sided. Pannenberg's argument against Barth – that to maintain that the invisible God spoke to man was only a figure of speech – can also be applied to his own assertion that God acts in history.[60] Both Pannenberg and Barth rejected the literal inspiration of the Bible. But whereas Barth still affirmed that the Word of God was to be found in Scripture, Pannenberg retreated, as he put it himself, into preverbal events.[61] Nonetheless, the difficulty of making assertions about the activity of the God of History persisted. Thus the activity of God as the active subject of history and of the Word has not yet reached adequate expression in Pannenberg's theology. But this is an area in which his thought is still in development and it may well be that, like Barth, he will later feel the need to integrate into his theology what he had first wanted to exclude.

BARTH'S POSITIVE RELATIONSHIP TO MODERN AUTONOMY: BARTH CRITICISM SINCE 1968

Barth and the modern era is the theme of a broad stream of Barth criticism since about 1968 which finds in Barth a positive reworking of the autonomy theme – whether it is the self-determining autonomy of the absolute subject or the autonomy of the sciences or the relative autonomy of the concrete human subject. In this section we outline the change in historical perspective which has made this new series of interpretations possible and present the most important contributions.

The new historical perspective on Barth

Current Barth interpretation builds on a reappraisal of modern intellectual history that began in the 1960s. Christof Gestrich, whose study of the relationship between dialectical theology and modern thought forms part of that reappraisal, pointed out that between the wars the specific nature of modernity was difficult to grasp and interpretations tended to be one-sided and to express themselves in the taking of personal stances both ethical and political. The general discussion that took place after the Second World War had placed the entire modern era in a new perspective.[62] Bonhoeffer's last writings had challenged the theologians in particular to find new answers to the problems posed by the modern era.

The spread of secularisation in modern culture, interpreted with Dilthey and Bonhoeffer in the sense of a growing autonomy of man, led Friedrich Gogarten to develop a new theology of secularisation.[63] Secularisation was now interpreted as a long-term effect of fundamental Christian principles, especially of the liberation of man from a mythical, sacral, religious world view. An offshoot of this theology was the wave of death-of-God theology in the 1960s with its associated theme of man's sole responsibility for his world. The Neomarxist revival was matched by a theology of Revolution. This and the political theology of the early 1970s took up the theme of man's responsibility for his world but qualified it by a revived eschatology in which the relation between man's action and God's in history was once again a subject for discussion.

The thesis of the Christian origins of secularisation and of a Christian affirmation of man's autonomy in the sense of a growing domination of his world did not remain without contradiction. For Hans Blumenberg the modern era derives its legitimacy from its revolt against Christian theology. The theological absolutism of the late Middle Ages provoked, in his view, a revolt of human self-assertion against the unworldly and therefore life-denying principles of Christianity. Blumenberg did not accept that the result of this revolt had to be an absolutism of the human subject, but claimed that the self-assertion of reason against Christianity implied the sober affirmation of man's responsibility for himself and his world and his ability to face this task.[64]

The wave of interest in new theological constructions led to a new interest in the theological revolution that Barth and his contemporaries had carried through after the First World War. Jürgen Moltmann's re-edition of important essays and documents from the early period of dialectical theology reopened for discussion many questions that had seemed closed.[65] There followed a re-evaluation of the role of Barth according to the different perspectives of the new theologians. Thus, for example, Moltmann himself, in his theology of Hope, noted positively that Barth, unlike Bultmann, had replaced the subjectivity of man as the starting-point of theology with that of God. But he complained that Barth's notion of the self-revelation of God remained lost in a transcendental eschatology that had too little to do with the reality of the historical world.[66] The death-of-God theologian Dorothee Sölle, however, found Barth's concept of Christ the Mediator to be entirely negative: it depersonalised man and deprived him of his autonomy.[67]

In 1968, the year in which Barth died just after the new sociopolitical ferment had exploded, the constructive reinterpretation of Barth in the new theological situation was the specific theme of a collection of essays by a group of younger theologians. A new and sceptical generation of scholars, the editors wrote, made sensitive to the dangers of ideological thinking, could not simply accept Barth's theology as it was. Barth's insistence on the Word of God, on Revelation in Christ, was to be qualified by the observation that responsibility for the message of the Bible had to be undertaken within the historical situation. Barth's answers to the questions posed in the 1920s could no longer be accepted without interpretation. Barth could not in any case be identified with the orthodox school of Barthianism.[68] In the subsequent essays the demand for a constructive reinterpretation of Barth was complemented by criticism of his theology of the Word of God and the attempt to find a convergence between Barth and the Bultmann school of hermeneutical theology.[69] However, the proponents of the theology of secularisation were equally insistent in laying claim to the heritage of Barth. Paul Hessert claimed to find in Barth's actualism the roots of the radical theology of the 1960s, which he wished to defend against the charge of Liberalism. James M. Robinson, on the other hand, held that the new radical theologians had abandoned Barth's theology under the influence of Bonhoeffer and the theology of secularisation.[70] In the light of secularisation there was a general consensus that Barth's theology allowed too little access to the real, empirical world, and his alleged neglect of natural science and technology received frequent mention.[71]

The Neomarxist theologians did not take long to stake their own claim to be the authentic heirs of Barth in the new theological era. This time it was Barth's socialism that was held up as the key to his theology. The hermeneutical debates were dismissed as irrelevant. Barth's attachment to socialism had been explicit up to the first edition of the Commentary on Romans. Thereafter, it was claimed, it had not atrophied but remained merely hidden behind the dogmatic language of his mature theology. It could easily be laid bare without doing violence to Barth's thought.[72]

A REVIVAL OF IDEALISM: TRUTZ RENDTORFF

The general change in historical perspective was accompanied by a revival of interest in German Idealism because of its peculiarly compelling combination of theoretical and historical speculation. The interest of Idealism in demonstrating the working of its formal speculative theories in the process of history, especially intellectual history, led at the end of the 1960s to new efforts to explain modern theology on the basis of a universal historical development. The revolt of Barth and the dialectical theologians against Liberal theology had been directed precisely against that identification of the essence of Christianity with modern intellectual culture which had been one of the triumphs of the Idealist philosophy of history. The success of dialectical theology over Liberalism had led to the general abandonment of the Idealist harmonisation of the Gospel and the world, even if the dialectical theologians subsequently disagreed on how to relate the one to the other.[73] The new attempt to identify the essence of Christianity with modern secular culture had to account for Barth's success. It had to be explained in a way consonant with the general thesis, that is Barth's theology could not be put aside as an anachronism but had to be understood as a part of the general development of modern culture itself.

Some of Pannenberg's colleagues in the Heidelberg discussion circle of the 1960s took up the challenge. Thus Dietrich Rössler, in a celebrated lecture delivered in 1969, characterised post-Enlightenment theology as a whole as a 'positional' theology. It was an expression of the religious subjectivity of the individual theologians, each of whom could claim to represent only one perspective in theology.[74] He called for a 'critical theology' which would represent a higher perspective, a 'meta-theory' which would make a theological pluralism itself its object. In doing so it would seek to explain the individual, ecclesiastical and confessional positions on the basis of modern intellectual history. Its theorem would be the identification of Christianity with the modern world, that is the claim that the theme of modern theology had been expanded until it had become the entire world of meaning and of praxis in its relation to the Christian tradition had in a word become the modern world itself. The new critical theology would therefore address itself to the theoretical and practical situation of contemporary 'Christendom'. Trutz Rendtorff, who had already (in *Offenbarung als Geschichte*) taken up the challenge of situating Revelation and the Church within the perspective of universal history, also adopted the term 'Christendom' for the identification of the essence of Christianity with that of modern culture. In collaboration with Rössler he began to develop a 'theory of Christendom'.[75]

It was therefore with a definite programme in mind that Rendtorff addressed himself to the problem of Barth. In a celebrated essay he stood Barth's reaction against Liberal theology on its head. Instead of the negative relationship between Barth and modern autonomy which had been the leitmotiv of Barth criticism both favourable and unfavourable up to that point, he posited a positive if paradoxical relationship. Barth had not rejected the autonomy theme. He had adopted it in a far more radical form than the half-hearted affirmations of the Liberal theologians had allowed: Barth had proclaimed the radical autonomy of God. Rendtorff's premise was the inevitability of modern intellectual history. Barth was willy-nilly confronted with the situation created by the Enlightenment and Idealism. He was compelled to provide answers that would carry forward and radicalise the historical positions, namely those of Liberal theology, that he wished to overcome. The laws of historical-systematic development could not be reversed and Barth was inevitably carried along by the inner dynamic of intellectual history.[76]

A BETTER ENLIGHTENMENT: EBERHARD JÜNGEL
AND K. G. STECK

Other critics of Barth who were more cautious than Rendtorff about reading an inherent and inevitable systematic development into intellectual history nonetheless began to perceive a positive relationship between Barth's theology and the Enlightenment and its aftermath. They included some of those who had been close to Barth during his lifetime. Thus Eberhard Jüngel, in a tribute delivered two days after Barth's death, applied the phrase 'Enlightenment in the light of the Gospel' to Barth's effect on both the Church and the world. He too distinguished between Barth and Barthianism, pointing out that Barth came into conflict not just with Liberal theology but with a positivist orthodoxy and with Church leadership. His theology could not be called reactionary. Instead, in Jüngel's view, Barth had accepted the challenge set by the modern consciousness of universal truth (das allgemeine Wahrheitsbewußtsein). (The phrase indicates that Jüngel too was influenced by the revival of interest in Idealism.) Jüngel emphasised that Barth retained his freedom in relation to the heritage of the Enlightenment and was able to question it. Nonetheless he had profited by that heritage and put it to good use; he was interested in more and better enlightenment rather than in less. Sin, for example, he treated as culpable *stupidity*. Theology, in Barth's view, called for the courageous exercise of one's own understanding. Barth's encounter with modern thought took place within dogmatics, a dogmatics in which he left no traditional doctrine unexamined and which was the very opposite of an orthodoxy that was exclusively faithful to tradition.[77]

Jüngel saw Barth's challenge to modern thought as a challenge both to modern theology and to modern atheism. Barth interpreted modern atheism as the logical consequence of modern theism. The 'supreme being' who is above all reason and beyond it, who is so defined that he is precisely what man is not, is the God against whom Reason in the later stages of the Enlightenment rebelled. Barth rejected this concept of God, in which both scholastic metaphysics and the anti-scholastic philosophy of the Enlightenment had concurred, because it was too anthropomorphic (allzu menschlich). It conceived God as the abstract antithesis of man, whose transcendence and supernatural character is really the reflection (or projection) of human pride, as the God that man would want to be rather than the God who willed to become man, the humble God of Christianity. This abstract God of traditional theism and of atheism is rather a devil, a supreme being that posits and wills only itself and wills in this sense to be 'absolute'.[78]

Barth's interest, as Jüngel shows, is concentrated principally on the nature (Wesen) of God, rather than on his existence, which receives passing attention. In this there is a parallel, not accidentally, with Nietzsche. The question is who or what God is, and the answer contradicts both theism and atheism. Jüngel understands the insistence of the early Barth on the tautological formula 'God is God' as a concentration on this question rather than the assertion of an authoritarian concept of God. Not, however, until the methodical principle of the *Church Dogmatics* − to conceive of God exclusively in terms of Revelation in Christ − is adopted is this tautology, is God, positively interpreted. Barth's early rejection of every determinate concept of God is replaced by the insistence that the concept of God be positively determined by Revelation in Christ.[79] God is conceived in terms of the Gospel as the God who in his freedom is the loving God and this concept leads to that of man as the one who is set free to love. In going beyond theism (and atheism) Barth had followed not only Luther but Hegel as well and had thus demonstrated his fearless commitment to the intellectual task and also his freedom to make use of Idealism without being absorbed by it.[80]

It was not merely the younger generation of Barth's disciples that now began to affirm a positive relationship between Barth's theology and the Enlightenment and its aftermath. In 1973, K. G. Steck published a reconsideration of Barth's rejection of modernity. Steck, who had been a student and close disciple of Barth since the early 1930s in Bonn, admitted that he and many interpreters of Barth had previously understood him to have followed a purely defensive strategy of delimitation in his insistence on the special object of theology – the Word of God. Reconsidering the matter now, Steck concluded that Barth's rejection of modernity had essentially been aimed at the developments *within* theology and the Church in the previous two centuries. It remained an open question how far he had thereby put himself in opposition to the essential characteristics of the modern era as such.[81]

Steck pointed out a number of ways in which Barth entered into discussion of the modern era in general. In his history of Protestant theology in the nineteenth century, he had characterised modernity as an absolutism in which man seeks to dominate his world and in which he does not stop short of trying to control Christianity. But, Steck observed, Barth did not dwell on the phenomenon of modernity nor devote much attention to features such as secularisation. His criticism was different in character to the attacks on the modern era in the papal manifestos since 1830 and to the sarcasm of many critics of modern civilisation. Barth found fault not with the evil world, but with the failure of the Church and of the theologians themselves. The sin of modern theologians lay in their abandonment of the standpoint proper to theology in favour of an accommodation to man's natural understanding of himself, to the humanist optimism of the Enlightenment.[82] Barth's own theology was not, however, an attempt to put the clock back to the Reformation. His argument, documented in the controversy with Harnack,[83] was that if theology only had the courage to insist on its proper theme, the Word of God, it would lead and dominate the movement of thought rather than follow and be subordinated to it. The theologians of the Reformation and of Protestant Orthodoxy were, according to Barth, the leaders of the movement of thought in their time.[84]

Steck finds that Barth remained linked with his Liberal predecessors – particularly with Schleiermacher – precisely because of his desire to contradict them. The core of Barth's dispute with the moderns lay not so much in the doctrine of God but in his anthropology. The claim that the theology of Revelation represented the exclusive truth about man brought him into conflict with philosophy – not indeed with a philosophy that kept within the limits recognised by Barth but with any philosophy that overstepped these limits in the direction of theosophy. The acceptance of such a philosophy as the basis of Liberal theology was the point at which Barth's deepest rejection of the modern spirit occurred. Barth rejected every attempt on the part of theology to canonise, as Bultmann did, some element taken from modern thought. Barth's insistence was on the Word of God that can speak for itself. It is on that point that every criticism made of him from the modern perspective is concentrated. But, Steck notes, here is no return to a premodern stance. Barth is modern in the sense that he rejects every appeal to security in dogmatics, to old orthodoxy or modern neo-orthodoxy, in favour of an appeal to the Spirit, to a prophetic objectivity.[85]

SUMMARY

With the change in intellectual perspective in the 1960s, Barth's position within modern intellectual history and that of the dialectical theologians in general began to be reappraised. Representatives of several new schools of theology claimed to be the legitimate heirs of Barth: hermeneutical theologians, proponents of the theology of secularisation, Neomarxists and Neoidealists. Trutz Rendtorff stood previous interpretations on their heads, claiming that Barth was willy-nilly fulfilling the programme of Liberal theology which coincided with the programme of the modern mind in general. Barth had appeared to overcome Liberalism by substituting the radical autonomy of God for the radical autonomy of man. But in each case the principle was the same: radical subjectivity. It could not have been any other in the wake of the Enlightenment and of Idealism.

Even close disciples of Barth joined in the re-evaluation. Eberhard Jüngel noted Barth's conflicts with positivist orthodoxy in theology and with Church leadership. Barth was interested in more enlightenment rather than less. In particular he moved beyond the concept of

God as self-sufficient subjectivity, common both to theism and to atheism. He understood the essence of God exclusively in terms of Revelation in Christ and therefore of freedom to love. K. G. Steck, a first-generation disciple of Barth, noted that Barth's ire had been directed not at the modern world as such but at the ineptitude of the Liberal theologians and churchmen who had responded to its challenge by abandoning the essence of theology itself.

Socialism or Idealism?

BARTH'S SOCIALISM AND HIS CRITICISM OF MODERNITY

Dieter Schellong agreed with Steck that Barth did not trouble to make a detailed analysis of the modern phenomenon nor to define his position in relation to modern thought as such. His interest lay in modern theology. The element in modern thought that had thrown theology into confusion was the tendency of man since Descartes to identify himself in his own self-consciousness with God. Schellong himself offered a diagnosis of the modern phenomenon, the essence of which he saw in the principle of self-conservation.

This principle was articulated by Spinoza (Schellong here followed an article by Hans Blumenberg) in direct opposition to the theological theme of the *conservatio Dei* and to the theology of Calvin in general. Schellong developed his analysis as a broad critique of modernity in general. The modern era contains so many contradictions in itself that criticism need not presuppose a standpoint from without but can come from within modern consciousness itself. Schellong believed that Barth's criticism of modernity was modern in this sense. The principle of self-conservation was, according to Schellong, the principle of the bourgeois subject who identified freedom with the exploitation of nature and of other human beings, with possessions and work to increase wealth.[86]

Schellong brought his own socialist analysis of the modern era into conjunction with Barth's own socialism. He did not, however, try to reduce Barth's theology to a shadow of socialism. Admitting, unlike F. W. Marquardt, that Barth's faith in socialism was destroyed by socialist support for the First World War, Schellong maintained that socialism and the social question remained relevant for Barth because of his commitment to reality – the reality both of God and of man.[87] Barth's criticism of religion, a criticism of its positive character of possessing and of putting things into practice, is in essence criticism of bourgeois religion. It is simultaneously criticism of the Church and (here Schellong appealed to Barth's rejection of sacrament in *KD* IV/4) not only a rejection of every claim to possess the divine but a rejection of whatever is particular. This is above all what is modern in Barth.

The modern era had rejected the claim of anything particular to represent the divine. Only the universal could be the ultimate truth. Barth had not, however, adopted an abstract universalism. He affirmed the immanent as energetically as he affirmed the universal and therefore faced the same problem that Spinoza and Hegel had posed – that of the reconciliation of the immanent and of the universal. What he rejected was the notion that this universal–immanent reconciliation might be achieved within the rational self-consciousness of the thinker as assumed by Spinoza and Hegel.[88]

The failure of modern thought to achieve reconciliation shows that it must be sought elsewhere. The principle of modernity was not that of a universal reconciliation but that of self-conservation. The evidence of the negative force of this principle struck Barth with full force at the outbreak of the First World War and made his judgement about the modern era a negation. Reconciliation could not be found in the Hegelian synthesis but only *extra nos* in the unique history of Jesus Christ. The negativity of modern history is countered by the Cross of Jesus Christ, in which the principle of self-conservation is broken through. The Resurrection of Jesus Christ is the realisation of the divine on earth, not as a process immanent in human consciousness, not as a spiritualisation, but as an earthly material event. That is a scandal for modern thought, yet here the modern sense of the reality of the world is taken more seriously than in much of the apologetics for the Resurrection in modern theology. Rather than translate God into self-consciousness Barth presents him as an alternative to what men normally call reality. This reality, that of Jesus Christ, is the true reality as opposed to the negative and distorted history of mankind.[89]

Barth was therefore not guilty of ignoring or passing over the reality of human history. But human history is not accepted as a fact: it is transformed into the place of struggle for the realisation of the new divine reality of the world. The reality of the given is put in question by the establishment within it of a counter-reality that is particular but has universal implications.[90] Christian praxis can therefore *not* follow the autonomy (Eigengesetzlichkeit) of what we call reality but must give witness to the counter-reality of God. Therefore Barth rejected the Lutheran doctrine of the Two Kingdoms, the distinction between faith and reason, and the notion of divinely established orders of Creation such as work, vocation, marriage, parenthood or the state. To accept these would be to capitulate before modern reality. This is also the characteristic of Barth's concept of freedom. He rejected an empty and formal freedom that consists in mere freedom of choice, which is simply a guise for an absolute self-assertion in the struggle for existence. Instead Barth insisted on a substantial notion of freedom that implies a bond. What is decisive is the kind of bond involved. The Spirit of God does not oppress but brings man into correspondence with the free world-transforming activity of God, so that the free man, autonomous and self-determining, becomes a witness of God's Kingdom.[91]

THE BIBLE OR IDEALISM? ADRIAAN GEENSE AND CHRISTOF GESTRICH

The new perspectives on the relationship of Barth's theology to modern thought did not go unchallenged by the established school of Barth interpretation. In a comprehensive review article on the reception of Barth's theology, the Dutch theologian Adriaan Geense recalled that for Barth the primacy belonged to the Word of God. Academic theology in Germany had always been concerned with its own history and continuity in relation to the general scientific consciousness, with its own place in intellectual history, with the relationship between the Reformation, the Enlightenment and Idealism, and with the unresolved questions of the nineteenth century. This had always led to an ambivalent reception of Barth's thought, from Harnack to the hermeneutical theologians to Pannenberg and his circle. Barth, however, had begun outside the academic field, had produced neither dissertation nor *Habilitation* and, however much he felt himself confronted by the Idealist tradition, had simply dispensed with the academic problematic to turn to the Word of God and the situation of the preacher. Barth could indeed claim that he had worked more on systematics than many others, but he did not see his priorities there. Geense asserted that academic theology today ought to be in the best position to recognise that the era of universal conceptualities is over, whether religious, metaphysical, ontological, anthropological or social.[92]

Instead of historical perspectives and universal systems, Geense saw the key to the *Church Dogmatics* in K. H. Miskotte's *regula nominis*, namely the replacement in theology of the method of deduction from a concept by induction from the Name of Jesus Christ. Like the Old Testament *shem*, the Name of Jesus Christ is the particular way in which the reality of God manifests itself. The movement is from the particular to the universal and not vice versa. Jüngel's interpretation, Geense noted with approval, moves from the Name, from the concrete history of Jesus and does not hesitate to draw the consequences for the being of God himself. This is a consequential exegesis. However, Geense rejects this school of interpretation as soon as the consequences are drawn to an ontological system. Thus he rejects Wilfried Härle's claim to find a unified, systematic ontology in Barth. Geense will accept that the *Church Dogmatics* contains a multiplicity of indications (not excluding conceptual ones) that converge on the Name of Jesus, but he will allow nothing more. The four critical points for Barth interpretation are summed up by Geense thus: the freedom of God, reference to Holy Scripture, the ecclesiastical character of theology and the goal of universality. The point of universality, however, is not to be discovered in systematic constructions or historical perspectives but in ever-new recourse to the Bible.[93]

Geense's attack on the new interpretations of Barth was parried immediately by Gerhard Sauter.[94] The new interpretations were not merely a case of the fascination of the German intellectual sciences with their own history. It was true that Barth, like Buber, had turned his back on the Idealist tradition. But both had nonetheless concentrated on a single Archimedian point from which they could either challenge every possible universal and conclusive view of reality or develop a new one themselves. This meant that they were faced with the claim of Idealism to represent such a view and obliged to provide their own answers to the basic questions that Idealism had claimed to solve – those of the nature of thought itself and of its relation to reality.

Christof Gestrich adopted a similar Idealist–historical perspective to that of Sauter. Barth's use of Idealist schemata and his interest in the problem of freedom as posed by Idealism was not a tactical choice that he might just as well not have taken, as in Hans Urs von Balthasar's interpretation, but was governed by historical necessity. It was Barth's fate to have to deal with the effects of Idealism in the history of theology and to be confronted with the questions that it had left unsolved. Gestrich affirmed with Rendtorff the thesis of the secularisation of elements of Christian thought in the social structures of the modern era and found that Barth in particular did not take adequate account of this phenomenon because of an overhasty identification of this secularisation with natural theology. Thus the historical phenomenon was distorted by Barth and reduced to a traditional dogmatic problem.[95] Gestrich differed with Rendtorff, however, in his evaluation of the historical development. Whereas Rendtorff saw in the historical development the distillation of the essence of Christianity in the question of freedom as such, Gestrich saw in modern intellectual history a shuttling back and forward of key problems between philosophy and theology. Thus Kierkegaard's objections to Hegel were made from a theological standpoint, but were taken up by the philosophers – Bultmann and the earlier Heidegger were closely related – and dialectical theology and existentialist philosophy handled the same problems in similar yet different ways. Affirming, like Schellong, the internal contradictions and problems of the Enlightenment, Gestrich saw in Barth not a reaction to, but a participation in, a debate within the tradition of the Enlightenment and to a great extent in its support.[96]

Barth did not believe that the Enlightenment brought anything fundamentally new. It confronted the theologians with the age-old conflict of the resistance of man to God but the problem did not lie here. Gestrich noted Barth's lapidary insistence that it is false to assume that any historical era is alienated more than others from Revelation. The problem lay for Barth, as Steck had pointed out, in the concessions made by the theologians to this resistance. Theology should disregard the agenda set for it by the modern era. Barth was not interested in any public debate in the sense of a discussion with a pluralist audience on any other basis than that of the proclamation of the Word of God. He had no desire to see the theologian lead the movement of thought in that sense. Nonetheless, Gestrich saw Barth practising *solidarity* with the modern era precisely here. His intention was to free the Enlightenment from the problems created by the theologians! The tendency of the Enlightenment to theosophy, its involvement in inner contradictions, should be corrected by the consequent insistence of the theologian on his own theme, and this insistence should be of benefit *ipso facto* for the health of modern thinking in general.[97] Gestrich thus underlined Barth's own claim that man is emancipated by defining his limits and freeing him from the burden imposed by philosophical speculation in the wake of the Enlightenment.

Nonetheless Gestrich claimed that Barth's theology stood not merely as a corrective but also to a great extent in continuity with Hegel's philosophy. Gestrich finds the common starting-point for both Barth and Hegel in Hegel's criticism of contemporary theology, of the false opposition between faith and knowledge which had led the theologians to neglect the basic teachings of Christianity. Barth shared with Hegel the same ontological question about God and reality. But Barth was concerned to offer something better than Hegel. He began by contradicting the identification of God and man in Idealism and therefore liberated man from the burden of having to play God. Barth did not just return to the same starting-point as Hegel and take a different track; he built on the criticisms of Hegel in Feuerbach, Marx, Kierkegaard and others. His was not a pre-Enlightenment but a post-Enlightenment criticism. On the basis of a renewed doctrine of the Word of God and of the ecclesiastical foundation of theology Barth offered a new onto-theology. In opposition to Hegel, Barth claimed for theology not only the competence to deal with the question of God but also competence in the area of ontology. He could claim all the more freedom to do so because philosophy since Hegel had destroyed any other form of ontology.[98]

Thus Barth could claim to have fulfilled Hegel's goals in a way in which neither Hegel nor any form of philosophy could do, for modern philosophy could no longer answer the classical questions about God, man and the world. In taking them up as a theologian, Barth had reversed Hegel's subordination of theology to philosophy. Here, according to Gestrich, Barth was more far-seeing and more rather than less modern than his companions and later rivals among the dialectical theologians. They tried to restore the question of God within a philosophical context shaped by the left-wing Hegelians and their successors, whether materialists, naturalists or existentialists. But this philosophical context was defined by the systematic exclusion of Hegel's onto-theological premises, whereas Barth took up the entire question of onto-theology anew. Thus their theology was short-lived, whereas Barth wrote a theology that took better account of the movement of intellectual history than any other in this century.[99]

SUMMARY

For the socialist interpreter, Barth's criticism of religion, of theology and of the Church reveals itself as a criticism of the bourgeois subject and his pretensions to possess, to act and to control. The Cross and Resurrection of Christ represent an alternative that is truer to reality: the realisation of the divine as an earthly material event. Barth therefore rejected an autonomy of earthly reality in terms of the Lutheran doctrine of the Two Kingdoms, the distinction between faith and reason and the concept of freedom as a mere freedom of choice. Instead the freedom and autonomy of man can only be affirmed as a positive freedom that implies a bond, namely a free and autonomous correspondence with the world-transforming activity of God.

Adriaan Geense dismissed the new interpretations of Barth as an instance of idle German fascination with intellectual history. But his answer went beyond Barth's appeal to the Word of God by insisting on a kind of biblical nominalism opposed to any attempt to answer the ontological questions. Gerhard Sauter and Christoph Gestrich replied that Barth had had no choice but to answer the questions posed by Idealism. Gestrich believed that Barth fulfilled Hegel's goals by providing a better answer to the classical ontological questions than Hegel himself had done. He had achieved this by reversing Hegel's subordination of theology to philosophy and establishing a clear distinction between theology and a philosophy shorn of the theosophical pretensions that were the plague of Idealism.

Conclusion

The new historical perspective on Barth presents on the whole a positive relationship between Barth and the modern era. The interpretations divide on the understanding of the modern era itself and on the reading of Barth's reaction to it. A revived Idealism understands Barth as a more or less conscious victim of historical process whose theology represents in one way or another the further development of the understanding of reality in terms of absolute self-consciousness. Other interpretations see Barth as compelled to provide alternative answers to the problems of the nature of thought and its relationship with reality as a whole. Here he was attempting to fulfil at least the aims that Idealism had set itself. For others, his contribution lies precisely in a refusal to admit such questions and in an insistence on the proper object of theology – Revelation in Christ. But even here a positive relationship, a solidarity with the modern era, is now affirmed. On the one hand the rejection of all universal theories of reality is welcomed as a modern reaction against a theosophical tendency that had long plagued modern philosophy. Barth's positivism in Revelation could be seen to have a healthy counterpart – and even complement – in a methodically restricted philosophy. On the other hand Barth's socialism is seen to have led him to a thoroughly modern unmasking of the true nature of modern philosophy: the principle of self-conservation or man's quest for domination over reality. Here the insistence on the Word of God over which man can have no control is welcomed as a modern liberation from modernity.

AUTONOMY AND IDEALISM IN BARTH

In this and the following section we examine in more detail recent interpretations of Barth that pay special attention to the relationship between the autonomy of man and the freedom and transcendence of God. To articulate this relationship is to pose the question of its ontological basis and therefore the question posed by the Roman Catholic reception of Barth from its beginning. The revived interest in Idealism led to a new interest in the Idealist elements in Barth's theology. The question was how far Barth had adopted or carried out the Idealist programme and whether his insistence on the sovereignty of God as revealed in Jesus Christ could or could not be reconciled with any of the variations on the autonomy theme in Idealism.

The radical autonomy of God: Trutz Rendtorff

For Trutz Rendtorff neither Barth's appeal to the Bible nor to the Church nor to God's action in Revelation is sufficient to explain the historical impact of his theology. In the Enlightenment and its aftermath Christianity had long emancipated itself from the Church with its institutional, heteronomous reception and transmission of Revelation in favour of the autonomous activity of the productive self-consciousness. The result was a freer and more universal Christianity, for which secularisation represented a gain in the free realisation of ethical and religious values outside the Church.[100] Barth could have had no hold on the attention of this Christianity unless he had more to offer than mere reaction.

Rendtorff understands Barth not as a reactionary who wished to return to a pre-Enlightenment theology but as a Liberal theologian who adopted a radically Liberal position, as a true follower of his teacher Wilhelm Herrmann. Barth went to the core of the dispute that lay behind the attempts of Liberal theology to mediate between traditional Christian theology and modern thought: the problem of autonomy. Radical autonomy reduced all other positions to the status of conditioned, contingent and secondary entities. Liberal theology's attempts to meet the challenge by means of ethical or historical arguments were doomed to failure. The Enlightenment, with its principle of autonomy, must be radically adopted or not at all. Barth chose to adopt the principle of autonomy in a radical sense, but instead of accommodating himself to the historical event of the Enlightenment, as Liberal theology had done, he presented the principle of autonomy in a new systematic construction as a challenge at every possible point to the accepted self-understanding of the Enlightenment. What Barth represented was a new Enlightenment that turned on the Enlightenment itself the same critical weaponry which the Enlightenment had formerly used against religion. He replaced the freedom and autonomy of man with the freedom and autonomy of God. On the one hand Bultmann's analysis (in his review of the second edition of the Commentary on Romans) that Barth was concerned with the independence of religion was correct, but on the other hand Barth's intention was more radical: the autonomy of God, or of religion, must relativise all other positions.[101]

By means of this change in the subject of autonomy – from man to God – Barth transformed the difficulties with which Liberal theology had struggled in vain. The epistemological problems that had been the daily bread of Barth's Neokantian theological schooling under Wilhelm Herrmann were turned in a deft dialectical reversal into evidence for the impossibility of speaking about God apart from Revelation. The thesis of the radical autonomy and freedom of God rendered all forms of human knowledge and life itself arbitrary, irrelevant and contingent. The first task of theology, according to Barth in his Commentary on Romans, was to expose the illusory character of human life and consciously to question every form of insight and knowledge that was not based in God's own Word of Revelation.[102]

In the *Church Dogmatics*, according to Rendtorff, the question of Christology is the dogmatic form in which Barth treated the problem of autonomy. Jesus Christ is the expression of God's autonomy. This means that theology must be reduced to Christology; indeed Rendtorff claims that Barth tended more and more in the later sections of the *Church Dogmatics* to qualify even his own theological explanations as doubtful and irrelevant and to insist on the simple formula 'Jesus Christ'. This betrays the radical nature of Barth's insistence on the pure autonomy of God, which is threatened as soon as explanation is attempted, since explanation implies mediation with the reality of man.[103]

The radical autonomy of God, now transformed into a demand for a radical Christology, enabled Barth to subject the whole of traditional theology to a radical revision. Barth's profession of adherence to an ecclesiastical theology is countered with the observation that Barth always preserved a critical independence of ecclesiastical institutions and adopted a style of biblical exegesis that did not follow the official criteria but those of a self-determining theological autonomy. Nor may Barth's theology be understood as a repristination of Reformation theology. Barth made use of the material of a precritical theology but he did so in order to dispose of the challenge posed by tradition. To leave this challenge unanswered, as Bultmann did, is to leave one's theology open to the charge of reductionism. Barth's aim was to overcome the burden of tradition by subjecting it to a radical systematic revision and so to 'liquidate' the liability imposed on modern autonomy by the history of Christian thought.[104]

Rendtorff proceeds to substantiate this thesis by means of three examples drawn from the *Church Dogmatics*.[105] In the first, he portrays Barth's doctrine on predestination as an attempt to avoid the concession that God and man might have to do with another instance alongside of God, namely with evil. God takes back the problem of double predestination into his divine self-determination and so removes it from the sphere of human life and reality. This doctrine shows a striking analogy with the axiomatic victory of good over evil in Enlightenment philosophy. The tendency of the doctrine of Election is even more marked in Barth's treatment of evil and sin. In speaking of these only in paradoxical terms (as 'the impossible possibility') Barth revealed his inability to concede them any reality in case that might diminish the unlimited and unconditioned sway of God's autonomy in the world.

In the third example, Rendtorff criticises Barth's inability to accord any substantial reality to the Church. Whereas in the Commentary on Romans it at least had the dignity of being the last bastion of religious man against God, at the end of the *Church Dogmatics* the Church has no more than a shadow existence: it is a mere reflection of the Christological principle of autonomy and nothing in itself. It is conceived in terms of decision; it is dissolved in a constant movement and thus prevented from developing any consistency of its own. This amounts to a 'liquidation' of the Church. This radical relativisation of the Church is topped by a further thesis: God's action in the world is not bound to the Church. The world would be lost without Christ, but it need not be lost without the Church. The Church, however, would be lost without the world because its right to existence is reduced to a functional relationship to the world. The result is that the Church is set an impossible task but that its success or failure in fulfilling this task is finally irrelevant since Jesus Christ can go his own autonomous way without reference to the Church.[106]

Far from attaining his aim of reversing the Enlightenment, Barth became the instrument by which the Enlightenment, with its boundless moral optimism and its separation of Christianity from the Church, pursued its conquering advance into the heart of Christianity. To adopt radical autonomy in a Christological form was to end the traditional opposition between dogmatic theology and modern autonomy. But it could do so only by a radical revision of traditional

Christian theology.[107] Why this must be so is explained by Rendtorff in the article 'Theologie als Kritik und Konstruktion'. In reaction to the challenge of autonomy, twentieth-century theology in general was compelled to take up the historical problem of autonomy as a systematic problem, that of radical subjectivity. Not only the contents of traditional theological teaching but scientific inquiry and the interest in religion can all be relativised as products of constructive or critical self-consciousness. Even the interest in an objective theology, in an 'object' supposedly outside of human subjectivity (such as is characteristic of Barth), is caught in the dilemma. It is forced endlessly to distinguish itself from philosophy or science and thus to betray itself as an act of reflective self-consciousness like any other.[108]

Modern theology dissolves apparent historical and religious objectivity into subjectivity, not in order to do away with its object, but to make evident that its root lies in productive and constructive self-consciousness. This pure, creative subjectivity becomes the real theme of modern theology and the more radical the theology the more it represents this pure autonomy in opposition to the modern bourgeois Western culture that claims to be the historical realisation of autonomy. Thus Rendtorff claims that theology is part of the dialogue of the world with itself at the sensitive point at which the transcendent quality of freedom becomes evident. The self-consciousness of autonomy is not ultimately based within the world that it creates. Theology is neither more nor less than a commentary on freedom itself; on that it can claim no monopoly but there it is really dealing with a new stage in historical consciousness.[109]

THE ETHICAL MEANING OF BARTH'S *DOGMATICS*

Trutz Rendtorff took up the problem of autonomy in Barth a second time in a consideration of Barth's doctrine of Baptism, which had proved so startling not just for its rejection of sacrament and of infant baptism but also for its insistence on the freedom of the human subject in undertaking baptism with water and on the ethical meaning of this act. Rendtorff reconsiders from this perspective the entire relationship between dogmatics and ethics in the *Church Dogmatics*. Barth had seen in the priority of ethics over religion in Liberal theology the surrender of the specific theme of theology. For the subjectivity of man he substituted the subjectivity of God and correspondingly asserted the priority of dogmatics over ethics. Rendtorff, however, argues that the reality which Barth seeks to repress returns in another form. Dogmatics must in fact now claim for itself the perception and the solution of the basic problems which constitute the importance of ethics and which ethics itself is unable to solve. Indeed Barth's doctrine of God can be said to derive its meaning as theology from the insoluble problems of ethics in that it poses the key question of how the subject of ethical action can be grasped in its purity, prior to the determinate subjectivity of the empirical human being. In modern philosophy and theology the ethical understanding of man had either become Promethean or had not been tackled sufficiently at the level of principle. Barth's answer to the problem is that the self-determination of man must follow on his predetermination by God, a predetermination that fundamentally consists in God's own self-determination.[110]

The weakness of this solution makes itself felt wherever Barth takes up the question of specific ethics. Here he has difficulty in explaining how theology can conceive of a properly human subject that is capable of action in distinction from God. Sin comes to mean that man makes his own ethic in competition with God; he seeks to explain himself, to confirm himself, to be independent of the grace of God. The change of subject has not eliminated the formal competition between the human and the divine subject.[111]

Nonetheless Rendtorff argues that this conflict is resolved in the broader context of the *Church Dogmatics*. The doctrine of God is explicated by Barth in *ethical* terms. God exists in that he acts; his action is his self-determination as the gracious God and this self-determination-for-man is the ethical meaning of the doctrine of God. But man also exists, according to Barth, in that he acts. The problem is thus concentrated on the relation of the divine to the human ethical action and can be formulated thus: the self-determination of man – his freedom – must be taken out of its formal competition with the divine subject and brought into material correspondence with him. Barth's solution is to construct in the doctrine of God an ethical framework sufficiently comprehensive to embrace and relativise the formal and abstract competition between the human subject and the divine. The overall purpose is to integrate human freedom and subjectivity into the ethical action, itself constitutive of reality, that is God's Love, Grace and Reconciliation.[112]

Rendtorff is therefore ready to revise his earlier judgement in which he had alleged that Barth was unable to ascribe any significance to human activity as such because that would allow for another instance alongside the autonomy of God. If, in the *Church Dogmatics* as a whole, God takes the place otherwise accorded to man as the autonomous subject, ethics is the point at which free subjectivity is restored for the sake of the Christian conduct of life. This becomes crystal-clear in the doctrine of Baptism. To the subordination of ethics under dogmatic statements about God there now corresponds the setting-aside of all dogmatic statements (such as the notion of sacrament) that might be held to take away from the setting of maximum ethical demands on man. Barth is therefore not properly understood if he is taken to affirm the permanent polarisation of God and man in which God alone is active and man's role is that of passive acceptance. The relation between the action of God and the action of man is not one of cause and effect but of correspondence. The methodical subordination of the human subject under the subjectivity of God does not intend a subjection or suppression by the one of the other but on the contrary the properly established, because henceforth universal and objective, recognition of the free subject. It is his own objective freedom that is confirmed by the Christian subject at his baptism.[113]

Rendtorff's re-evaluation of Barth's treatment of human freedom and autonomy built on Wilfried Groll's comparison between Barth and Troeltsch.[114] Troeltsch had regarded ethics rather than dogmatics as the fundamental science. But he had not understood ethics as unproblematic, and had seen in Nietzschean individualism the symptoms of an ethical crisis brought about by the abandonment of God and of the religious thematic. The autonomy of the subject seemed to Troeltsch to have the character of an insoluble problem. He looked to the scientific treatment of religion to provide a sense of objective goals and a gradation of values. Barth's procedure was to reverse the priorities and decide the question of the objectivity of ethics on the basis of the subject of all reality, namely God. This absolute subject, the ground of all objectivity, could then determine the objectivity of ethics. In Troeltsch's terms, religion could now determine the subject of the objective good. The content of ethics – the objective good – is now established by the relationship in which the human subject stands to the subject God.[115]

Rendtorff thus accepts Barth's account of God and man in terms of a religious ethic. It is religious not only in its style and language but even more so because it resolves a fundamental ethical problem in theological terms. Barth's theology cannot claim to solve the detailed questions of objective morality nor even to have tackled them in a more than arbitrary fashion at the material level. These were the questions that Troeltsch and others referred to non-theological science for clarification. But, in referring ethics to the question of the relationship between God and man, it raises the question of the subject, without which the moral character of ethics cannot be established. Religious ethics cuts across the 'horizontal' dimension of the empirical world and places everything in the special perspective that is accessible to itself alone.[116]

In a lecture delivered in 1981, Rendtorff could look back at the reception given to his thesis that Karl Barth took up modern autonomy in the guise of the 'radical autonomy of God' and claim that no one had been able seriously to refute it.[117] What was disputed was Rendtorff's articulation of theology itself as a commentary on freedom and of its task as the construction of a paradigm that might guide and channel man's understanding of his own freedom in the historical world that his freedom had produced. This understanding of theology disregards too many questions that are essential to the theology of Barth. Rudolf Weth points out that in Rendtorff's interpretation Barth's identification with the Church is presented as a mere historical accident caused by the peculiar circumstances of the ecclesiastical struggle with the 'German Christians'. Weth also observes that, if theology is not to be dissolved in the general theme of modern autonomy, the Word of God must be retained in a sense not allowed for by Rendtorff.[118] Similarly, Dietrich Korsch draws attention to the two complementary aspects of Revelation in Barth. On the one hand it is a self-sufficient principle; on the other it is a contingent historical fact. Once the factual–historical element is ruled out of court, as it is by Rendtorff, there remains only a theological variation of Idealism with all its unresolved problems. Barth's concept is not understood if the unity between abstract principle and historical fact is destroyed.[119] Konrad Stock finds that Rendtorff neglects Barth's theology of the Covenant between God and man and so fails to do justice to the relationship posited by Barth between the autonomy of God and that of man and to Barth's criticisms of the philosophical theory of freedom. He also fails to mention the positive presentation of ecclesiology in Barth in terms of Justification and Sanctification. Stock also observes that the autonomy theme itself remains far too undefined in Rendtorff's original essay on Barth.[120]

Rendtorff, however, admits that his interpretation of Barth is controversial. Barth did in fact resist every attempt to integrate his theology into the horizon of modern thought. No interpretation of Barth can be accepted without reserve. Barth's reconciliation between the sovereignty of God and modern autonomy was not free of ambiguity.[121] The difference ultimately lies in a radically different dogmatic standpoint. In Rendtorff's view, the radical autonomy of God has a radical *function*, that of affirming pure freedom against every claim of a historical structure to be the realisation of freedom. This radicalism may lead to the statement that the self-consciousness of autonomy is not ultimately grounded in the world that it creates. Such a statement points in the same direction as the later Fichte. But, like the later Fichte, Rendtorff does not clearly distinguish between the divine subject and the human. He may speak of the distinction between the divine (universal) and the human (particular) subject. But then he also understands the correspondence in Barth's doctrine of Baptism to take place between *man* as the free subject, ideally conceived, and *man* the empirical subject. God may be spoken of as the 'subject of all reality' and again as 'the freedom that constitutes all subjectivity',[122] but it is not clear how far it is a question of a living subject that confronts man. This sensitive interpreter of the interrelationship between the theological problematic and that of the modern thematic of freedom and autonomy remains selective in his interpretation of Barth. The theme of the Word of God must be tackled more boldly if the full breadth of Barth's theology is to be covered.

SUMMARY

Trutz Rendtorff holds that modern Christianity has long since emancipated itself from the Church and from the heteronomous transmission of Revelation. Barth's appeal for modern Christianity was not based on heteronomy but on his appeal to radical autonomy. He simply replaced the radical autonomy of man by the radical autonomy of God. His assertion of the freedom and autonomy of God represented a new systematic construction that challenged the humanism of the Enlightenment at every point. In taking up the Enlightenment's own weapon – radical subjectivity – Barth compelled himself to present his own theology in the same terms. The result was a radical revision of the entire tradition in Christological terms because it was Jesus Christ who represented for Barth the radical autonomy of God. Rendtorff cites Barth's treatment of Predestination, Election and of the Church as proof that Barth makes himself the instrument of the Enlightenment theme of radical subjectivity. This theme is understood by Rendtorff in Idealist terms: for him it represents the transcendent freedom of the productive self-consciousness.

In a second essay – on the ethical meaning of Barth's theology – Rendtorff made a very positive evaluation of Barth's achievement. Barth had rejected the subordination of dogmatics to ethics in Liberal theology. But in taking the ethical problematic on board, Barth ended by giving a fundamentally ethical meaning to dogmatics. God is now conceived in ethical terms: he exists in that he acts and his action is his self-determination as the gracious God for man. This divine self-determination becomes a predetermination of the being of man. But instead of being heteronomous it is the source of the ethical self-determination of man himself. Instead of competition between God and autonomous man, a correspondence with God's freedom is established in which man's objective freedom is affirmed and he is exposed to maximum ethical demands. The positive ethical consequence of Barth's rejection of sacrament is the affirmation of the ethical subject, man. The fundamental theoretical problem of ethics – the constitution of the ethical subject – is resolved in Barth's account of the relationship of the ultimate subject – God – to the human subject of ethics. The fundamental limitation of Rendtorff's penetrating interpretation of Barth remains, however, its disregard of Barth's insistence on the historical and factual character of the Word of God and its involvement in the unresolved dilemmas of Idealism.

Was Barth an Idealist?

Three years after the publication of Rendtorff's essay on the 'radical autonomy of God' there appeared a collection of essays by Rendtorff and some Idealist colleagues of his in which his critique of Barth's treatment of autonomy is developed. We have already dealt with Rendtorff's own contribution to this volume – on Barth's ethical understanding of Baptism. The other contributors retain the same format as Rendtorff – analysis of the formal structure of Barth's theological argument, with an evaluation of its positive as well as its negative treatment of the problem of freedom and autonomy in Idealist terms to the exclusion of Barth's concern with the historicity and facticity of the Word of God.

Falk Wagner presupposes a much more stringent theoretical framework than that of Rendtorff.[123] Whereas Rendtorff's chief interest lay in the explication of freedom in history, Wagner's is the construction of a systematic theory of reality on the basis of the Idealist philosophy of self-consciousness. Barth's theology must first be stripped of its positivism and objectification. Wagner credits F. W. Marquardt with the first successful attempt to 'reconstruct' Barth's theology in this way, namely to lay bare its inner structure and to demonstrate what function particular dogmatic material plays in the whole. The aim is to relativise the importance of the particular dogmatic content affirmed by Barth and even to substitute other content without destroying the overall structure. Wagner speaks in this context of 'encoding' and 'decoding' theology.[124] As both Dieter Korsch and Wolf Krötke point out, Wagner thus imposes on Barth's theology an interpretative framework in which Barth's real concern, the factual–historical event of Revelation, is methodically excluded and the only possibility allowed is the position for which Wagner himself is pleading, an 'apologetic Idealism' (Krötke), or 'a theological variation on the philosophy of identity' (Korsch).[125]

Friedrich Wilhelm Graf's contribution to *Die Realisierung der Freiheit* shows the same theoretical concern as Wagner's essays. The main point of attack by both authors is Barth's failure to solve the theoretical dilemma of self-determining subjectivity and indeed Barth's argument in his criticism of alternative anthropologies that this dilemma is insoluble.[126] Barth's concept of God fails to take account of the other as such, the abstract other of Idealism. But the argument as presented by Wagner and Graf is of limited interest except perhaps to specialists in Idealism. Walter Sparn, in his study of the doctrine of Election in the same book, makes a similar charge. Barth neglects the other, but for Sparn it is the empirical human subject that is the neglected 'other'.

The individual human subject of religious experience that is presupposed by the dogmatic tradition is dissolved in the kind of exclusively Christological theonomy proposed by Barth. But Sparn does not find conclusive evidence for this charge without taking further account of the doctrine of Reconciliation. On the whole, Sparn vindicates the systematic consistency of Barth's theology, a consistency that is obtained by adhesion to a single methodological and epistemological principle: God's self-determination as exclusively revealed in his self-revelation in the Scriptures. The means of knowledge and its object coincide.[127]

In a dissertation on the doctrine of Reconciliation in Barth and Hegel, Christophe Freyd took up the challenge posed by the work of Trutz Rendtorff and his collaborators. He attempted to show that Barth succeeded in reconciling the freedom and autonomy of God and man in an Idealist framework. Freyd too felt entitled to disregard Barth's categorical rejection of the systematic principle of Idealism because he believed that Barth fell victim willy-nilly to the Idealist systematic. The autonomy and priority of God was the principle on which his theology was constructed and its scope was universal. Therefore the only question could be whether Barth had failed to reconcile divine and human freedom (as Graf and Wagner had claimed) or whether he had succeeded. That he did succeed was due in Freyd's view to the parallels between Barth's system and that of Hegel.[128]

Freyd admits that there is no question of a direct literary dependence of Barth on Hegel. Michael Welker has since abundantly confirmed this point: Barth had read no more of Hegel than two hundred pages of the *Philosophy of Religion*. Freyd uncovers some clues to an interest in Hegel on the part of Barth, such as Barth's admission that he had a weakness for Hegel. (Barth made the remark, however, only as an illustration of his eclecticism.)[129] Another clue, welcome to Hegelian interpreters of Barth, is contained in the postscript to a selection of readings from Schleiermacher. There Barth revealed that he had thought of writing a theology of the Holy Spirit in which the whole of God's work for the creature would be presented completely, 'in a teleology that would exclude every element of chance'. Freyd's claim is that it was Barth's more or less conscious intention to produce such a complete system in *KD* IV, that he in fact did so and that this system of Reconciliation structurally coincided with Hegel's system of 'unity in distinction'. The difference between Barth and Hegel, as Freyd's constant refrain has it, is only a matter of emphasis.[130]

Freyd therefore remains closer to Barth's text and intention than Wagner and Graf. He explicitly attaches himself to the right-wing Hegelians and rejects the left-wing interpretation of Hegel. He is especially anxious to emphasise that Hegel did not understand God to arrive at his true reality in man but to possess his identity in himself. Neither did Hegel identify the Holy Spirit with the human subject. Freyd is therefore anxious to correct a number of negative judgements that Barth made about Hegel. The evident difference between Barth and Hegel is explained by Freyd as a greater emphasis on the priority and freedom of God on the part of Barth. This emphasis on God's freedom and priority means that all statements about the relationship between God and man are based by Barth in God rather than in a reciprocal relationship in which neither side would have priority. Man has his being only in union with God; he becomes a subject only in the act in which God reconciles himself with him. That is the constitutive moment in Barth's anthropology. Man exists therefore only as a moment in the divine history.[131]

However, this is the point at which Freyd turns the tables on Barth. For even if, as Freyd concedes, Barth affirms a real autonomy in which man's own free decision confirms and activates the divine decision, this freedom is clearly secondary. This means not only that the prior activity of the divine subject and the secondary activity of the human subject are established but that the unity of both is included, a unity in difference but a unity nonetheless. Thus Baptism with the Spirit and baptism with water in *KD* IV/4 must not merely be distinguished; they must also be grasped as a unity. The subject of the Christian life is simultaneously God and man.[132] Freyd does not conclude that man's freedom is nullified because man is a secondary subject. Instead he claims that Barth is affirming a 'dialectical unity' of God and man.

Freyd explicitly dismisses some elements in Barth's thinking that do not fit in with this thesis. Thus he rejects Barth's occasional use of the Platonic scheme of prototype and antitype on the grounds that it does not do justice to the Incarnation. Instead of a parallelism of prototype and antitype, Barth's correspondence (Entsprechung) between the human and the divine subject must be understood as a genuine human participation in the divine, resulting in a unity of the two subjects. Freyd's treatment of Barth's use of analogy betrays embarrassment. On the one hand he is anxious to establish that Hegel made use of analogy and that Barth's use of it is precisely because of, rather than in spite of, his use of dialectic. On the other hand the whole tenor of Freyd's argument calls for the abandonment of analogy. Analogy is 'insufficient' for that which Barth wishes to express. The reconciliation between God and man in the *Church Dogmatics* is more than an analogy: it is identical with God's being. As God's self-revelation is a repetition of his entire being in time and space, the 'proportion' Barth speaks of between God in himself and God in his relation to the world is really an identity. The analogy becomes identity.[133]

Because analogy becomes identity, Barth must be considered to have finally revealed the mystery of the Incarnation. In Barth's inference from the history of Incarnation and Reconciliation to the immanent Trinity he can be shown to have overstepped the limits he had formerly set himself and to have created a structure equivalent to that of Hegel's Idea.[134] God takes the 'other', takes contradiction and death into his own being. As against the axiom of immutability God becomes free to be conditioned.[135] Incarnation and Reconciliation are the outwardly directed aspect of God's own being and are the *joint* realisation of the being of both God and man (even though this is exclusively grounded in God). According to Freyd this must necessarily be so: otherwise God would have no meaning for the world.[136] God must be thought of as a comprehensive unity that includes himself and the world even in his inner being.

Thus Freyd urges the systematic consequence of the Idealist elements adopted by Barth against what he presents as Barth's failure of nerve. Barth should have accepted that his systematic explanations had abolished the category of mystery.[137] He should have recognised that he had really shown that sin was not an absurdity but a necessary part of the history of Reconciliation and was ultimately founded on the trinitarian distinctions.[138] Freedom and necessity were in this system not mutually exclusive in God, so that, once God's eternal free decision for universal reconciliation had been made, pure transcendence was no longer possible and the Incarnation, the Resurrection and universal salvation (*apocatastasis panton*) were a logical necessity.[139] Christ became the Hegelian Idea,[140] and the divinisation of man, the identity of the being of Christ with the being of the Church, of his mission with hers, and the secularisation theology of Gogarten and Metz, were necessary consequences.[141] A Christian philosophy of history such as

Hegel's becomes possible and necessary; world history and the history of Salvation run parallel.[142] Christ becomes an exemplar whereas the Spirit is revealed as the primary figure whose 'inclusive power' is the real motor of the history of Reconciliation. Barth's concentration on Christology would therefore have to yield to pneumatology.[143] The 'truths of the world' are forms in which the truth of Christ manifests itself; Revelation becomes the key to all knowledge in the world; the *theatrum* becomes itself a part of the *gloria Dei* and the bearer of Revelation.[144]

That Barth had toyed with all of these ideas is amply demonstrated by Freyd. That they really represent his theology is another question. It is clear that Barth had sound theological reasons for what Freyd presents as his 'failure of nerve'. The affirmation of these consequences of the Idealist elements in his thought would have carried him beyond the bounds of what he knew to be sound Christian theology as witnessed by the Bible and the Christian tradition. In particular, the step beyond analogy into the affirmation of an identity of God and man, however qualified, would have completely reversed the whole programme of Barth's theology from its origins. The idea of a systematic unity that embraced both God and man and which was given to man to grasp was the heresy that he thought he could identify in the analogy of being. Freyd understands Barth's system to be based on God alone and therefore to avoid the pitfalls that Barth saw in the analogy of being. But where the inner being of God enters into a system of Reconciliation, where nature is so unproblematically integrated with and identified with grace, where the divinisation of man is affirmed, the limits set by Barth are disregarded. Despite a nuanced and balanced approach to Barth's thinking, Freyd does not pay sufficient attention to the anti-Idealist and non-systematic elements in Barth. That he fails to do so is due to an overemphasis on the importance of system in theology and an insufficient respect for the reasons behind Barth's eclecticism – the priority of the history of the Word of God in all its complexity over the systematic efforts of the dogmatic theologian.

A SYNTHESIS OF REVELATION AND EXTRA-THEOLOGICAL KNOWLEDGE?

The possibility of a new theology of the Holy Spirit that might overcome the limitation of Barth's 'Christological constriction' and integrate the whole of human knowledge was raised again by Christof

Gestrich. Again the remarks of Barth in his postscript to the edition of Schleiermacher were the starting-point. Gestrich took up the open question to which he had pointed at the conclusion of his work on dialectical theology and modern thought: whether Barth's doctrine of Revelation might meet the need for a modern and pertinent *verification* of discourse about God. This demand, originating in the discussion about the nature of science that had been launched by the Neopositivists and by linguistic philosophy, was here integrated with the demand for a synthesis of all reality as in Pannenberg's theology.[145]

Barth had admitted that he had never been able to decide whether Schleiermacher's anthropological theology was intended or could be understood to be a theology of the Holy Spirit. In conjunction with Barth's own remark that he himself had thought of writing a theology of the Holy Spirit in which the entire work of God for man would be presented, Gestrich claims that Barth, had he lived, would have attempted a synthesis between his own ecclesial dogmatics and Schleiermacher's intention. The characteristic of Schleiermacher, according to Gestrich, was 'the acknowledgement of a debt to extra-theological knowledge of the truth'. Here, however, the critical questions that Barth posed about Schleiermacher have been omitted. In four pairs of questions Barth had asked: Was Schleiermacher writing theology or philosophy? Is God in Schleiermacher's writings clearly distinct from man or not? Is man related primarily to a particular and concrete reality or to a universal essence of reality? Is the Spirit that moves man particular, distinct from other spirits, or a universal, diffuse, dynamic power? Barth could only accept a dialogue with Schleiermacher when all these questions had been answered in the sense of the first alternative. It is only in this sense that his open question about a theology of the Holy Spirit can be understood. Gestrich does not make this clear.[146]

Gestrich takes up Barth's theme of the universal rule of Christ. Here Barth left unanswered the question of how far all truth and goodness in the world comes from the Spirit of Christ. Does not Barth's separation of the truth taught in the Church from truth in general amount to a failure? Should not Barth have revised many of his judgements on modern intellectual history in the light of the universal rule of Christ? In the later Barth, Gestrich claims, two theological conceptions are in conflict. The one awards the primacy to the Church and its doctrine as an exemplar from which society or the world must learn. The other, so Gestrich claims, allowed an immediate, analogy between the general secular quest for truth, justice or order and the order of the Kingdom of God. In this second conception the Church would stand on the same footing as the world and the one would complement the other in the search for the truth. If Barth had actually adopted this model (the implication is that he had failed to do so) he could not have maintained that prior to faith man merely had to do with idols. The world could then claim to be the historical work of the Holy Spirit just as the Church did.[147]

Trutz Rendtorff's concern with Christendom might thus be taken up. At least, Gestrich argues, Barth might have recognised a potential and sometimes actual Christianity in the world outside the Church. The result would not be a secularisation nor a dissolution or sublation of the Church in a larger unity. Instead, 'Church' and 'world' might remain, independently of one another, two 'predicates' of the one being of Jesus Christ. The Church would be freed from the burden of being the sole representative of Christ. Theology could learn to address itself not only to the truth mediated by Christ within the Church but also to that mediated by him in the world. Such a theology would not represent a total reversal of Barth's position – evidently Gestrich's judgement on Rendtorff's theory of Christendom – but would at the same time seek to do justice to Schleiermacher's intention.[148]

The difficulty with this argument is that it confuses Barth's insistence on the service which theology and the Church is to perform for the world with the source of knowledge on which theology is to draw. In the latter area it too evidently overthrows the fundamental thrust of Barth's theology to which he bore witness to the end. It would establish a source of truth for theology alongside and equal to the proclamation of the Word of God in the Church. The statement that Barth made was Christological: the universal rule of Christ means that 'true words' of Revelation can occasionally be found in the world outside the limits of the Church. He never allowed that they might form a source of truth on which theology could systematically draw. He had good reasons for never specifying what they were.

He did of course leave a question open. Barth was not able to give an adequate place to the reality of truth in the world as distinct from

Revelation in Christ. He affirmed its relative value without being able adequately to relate it to Revelation. For this reason Gestrich's search for a more adequate relationship is understandable, but his attempt too easily brushes aside the problematic with which Barth had struggled all his life: the priority of the Word of God.

SUMMARY

Trutz Rendtorff's seminal essay on the radical autonomy of God sparked off a series of Idealist interpretations of Barth that were concerned with the formal structure of Barthian systematics and the extent to which it consciously or unconsciously attempted to fulfil the Idealist programme. The main point of attack for Falk Wagner and F. W. Graf is Barth's failure to resolve the theoretical dilemmas of self-determining subjectivity in its relationship to the abstract other. Walter Sparn accused Barth of a neglect of the concrete subject of individual religious experience. Christophe Freyd, however, considers that Barth did in fact fulfil the Idealist programme. The difference between Barth and Hegel is for him only a matter of emphasis. Barth is alleged to have affirmed a dialectical unity between the human and divine subject. The Reconciliation between God and man in the *Church Dogmatics* is said to pass beyond analogy into an identity with God's own being. The structure of Barth's Christology is equivalent to the structure of Hegel's Idea. God takes the 'other', takes contradiction and death, into his own being. It was only Barth's failure of nerve that prevented him from drawing the consequences. These are: the logical necessity of the Incarnation, the Resurrection and universal salvation (*apocatastasis panton*), the replacement of Christology by a universal pneumatology, and the construction of a Christian philosophy of history on Hegelian lines.

Christoph Gestrich also looked to a development of Barth's pneumatology on Idealist lines. Had Barth lived longer he would surely have attempted a synthesis between his ecclesial dogmatics and Schleiermacher's intentions. Gestrich believes that he would have affirmed the world as a source of truth on the same footing as the Church, complementing the Church's efforts in the search for the truth. Church and world would remain as two independent predicates of the one being of Christ. The Church would be freed from the burden of being the sole representative of Christ and theology would address itself also to the truth mediated by Christ in the world.

Conclusion

The current Idealist reinterpretation of Barth reflects the many-sidedness of Idealism itself. What it best underlines is Barth's concern with the freedom and subjectivity of God and with the affirmation of the relative but real autonomy and freedom of man. It also reveals and pays tribute to Barth the systematic thinker. Here, however, the Idealist programme and Barth's theology sooner or later part company. Barth is either castigated for his failure to realise a philosophy of absolute identity or he is accused of a lack of courage in carrying through such a philosophy.

Another interpretation claims the authority of the later Barth for the quest for a universal synthesis of secular knowledge and Christian Revelation. Barth's claims for the universal validity of Revelation in Christ are extrapolated into an explicit denial of the restrictive theses with which he tied his theology to the Word of God. Simultaneously his passion for unity, consistency and order in the presentation of his theology is extrapolated into an implicit denial of the priority of the Word of God over system and of his rejection of system as the ultimate criterion for his work.

The Idealist reinterpretation of Barth also overlooks those other elements of Barth's critique and correction of Idealism to which Dieter Becker has recently drawn attention in his dissertation on Barth and Buber. Barth adopted elements of the I–Thou philosophy that modified the radical subjectivism with which the Idealist philosophy of the absolute subject had previously been identified,[149] and qualified its compulsion for system-building. Becker admits that one strand in Barth's thought is the radical subjectivity of God as outlined by Rendtorff and those who followed him, including Falk Wagner, Friedrich Wilhelm Graf and more recently Pannenberg and Moltmann.[150] The concept of God as the absolute subject dominates Barth's account of the vertical relationship from God to man and the much-admired systematic construction of the *Church Dogmatics*. But alongside this train of thought and in tension with it runs Barth's account of subjectivity in terms of the personalist I–Thou philosophy. This is most marked in his treatment of human subjectivity as intersubjectivity, but it is also decisive for the relationships between God and man and between God and Christ and Christ and man. Indeed the account of human intersubjectivity itself appeals to a Christological and ultimately trinitarian foundation.

Barth characterises the relationship of God and man as an I–Thou relationship. Primarily God is subject and man object, but in knowing God man is also subject and God the known object. Man's act is his own free spontaneous act. The freedom of man and the self-determination of God are brought together in the formula of man's being as gratitude. From God, man's being is an object in pure receptivity but towards God it is a subject in pure spontaneity. God's being-in-himself is a being-in-relationship characterised by genuine encounter and this relationship finds analogy and correspondence in God's relationship to man. The principle of correspondence is also the foundation for the possibility of God's relationship with man. The movement from God to man is primary; that from man to God is complementary. Becker shows that the current emphasis on Barth's Idealism overlooks Barth's anti-Idealism, which consists in a marked relational and personalist thinking. It finds expression in Barth's tendency to use the concepts history and encounter synonymously. Barth's understanding of the inner-trinitarian relationships as a confrontation of I and Thou can partly be explained in terms of a subjectivist philosophy of reflection on the self but it also envisages a genuine encounter of persons. Barth's concern for the absolute subjectivity of God is complemented by thinking in terms of relationships, duality, reciprocity, dialogue, (inter-)subjectivity, analogy and perspectivity.[151]

Becker shows that Barth's theology is not characterised by the absolute consistency of a perfect system, but that at least two streams of thought run together. The current critical perspective on Barth from the Idealist standpoint simply disregards the relational elements in Barth's thinking.

AUTONOMY AND ONTOLOGY: EBERHARD JÜNGEL

Analogy and anthropology

Eberhard Jüngel's interpretation of the relationship between God and man and the relative autonomy of man in Barth's theology pays close attention to the problems of analogy and ontology while maintaining a strict adherence to the Reformation principles of *sola fide* and *solo verbo*.

Early in his academic career, Jüngel took care to clarify the relationship between God and man expressed in Barth's doctrine of analogy. He did so in dialogue with Hans Urs von Balthasar, Gottlieb Söhngen, Erich Przywara and Wolfhart Pannenberg.[152] Jüngel criticised Pannenberg's rejection of analogy, especially his assertion of a univocal element in all analogy. Jüngel sees in this assertion an abstract concern with the epistemological aspect of analogy. This abstract concern reveals that the subject man is still being treated as the starting-point of analogy. The criticism that Jüngel made of Pannenberg's rejection of analogy he applied equally to the Catholic insistence on the analogy of being. Jüngel rejects all concern with the human subject in analogy. Therefore the epistemological point of view is as irrelevant as the ontological. It is not a matter of similarity within a greater dissimilarity, nor of a dialectic between similarity and dissimilarity nor of a third term between univocity and equivocation.[153]

Whereas Pannenberg's understanding of the traditional doctrine of analogy had overlooked the negative aspect (*via negativa*) and exaggerated the positive element (*via positiva* understood as univocity), Jüngel's interpretation is the opposite: he can see only the negative aspect, the 'greater dissimilarity' asserted by the Fourth Lateran Council. Whereas most Protestant theologians had believed with the early Barth that the Catholic notion of analogy did away with the distinction between God and man, Jüngel now alleged with the later Barth that it made the distinction greater. As a merely human utterance it said nothing about God.[154] Jüngel's criticism of the *via positiva* in the light of the *via negativa* is complemented by a criticism of the *via eminentiae* (the application of open-ended superlatives to God) as an alleged attempt of man to ascribe to God a maximum of advantages and to exclude what appears to him to be deficiency from the divine being. This criticism rests on a contrast made by Jüngel between the theological tradition, whose theism is presented as a merely human effort to conceive of God, and the principle of God's self-revelation, which alone can establish the correct use of analogical language.[155]

The principle of Revelation alone is Jüngel's guide in his attempt to show that Barth's use of the analogy of relation in the later parts of the

Church Dogmatics must be understood exclusively in the sense of the analogy of faith. It is radically opposed to the adoption of an analogy of being even in the form of that presupposition for grace proposed by Söhngen which Urs von Balthasar had claimed was implicit in the *Church Dogmatics*.[156] According to the principle of Revelation alone, all valid analogy is founded on and to be known in the being of the man Jesus Christ. That God reveals himself in Christ means that the being of Christ corresponds to the inner being of God himself. This is the primal correspondence or similarity on which all other analogies are based. 'Correspondence' (Entsprechung) rather than similarity is the key term for Jüngel in interpreting analogy. It bears both a noetic and an ontological significance. It is in the coincidence of the noetic and the ontological that Barth's use of analogy must be grasped and distinguished from all other analogy. All created being, including reason itself, comes from grace and cannot be understood without it. The primacy of grace in the ontological order is reflected in its primacy in the noetic order.[157]

The analogies that Barth uses in his anthropology are therefore not freely invented but are based on a Christological foundation. Analogy is not a tool that Barth uses to develop a theological doctrine of man, but the analogy of relation founded in Revelation alone is the only basis on which a Christian anthropology is possible. It articulates the being of man in terms of a ladder of relationships beginning with God's inner being, descending to the relationship with the man Jesus, further to Jesus' relationship with all men, and further still to man's relationship with his fellow-man. In each God corresponds to himself – in his inner being, in his relationship to the man Jesus, in that of Jesus to man, and in man's relationship to his fellow-man. God, not man, is in every case the subject of the relationship or correspondence. But the correspondence does not extend beyond the relationship. Here the restrictive theses of Barth come into play: the correspondence consists indeed in a repetition of the being of God, but this being is event and as event it is pure relation. This being (Sein) is not a concrete existent (Seiendes) and can therefore not be thought of in terms of the analogy of being.[158]

As opposed to Söhngen, Jüngel does not even accept that Barth affirms a series of analogies or correspondences between God and himself, God in relation to man, man and man. The relationships *do not exist* except in the concrete 'yes' in which God, who is always the subject, corresponds to himself and so *simultaneously* posits other being. Jüngel can speak of the analogy of being (analogia entis) but only in the verbal form (analogia tou einai) not in the nominal (analogia tou ontos). The 'yes' of God grounds all creaturely being only as an external Word. The phenomenon of analogy belongs only on the side of the constitutive element, not of the constituted element. Analogy is a formula that expresses simultaneously the foundation and relationship in which the creature exists, namely God's 'yes'. It does not mean a common being, similarity or participation in God. The being of the creature is posited simultaneously with the relationship. The creature is not real in itself but real only in its relationship with God. Insofar as man exists, he exists outside of himself in that relationship.[159]

Anthropology, autonomy and freedom

God's self-determination as the God of man means that man can never be totally without God. The result of this bond is not, however, identity but distinction. Properly understood, it makes it possible for man to be man rather than to aspire to be God. Consequently, obedience is not an act of subjection that God demands of man so that he may himself rule (as in Falk Wagner's interpretation) but is something which is alien neither to God nor to man as he should be. One must not stop with Barth's insistence on obedience to God but pay attention to how he speaks of this obedience. Freedom and joy correspond on man's side to Barth's concept of God. A free obedience is the affirmation of the meaning and significance that is awarded to one's own being. Man is self-determining, not absolutely but within the context of his predetermination by God, a predetermination that corresponds to God's self-determination as the God of man.[160]

The relationship of God to man is ontologically prior to man's relationship to himself. It is opposed to that will of man to be the author of his own being in which Jüngel sees the essence of sin. Man comes to himself not in himself but in another, Jesus Christ. It is the denial of man's divinity that is the strictest definition of man's humanity. There is therefore only one freedom for man: that granted by God in Christ. It is opposed to the Liberal concept of freedom as an immanent characteristic of the human individual and of society.[161]

Man is not free; he is set free, set free especially from the compulsion to himself that makes him want to be God and so causes him to tyrannise others. Liberation consists in God's justification of man, which establishes God's right to man's freedom and renders impossible any natural right to freedom based on natural law. Thus man has no other right to freedom, not even one based in conscience, than God's right to man's freedom, which is expressed not in terms of law but in those of the Gospel. There are thus no absolute legal claims to freedom, only those granted in relation to God's justice.[162]

What human law must do is to respect this claim of God and it does so insofar as it respects man's freedom to live according to the freedom granted him by God. It is only through analogy, the analogy of relation based in Revelation alone, that Jüngel establishes criteria for freedom in relations between man and man that correspond to the freedom of the Gospel and coincide in large part with the freedoms proclaimed and realised by the Enlightenment. These are freedom to believe (which implies the freedom to live), freedom to communicate, freedom to proclaim the Gospel, freedom of information (about the Gospel), freedom for the future (implying freedom to criticise and to change). These are not legal demands but a challenge to the law-maker on the basis of purely theological reflections that refrain from establishing a legal demand that must inevitably confuse the law of God with laws made by man.[163]

Ontology, correspondence and relationship

This account of man's being as consisting exclusively in his relationship to God forms the interpretative framework for Jüngel's enthusiastic reception of Barth's doctrine of Baptism in *KD* IV/4. Barth's new insistence on the distinction of the human subject from the divine is explained as consistent with the notion of correspondence. For correspondence distinguishes man from God as well as it relates him to God. The activity of the human subject can thus be affirmed by Barth without adopting synergism or presupposing concurrence.[164]

The claim that Jüngel makes here is at first sight paradoxical. For the far-reaching parallels between God and man established by the category of correspondence − including even the repetition of God's inner being in his outward action in the ladder of relationships – as well as the denial to man of any existence distinct from the pure relationship to God, must indeed give the impression that Jüngel's Barth interpretation treats man as an epiphenomenon of the divine activity. But in Jüngel's view the movement of Barth's theology in its final phase is the opposite. Its premise is not the Idealist scheme in which the distinction between God and man is overcome by a stronger identity in Reconciliation. Instead the starting-point is the togetherness of God and man in the Covenant, which alone makes being possible in the first place. It is only this togetherness that subsequently reveals and establishes a lasting distinction between God and man. It is a question of that order of being that corresponds to the salvific action of God. The movement is not towards unity but from unity to distinction.[165]

The distinction between God and man has as its consequence Barth's rejection of the notion of sacrament. Jüngel traces this rejection to a radical insistence by Barth on the Christological restriction: Jesus Christ alone is sacrament. This restriction applies not only to the doctrine of Baptism. Barth also abandoned his own theology in *KD* I/1, written before his development of the Christological principle, and no longer held to the sacramental character of the Word of God in its proclamation in the Church. Like Baptism, this proclamation now possesses simply ethical character. The doctrine of the different forms of the Word of God is now dismissed as an Idealist concept that has long been replaced by the notion of correspondence. Similarly the Eucharist and the Church must now be understood in a non-sacramental, merely ethical sense. The criterion of the Reformation, *solo verbo – sola fide*, is fulfulled, following Calvin's formulation: *externis mediis non est alligatus Dei virtus* (God's power is not bound by external means).[166] Thus in Jüngel's interpretation too the old axiom *finitum non capax infiniti* returns to throw its shadow on the work of the later Barth.

What, then, is the reality of the being and activity of man in his correspondence to the action of God? What is the ontological basis of his autonomy? Jüngel qualifies Barth's interpretation of Baptism as ethical and as existential. Barth's is, according to Jüngel, probably the first existentialism that did not presuppose a natural possibility in man, a Catholic *potentia oboedientialis*. Man has no possibility, man is himself no possibility for the foundation of the Christian life. It is solely on the basis of God's action that the corresponding action of man occurs. Both actions together make one event. Man corresponds to God's subjectivity with a subjectivity of his own. He is not merely the passive impression of the divine activity, not the concave that corresponds to a convex. He is himself.[167]

Man is enabled to be himself, however, only insofar as he is constituted in his innermost being by his relationship with God. The Word of God posits man from within and thus, working from within, enables man to become himself. Therefore the Word of God has become the core of man in his new life and integrates him. Jüngel cannot accept that man is already constituted when Jesus Christ takes up his abode in him. That would mean that Christ in us would be outside of himself (außer sich). He is within us and simultaneously himself because he posits us outside of ourselves (extra nos). Man is therefore posited from within but outside of himself (von innen herausgesetzt). Christ in us must be understood with final consequence as our being posited outside of ourselves (poni nos extra nos), that is exclusively in the being of Jesus Christ.[168]

Jüngel's interest lies in a theology that combines linguistic and hermeneutical word-categories with the ontological and actualist categories employed by Barth. It is there that he situates Barth's 'existentialism'. Jüngel refers to his essay 'Jesu Wort und Jesus als Wort Gottes' for an account of the relationship between word, being and action.[169] Here Jüngel applies the Christological doctrine of anhypostasis and enhypostasis both to the existence of Jesus Christ and to that of the Christian. The anhypostasis of the human nature of Christ means, according to Jüngel, that without the Word spoken about the Kingdom of God Jesus' humanity would not possess any existence at all, much less an independent one (keine selbständige Existenz, sondern nur Nichtsein). Parallel to this statement he states that Jesus in his earthly life is nothing for himself and not himself without the Word of the Kingdom of God (ohne das Zur-Sprache-Kommen der Gottesherrschaft). Thus the classical an- and enhypostasis doctrine, which refers to the one person of Christ, is put aside and the terms are reapplied to a new problematic. They now refer to the relational being (Sein) that constitutes the existence (Existenz) of historical being (Dasein). The enhypostasis is the ontological foundation of the being of Jesus Christ in the being of God. The anhypostasis is the historical form in which the earthly Jesus lives out his being in Christological poverty. In the Resurrection he then manifestly lives out in glory the being of the enhypostasis. The an- and enhypostasis doctrine relates historical being to the ground of all being in its relationship to God.[170]

These statements about the being and existence of Jesus Christ are applied to the eschatological existence (Existenz) of the Christian in Christ. This too is an enhypostasis. In his earthly life the Christian lives out his anhypostasis as a freedom from the compulsive concern with himself. The ground of his being (Seinsgrund) is his enhypostasis in Christ. In his earthly life he lives out only the anhypostasis. To claim that he already lived out the enhypostasis in Christ would be a 'sacramental misunderstanding' not just confined to Catholics. Only in the eschatological future will the enhypostatic being of the glorified Christ, which is the only real being (Sein), be lived out in the existence of the Christian.[171] Here all statements about being (Sein) are withheld for the glorified existence of Christ in which alone the relationship with God that constitutes all being subsists. Both the earthly Jesus and the Christian merely live out an existence related to this being. They do not in themselves have being (Sein) but only non-being (Nichtsein).

In a study of Barth's an- and enhypostasis doctrine, Hans Stickelberger enthusiastically adopted this position of Jüngel's. The traditional ontological questions that had been addressed to Barth by his Catholic critics are here treated as an expression of man's will to be something in himself (in se) apart from God, of his fear of being dispossessed and made into a mere accident. The anhypostasis deprives man only of his egocentric and autocratic being (Dasein), his autarchy. The question of man's being as such is therefore assimilated to the modern quest for absolute self-determination.[172] As regards the enhypostasis, Stickelberger adopts the ancient Christological formula of Maximus Confessor, which has received a wide reception in recent Catholic theology, according to which the greater union of Christ with God means his greater independence (Eigenständigkeit). Thus the problem of simultaneously asserting that man's existence is to be articulated in terms of pure relationship to God and that he is nonetheless free and distinct from God seems to be solved.

Yet here an all-important difference can be observed. Stickelberger is not in fact saying exactly the same as von Balthasar, whom he quotes at this point. Von Balthasar says that when God and man meet in a single person, in the hypostatic union, it becomes clear that God is eternally and irrevocably other than man and that man therefore need not seek his salvation in the sacrifice of his nature. In its being exalted by grace, nature is strengthened and completed in itself. Here von Balthasar presupposes a sound distinction as the basis for the fruitful relationship of nature and grace.[173] But Jüngel's position as taken up by Stickelberger is that of a simultaneity of grace and nature, Creation and Reconciliation. Man is not created for Christ, in view of him, but simultaneously in Christ and exists only in relationship with him. Barth's Christological constriction is formalised in ontological terms.

Summary

Eberhard Jüngel's sensitive and accurate interpretation of Barth's analogy of relation shows how Barth remained faithful to the restrictive theses by which he tied his theology exclusively to the Word of God. Jüngel rejects all concern with the human subject and his claim to know anything or have any existence on the basis of analogy with God. The classical doctrine of analogy he dismisses on the basis of its negative aspect (via negativa). It can tell us nothing about God. Only God's Revelation can establish an analogy, one based exclusively in Jesus Christ. Revelation establishes a ladder of correspondences on which all analogies must be based, correspondences between the inner being of God and that of Christ, between the being of Christ and that of man. This is the only basis on which a Christian anthropology is possible. But these correspondences are to be understood exclusively in actualist terms, in terms of verbs rather than nouns. The creature has no reality in itself, only the paradoxical reality of God's pure relationship with him.

Consequently, the human being can never be without God and his self-determination occurs only within the context of God's relationship with him. Man has no natural rights and no natural freedom; there is only God's right to man's freedom, the claim of God's justice on him. This claim does, however, have consequences for the establishment of political and legal freedom.

Jüngel explains Barth's doctrine of Baptism in *KD* IV/4 in terms of correspondence. Correspondence distinguishes the human being from

God as well as relating him to God. The movement is, according to Jüngel, from a prior unity to distinct operations. Distinct operations mean that water baptism and Spirit Baptism are distinct because God's action and man's ethical activity remain distinct. God's power is not linked to human action. Human ethical and existential action does not, however, presuppose any human substance. The human being is posited outside of himself in the being of Jesus Christ. Jüngel explains this as a Christian existentialism. In this life man lives only an existential freedom from himself. Only in the eschatological future will he live out existentially the being of Christ. Jüngel's anthropology, a restrictive but accurate interpretation of Barth's, however attractive it may be in existential terms, is inadequate as an ontology. It formalises Barth's Christological constriction in ontological terms.

Conclusion

The reduction of Creation to an epiphenomenon of Reconciliation, of nature to an empty theatre, an insubstantial foil for grace, to be conceived purely in terms of a relationship to the latter leads Wilfried Härle to characterise Barth's ontology as an 'ontology of grace'.[174] Härle shows that what Barth says of God's being and of man's and even of the being of nothingness (das Nichtige) corresponds very well to the term 'ontology of grace'. God's being itself is grace, that is the connection between God's being and grace is an identity. Otherwise, Barth says, God would be an evil, a non-existent God. Its relationship to grace is constitutive for the being of being. The being of the creature is a being that needs and participates in grace. It exists only insofar as it is the recipient of grace and corresponds to grace. Even nothingness exists only insofar as it is a contradiction of grace, and thus, Härle argues, the contradiction must be thought of as being posited by grace itself. The presupposition of grace, namely created reality, is reduced by Barth to the historical possibility of the historical realisation of grace.[175]

Härle points out that Barth is not interested in the ontological question in the philosophical sense or in the abstract, but only in terms of a relationship to grace. Nor is he interested in a Hegelian system of mediation in which identity and opposition are reconciled in a higher sublation. For Barth, overcoming opposition means removing it, not preserving it in a dialectical scheme. The ontological question is expressed only in concrete terms, whereby 'concrete' for Barth means in terms of act and 'act' refers to the mode of relationship to God. There are as many concepts of being in Barth as there are relationships to God. Barth does not attempt to build a univocal concept of being but even his understanding of analogy is exclusively an analogy of grace.[176]

Härle rejects Barth's ontology. It fails the test of scientific statements in general. It is not non-contradictory, since its account of sin and evil includes a formal contradiction. It is neither verifiable nor existentially relevant because it abstracts too much from experience and does not give an adequate account of the factual elements that it tacitly absorbs. The deepest objection made by Härle is, however, theological: it does not allow sufficiently for the contingent character of sin and Reconciliation.[177]

The latter point is also the key objection of Konrad Stock against Barth's anthropology. The contingency of sin and Reconciliation must imply the relative priority of Creation. Barth's statements on the ontological meaning of the man Jesus Christ for the being of all men ought to have been referred to God's Word of Creation. Instead Barth is guilty of withdrawing them into a 'Christological concentration' in which they are identical with the Word of Reconciliation. Barth is in fact inconsistent. He makes the distinction between Creation and Reconciliation but then fails to carry it through, so that it remains inchoative. For Barth, the doctrine of Election is decisive, yet he must also allow for a resistance on man's part, a resistance that ought logically to be prior to Reconciliation. Barth does occasionally speak of grace as a new beginning in relation to sin, which implies a priority of Creation. But this admission is not consistently followed up. Stock believes that Barth was aware that this exclusively Christological anthropology could not be maintained and sees in Barth's concessions to Calvin's natural theology in his final lectures on the ethics of Reconciliation a concession, an implicit admission that this was so.[178]

3

Conclusions

The autonomy theme was originally Kant's application to ethics of a legal metaphor, implying the proper rights, duties and operations of a subordinate legal entity within the broader legal context of sovereignty. Kant applied the metaphor to the role of the individual human subject in accepting, excogitating and applying the universal moral law of reason. In doing so, Kant abstracted from the role of society, of culture and of religion in forming and maintaining moral norms and fostering moral insights. As a result the moral individual appeared in artificial isolation.

Both Fichte's theory of the absolute subject practising absolute self-determination and his principle of freedom meant that the original Kantian metaphor was abandoned. Fichte identified the autonomy theme with absolute self-determination and proclaimed an ideal of freedom that was expressly superhuman. Yet Fichte attempted not only to develop a comprehensive theory of freedom in the abstract but also to come to terms with the limitations of its realisation in the world, particularly in view of a plurality of free subjects. In this he was only partially successful. The romantic pathos of freedom and the notion of self-determination subsequently became a powerful catalyst in the clash of political, economic, ideological and cultural forces in the nineteenth century. The autonomy theme was adopted by many political and social causes. We find it being taken up by modern atheism as a polemical assertion of the autarchy or absolute self-sufficiency of the human subject in history, as a positive counterpart to the denial of God. Nineteenth-century Liberal theology attempted a reply and was drawn into an almost exclusive preoccupation with the human subject to the neglect of the identity, freedom and activity of the divine subject.

Karl Barth reacted against Liberal theology by affirming the absolute claims of the divine subject. Here the traditional Calvinist theme of the sovereignty and sole rule of God took on the overtones of modern subjectivity: it became the radical autonomy of God. God was represented as the absolute and supreme subject, the subject that determines all others. This affirmation corresponded in the early Barth with a massive rejection of the claims of human subjectivity. The force of the affirmation of divine subjectivity was to question and indeed negate all expressions of the human will. That rejection characterised the first decade of Barth's theology and formed the popular image of Barth that persisted until after the Second World War and still lingers in some quarters up to the present day. Barth had, however, begun to move away from this early dialectical theology as early as the mid-1920s as he faced the task of articulating his theology in more positive terms. The adoption of a positive principle of analogy, complete with his work on Anselm, *Fides quaerens intellectum* in 1928, paved the way for the first volumes of the *Church Dogmatics*.

The *Church Dogmatics* shows a progressive affirmation of human subjectivity which can readily be traced by following the autonomy theme. Barth first took up Tillich's terms – autonomy, heteronomy and theonomy – and applied them to the Protestant Scripture principle. Man is called to a personal encounter with the divine subject in which he hears the divine Word and responds to it in full and free obedience. This obedience is autonomy. Barth immediately saw the danger of a return to anthropocentrism and sought to head it off by formulating the 'otherness' of God's Word as a heteronomy that confronts man from without, a heteronomy to which Barth intended to give the priority over autonomy. But Barth's insistence on the transcendence of God and his consequent criticism of all human claims to possess God or his Revelation, most especially the claim to possess Christian Revelation objectively in the Church and to put it into practice, did not allow him to give the same importance to heteronomy as to autonomy. His account of heteronomy dissolves almost entirely into subjective categories (biblical, ecclesiastical and confessional 'attitude') and it does not surprise us to find that the term 'heteronomy' is quietly dropped in the remainder of the *Church Dogmatics* while the concept of 'autonomy' in the sense of a subjective obedience and correspondence to God's Word and his action is retained and developed.

Barth's new definition of autonomy must be applied to the theologian himself. He must not try to control the divine subject who is the author of the Word of God but instead abandon the 'will to system', that is the ambition to create a system of his own and to subject all theological material to its constraints. The claim of the human subject to control the process of inquiry must be abandoned in theology. The divine subject remains free. The theologian must let the Word of God speak for itself. Instead of a single comprehensive system, Barth proposed the retention of the classical *loci* of theology: God, Creation, Reconciliation and Redemption. None of these can form the basis of a systematic unity that integrates all the others. Thus the human compulsion to control material by creating a system can be thwarted, that is the theologian is compelled to leave his system open or incomplete to allow room for the Word of God.

Barth took a further step in affirming human subjectivity and its role when he adopted his Christocentric principle. It is Christ who is the true human being. Anthropology must be conceived in terms of analogy to Jesus Christ. Barth can predicate the autonomy of Jesus Christ without difficulty. Jesus' spontaneous and free receptivity for the Father's Word is the perfect autonomy. It is manifest especially in Christ's prayer and even in the Agony of Jesus in Gethsemane, where the struggle reflects God's own struggle and the outcome is a triumphant 'yes'. Jesus Christ is the true autonomous subject, the model for all human existence.

Barth discusses alternative anthropologies in his treatment of Creation such as Fichtean Idealism and the existentialism of Karl Jaspers. Barth's conviction about the reality of the divine–human dialogue leads him to accuse Fichte of arbitrarily excluding the divine subject manifest in Revelation from his philosophy. Jaspers he charges with formulating the encounter with the other in such terms that there is no encounter with a genuinely other subject. Instead there is merely a projection of a sense of otherness immanent to the restless human subject himself. Barth is unwilling to affirm any such immanent perspective, including any autonomy based in human nature itself. Instead he holds to a theological, a Christocentric understanding of humanity.

In Barth's understanding, the human subject is first of all an object posited by God. But the character of this object is in turn to posit itself and become a subject. Barth shares the Idealist and existentialist definition of being as act and decision. But he will allow that it can be true of humanity only within the dynamic relationship in which God establishes the human subject. Humanity has no existence prior to or apart from this relationship. Our autonomy and freedom is a reality, but it is established only at God's summons and only insofar as it is a reflection of the perfect autonomy, the perfect correspondence between Jesus and God.

Barth places the human subject on a ladder of relationships, analogies or correspondences beginning in the inner life of the Trinity, extending to God's outward relationship with the humanity of Christ, then to Christ's relationships with his fellow human beings, then to their relationships with one another. The point of comparison or rather the ontological reality constitutive of all these relationships is not being as such but the freedom and love that is rooted in the subjectivity of God. The relationships are constitutive of the respective subjects, not vice versa. The basic act of human subjectivity coincides with its relationship to God, in prayer. Barth can be said to make a genuine affirmation of the autonomy of the human subject in these theological terms.

Many of Barth's critics take issue with such a statement, accusing him of a deficient notion of freedom in which a genuine otherness is not allowed and all is mere conformity with an absolute divine will. But once this argument is pursued in the abstract the case is lost, for the 'other' becomes an abstraction and, as otherness to God, becomes identified with the pure negation of the Idealists or perhaps with sin or evil. Closer to the bone is the accusation that Karl Barth neglects the empirical human subject of faith and of history and does not accord him substance and weight, treating him instead as a mere epiphenomenon of divine grace and of the divine will.

Barth does indeed wrestle with this latter accusation. His answer is to develop what has rightly been called an 'ontology of grace'. This ontology of grace corresponds to the priority of Revelation and the absolute priority of the divine subject. It is opposed in the first place to any ontological statements that might conceivably provide the foundation for natural theology, to any consideration of God or of man apart from Revelation. The startling consequence is that nature is never said to possess any real substance. It is never said to be more than a shadow, an insubstantial outer shell, an empty theatre, a foil for grace.

Is the existence of nature, then, coterminous or coextensive with the action of grace? Barth's resistance to anything remotely suggesting a natural theology is such that he hesitates to give either a positive or a negative answer to that question. Were nature coterminous with grace, then it might have to be reckoned with as a source of Revelation. Were it not coterminous with grace, then it might have to be allowed an independent existence or an independent voice alongside Revelation. To the end of Barth's life, he continued to struggle with this problem without arriving at an answer. In offering some tentative hints, he laid himself open to subsequent speculation about a reconciliation between Barthian and Liberal theology. He is now claimed to have nourished a desire to fulfil the programmes of Schleiermacher or of Hegel or to have been on the point of abandoning Christocentric theology for a universalist theology of the Spirit. But none of these possibilities would have been consistent with his theology up to that point.

Within the ontology of grace, therefore, and never apart from it, Barth affirms an autonomy of man. This affirmation reflects the mutual determination and convergence of Christology and anthropology. Von Balthasar used the image of the sand in the hour-glass to describe the relationship between theology and anthropology in the *Church Dogmatics*: the primary movement is downwards, from God to man. But this movement makes possible a secondary upward movement from man to God. Once this secondary movement is characterised as a free and spontaneous response, one may speak of it as autonomous.

In his doctrine of Baptism, however, Barth moved beyond this strict mirror correspondence between divine and human action to affirm the distinct actions of two distinct subjects, God and man. The distinction is now employed axiomatically to mean that the action of the one cannot be the action of the other. What in terms of the proper understanding of Baptism itself must be considered a retrograde step has its positive aspect in Barth's more generous recognition of the autonomy of the human ethical subject. Human action is now affirmed to have a substantial reality of its own. The human sphere is of course sharply limited in its importance but within it man has his own proper tasks and activity. He can be said, moreover, to be intrinsically transformed and affirmed by grace, a statement that Barth had been slow to make and which had been urged by authors such as Söhngen and von Balthasar.

These positive gains are, however, offset by some typically Barthian denials to balance the affirmations. The main attack is directed against the notion of sacrament. The mediation between God and man is restricted to narrow categories of word and witness, command and obedience. The biblical testimony to other categories – to the reality of God's sacramental presence in the body of Christ and in the Christian Church, and to his mysterious presence in the world – is disregarded. The corresponding ontology, ably analysed and developed by Jüngel, is excessively limited by the Christological constriction and by the ontology of grace. Barth's affirmation of autonomy, therefore, while substantial and generous in its own terms, remains unduly qualified by a defensive and negative affirmation of God's transcendence.

CRITICAL QUESTIONS

Barth's Christocentric treatment of the autonomy theme raises many further questions. As we followed the convoluted paths of current Barth criticism in chapter 2, we saw how these were teased out in the extensive secondary literature. It remains to draw together what can be said by way of conclusion on these points, each of which opens up fascinating vistas for further reflection and research.

The change of subject from man to God

Looking back on his violent reaction against anthropocentric theology forty years earlier, Barth saw grounds for the thesis later put forward by Trutz Rendtorff:

Was the impression of many contemporaries wholly unfounded, who felt that the final result might be to stand Schleiermacher on his head, that is to make *God* great for a change at the cost of *man*? Were they wrong in thinking . . . that perhaps . . . it was only a new Titanism at work?[1]

Such was not Barth's intention, yet he admits having been so fascinated with God as the 'wholly other' and with having seen him in such isolation, abstraction and absoluteness in contrast with man that he might have provided 'a new justification of the autonomy of man and thus of secularism in the sense of the Lutheran doctrine of the two kingdoms'.[2] Barth's reaction against anthropocentric theology was negative; this negativity was, he admits, reinforced at first by the sources to which he turned for inspiration (Barth mentions especially Calvin's negative influence here). It bound Barth to a permanent controversy with the position that he had rejected, namely with anthropocentrism in theology. This dispute led to his draconian insistence on the principle of Revelation in Scripture, more precisely in Jesus Christ, and his absolute rejection of anything that might appear to compete with that Revelation, especially of natural theology in any form.

If Barth's change of subject from man to God were not to rest in an absolute negation of man that would provide a new justification for the autonomy of man in the sense of polemical self-assertion, the positive integration of man into the sphere constituted by divine subjectivity had to be achieved. That was one of the motives that drove Barth from dialectical theology to the adoption of analogy and on to a Christocentric position. It also prompted the efforts that Barth continually made throughout the *Church Dogmatics* to conceive of the human subject in its distinctness and reality without departing for an instant from the primacy of the divine subject and the absolute claims of grace.

Barth's fear and mistrust of heteronomy was a fear and mistrust of the claim to objective knowledge of Revelation in the Church. It was not a mistrust of the subjectivity of the individual but mistrust of the claims of collective religious intersubjectivity to determine the Word of God. The letter of the biblical text, the Confessions and the teaching authority of the Church could all become instruments in the hand of the collective human subject with which he could seek control over the Word of God.[3] Here, too, Trutz Rendtorff's observation is apt: Barth sought objectivity on the side of the divine subject. But the divine subject was not to be reduced to a projection of the human subject nor to an abstraction corresponding to subjectivity in general. Barth held to the reality of the divine subject in a sense that had long since been dismissed by Liberal theology as naive. Objectivity was to be sought in the greatest possible immediacy to the divine subject on the part of the individual.

The autonomy of the theologian

The question of the interaction of the divine and human subject becomes acute once the theologian has to specify in what divine Revelation consists. It is at its most delicate when one addresses oneself to dogmatic *system*. Barth clearly saw here the Idealist demand that all theological content must be conceived as due to the constructive activity of the thinking subject that is explicating itself in its own constructions. A concession at this decisive point implied a capitulation to anthropocentrism in theology. Barth carried through the change of subject from man to God in this delicate area as well. System was rejected not in the sense of order and coherence but in that of the human 'will to system', conceived on the analogy of the Nietzschean 'will to power'. The human subject must make a systematic effort to be non-systematic, to allow the Word of God to speak for itself, to expose himself to the power of the divine subject rather than to exercise control over the Word of God.

As Rendtorff observed, Barth turns the weapons of the Enlightenment on its champions. He appeals to the pathos of openness for the truth that the Enlightenment had used as a weapon against dogmatic authority. Now it is turned against the new dogmatism that followed the systematic rejection of authority in the Enlightenment: the argument from the systematic unity of knowledge to a radical subjectivity. Against the claim that all knowledge must be explained as the activity of the one knowing subject, identified with man, Barth makes neither the systematic subjectivity of the human subject nor the systematic unity of knowledge the first principle of dogmatics. Its first principle is the systematic subordination of the activity of the thinking human subject to the Word of God.

This subordination is a dynamic openness to the activity, to the freedom and sovereignty, of the divine subject. The divine subject is the originating subject and the human subject is the receptive subject. It is the unity of the divine subject, not the ordering activity of the human subject, that is the cause of the unity of the divine Word and consequently of the unity that may be perceived and affirmed by the dogmatician. His autonomy is only a function of theonomy, which is the autonomy of the divine subject.

Theology as a theoretical science does not claim, in Barth's view, to carry in itself the source or ground of the truth it acknowledges. It posits a distinction between its principle, Revelation in Christ, and its own perception and conceptualisation of this principle. In order that theological knowledge should really occur, theological theory must be granted a participation in the self-revelation of Jesus Christ. As pure theory, as the constructive activity of the theologian, theology denies that it is of itself capable of realising its object, true knowledge of God, while at the same time pointing to the one condition, Revelation, that makes this knowledge possible and actual. It is in this distinction and relationship between the theological theory and the principle of theological knowledge that the theme of analogy becomes essential for a systematic account of theological method. Rendtorff, and more especially Wagner and Graf, deny the possibility of this distinction between the constructive activity of the theologian and the truth he claims to perceive and affirm as coming to him from divine Revelation. The truth of Revelation is reduced to the creativity of the theologian's intelligence. Against this argument, Barth appeals to the material witness of the Scripture and of the Confessions and to the witness of the Church. In his own practice he makes use of this material witness and feels himself obliged to answer to it.[4]

This position is nonetheless open to the challenge of Rendtorff that the activity of the divine subject is no more than an alibi for the uncontrolled autonomy – or rather autarchy – of the theologian. Härle makes the criticism that for Barth it is not what man perceives 'here below' that is valid but only Revelation *as Barth understands it*. Becker observes that Barth did not include himself among the subjects that produce theology but identified his own theology with the sum and substance of theology itself. There exists a broad consensus that Barth's theological stance was a radically autonomous one, at least in the sense that it was emancipated from tradition and from the control of Church authorities.[5]

While this verdict is in part an attempt to correct the popular impression of Barth as a biblical and ecclesiastical dogmatist who was hostile to modern autonomy, it contains its core of truth. Barth's assertion of the immediacy of the divine subject in his Word to the individual human subject, together with his certainty that this Word has infallibly been spoken, tends to constitute an autarchy in relation to every other instance. In particular, as we have seen, he reduces the Confessions and actual decisions of the Church in principle to the same basis as the statements of the individual. All are challenge, suggestion or counsel and the decision between them is left to the inward or subjective autonomy–obedience of the individual. Here Barth does appear to prepare the ground for that destruction or 'liquidation' of the tradition that Rendtorff asserts to have been his conscious or unconscious aim.

However, one can hardly speak of an absolute autarchy here even in relation to other human subjects. It is not an absolute self-positing autonomy, nor is it the source of its own constructs. The Word that will speak is the Word that has spoken. This autonomy is placed in the context of the material witness of Scripture and the Confessions and living witness of the Church, even if in the last resort it is placed above them in direct relationship with the divine subject that is their source. The tradition has its say and the theologian must respond to it. Individual autonomy is the final arbiter of truth only for the individual. The activity of the divine subject is broader than the individual, broader even than the confines of the Church. Barth's reflections on the Prophetic Office of Christ in the course of the *Church Dogmatics* led to an increasing insistence that the Word of God would establish itself no matter what man might do. There is here a parallel with the Enlightenment belief that the truth would assert itself if the autonomy of the rational individual were given free play. The basis of trust is, however, transferred by Barth from the autonomy of the human subject to the activity of the divine subject. The activity of the divine subject also grounds the autonomy of the human subject, but not of the one individual subject alone. Individual autonomy is complemented by the multiplicity of witness to the Word, and the centre of attention is not the perceptions of the individual but the self-communicating activity of the Word of God.

Nonetheless one can agree with Walter Lindemann[6] that Barth does not do justice to the fragmentary character of historical Revelation in his insistence on the self-revelation of God. The realisation of God's self-revelation in his encounter with man is allowed to eclipse and even polemically to exclude consideration of the mediation by which God's self-revelation actually reaches man in his historical situation. In this sense Pannenberg's criticism of Barth can be accepted, even if his reaction against the theology of the Word of God went too far in the opposite direction. What is needed is a theology in which a real interpersonal communication[7] can be affirmed in and beyond the multiplicity and multiformity of historical mediation. The question of natural theology need not then be the embarrassment that it was for Barth, but can be understood as a presupposition that faith itself demands and posits.

Revelation and the question of system

Barth's formula for the presentation of dogmatics, the return to the classical *loci* of Protestant Orthodoxy, has primarily the intention of binding the theologian to the Word of God, since the four classical *loci* do not allow of the construction of a single system based on any one of them. Here Barth takes a decisive step that leaves many of his critics behind. For the demonstration that dogmatics cannot be reduced to the *locus theologicus* of the doctrine of God means that Barth rejects 'theomonism', rejects the abstract 'radical autonomy of God' that Rendtorff originally charged him with, in favour of a doctrine of God that is specified in terms of concrete Revelation, that is in terms of Creation, Reconciliation and Redemption. The insistence on the divinity of God, on the absolute priority of his subjectivity, now ceases to have a purely negative force and, as Jüngel says, becomes capable of a positive interpretation. God's freedom retains its priority, but the force of negative theology, with its ability to relativise every theological statement by appealing to the indeterminate subjectivity of God, is broken. The doctrine of Election is the doctrine of God's free self-determination as the God of man. Karl Barth himself saw in this the decisive change from the negative tendency of his Commentary on Romans: God is positively to be interpreted in terms of Revelation, more specifically in Jesus Christ. The priority of the divine subject in dogmatics is respected only when exclusive attention is paid to this. The autonomy of the human subject of dogmatics consists in his paying that attention to Revelation in Christ alone.

'Revelation alone', however, means the return of system via the demand for consistency and consequence. Attention to Revelation alone means the systematic exclusion from dogmatics of attention to any other source of knowledge. Every other source of knowledge must be treated as problematic and relative in relation to Revelation. Barth accepts and makes positive use of the negative restrictions that Kant had laid on reason in the religious sphere. Kant, he claimed, had seen and set aside the possibility of Revelation outside the bounds of reason alone. It is with the actualisation of this possibility in the Word of God that the dogmatic theologian has to do. Barth employs Feuerbach's projection thesis against every attempt to found knowledge of God on anything other than Revelation alone.[8]

But it is knowledge of God that grounds knowledge of man. Christof Gestrich is justified in his observation that for Barth the real battleground of the struggle against natural theology lay at what we may call the centre of anthropocentrism – the knowledge of man. Barth was driven to attack anthropocentrism in its historical expression, namely within the philosophical tradition since the Enlightenment, and to show the inner impossibility of man's constituting the centre of the universe. Therefore he was ready to leave the sphere of a pure theology of Revelation in order to demonstrate the inadequacy of naturalism, to unmask the inner ambiguity that marks the incompleteness and lack of consequence in Fichte's Idealism and to point to the final immanence of what Karl Jaspers called transcendence.

This does not mean that Barth must be compelled to construct an alternative theory of absolute self-consciousness as demanded by Rendtorff, Wagner and Graf. His criticism is negative; it confines itself to showing the internal dilemmas in which such systems must end if they bypass the only available knowledge of God – Revelation in Christ. Revelation here becomes a unique principle, the one presupposition for which all other presuppositions must be sacrificed, and which thus attains all the force of an axiom. Its logical and conceptual value is expressed in its sufficiency, exclusivity and non-derivation. It demands a unique status in reality and Barth is therefore compelled to articulate its significance in universal terms.

Consistency and the systematic principle: Barth's ontology

In order to safeguard the primacy of Revelation Barth is compelled to reconstruct reality from this central point. He has to show, in a logical scheme or system constructed by himself, how Revelation can include or account for all human realities and all human knowledge without yielding its claim to be the unique source of knowledge about God and man. He is thus compelled to take up the metaphysical question, the question of ontology. Barth's ontology reverses the usual metaphysical order by giving priority to the concrete, not, however, in the sense of a pure actualism (an accusation often raised against Barth on account of the actualism of his early dialectical phase) but of the concrete as the event of Revelation in Jesus Christ. This is a concrete event that has universal significance. Hans Urs von Balthasar sees in Barth's decision to explicate reality from this concrete event the decisive step beyond the Hegelian dialectic. Dieter Korsch describes Barth's theology as a theory in which the particular fact and the universal principle coincide.

Wilfried Härle shows how Barth's concept of being is dogmatic in its content: the being of the creature is identical with its act of relationship to God. Barth defines being exclusively in terms of relationship to Jesus Christ. His is a Christological ontology. The conceptual interpretation and formulation of the ontological principle Jesus Christ is grace. Therefore Barth's ontology can be characterised as an ontology of grace.[9]

At this point the arguments of the Idealist interpreters of Barth carry some weight. Not only consequence and consistency, but the Idealist-inspired demand for a unique principle on which to reconstruct all reality, haunts Barth's thinking in his insistence on Revelation alone. This does not mean, however, that Barth adopts the construction of a system as his primary aim. It is at the most a secondary objective, a 'sin forgiven'. He is even further removed from an interest in perfecting a system of absolute self-consciousness. Furthermore, while Jesus Christ may be conceptually interpreted in terms of grace, Barth insists that he may not be exchanged for a universal concept and thus be deprived of his historical uniqueness (as appears to be the case in Falk Wagner's sketch of Christology as an exemplar of the theory of self-consciousness). Härle notes Barth's reservations in the later volumes of the *Church Dogmatics* about the term 'principle'. It is not a question of a Christ principle, but of Jesus Christ himself.[10]

Barth's interest in system was determined by his reaction against the use of the Idealist systematic principle in Liberal theology. His criticism of that theology always concentrated on one point: it gave the central place to man and constructed reality systematically, including statements about God, from this point. Thus it made man the measure of statements about God and reduced God to a complement or converse of statements about man. Barth went behind anthropocentric theology in order to attack various systematic principles adopted by post-Idealist philosophies that had the effect of making something else the measure of man and of God – the theory of absolute self-consciousness in Fichte, naturalism and evolutionism (Vitalismus), or 'a common denominator which can then be proclaimed as the world *logos*, whether it is matter, spirit, energy, act or existence'.[11] Natural theology was for Barth a systematic construction whose basis was something other than Revelation in Christ.

It was therefore in order to protect his theology from being infiltrated by any elements that might compromise the exclusivity of his one presupposition, Revelation, that Barth constructed an ontology subservient, certainly in his intention, to the freedom of the Word of God but consistent and systematic enough to exclude any systematic starting-point other than Revelation in Christ.

Ontology and autonomy: Jesus Christ and other men

Barth's anthropology is embedded in an ontology conceived in terms of relationship to Jesus Christ. In other words, man must be understood in relation to this unique historical–universal principle. What man is is primary in Christ, secondary in other human beings. Thus man's autonomy is defined in terms of the autonomy of Jesus Christ. Christ's autonomy is obedience, but it is not an obedience laid on him heteronomously from without. His being is exclusively being in relationship to God. God elects man in Jesus Christ and Christ correspondingly elects God in a free decision of his own for God.

Barth's Christological anthropology answers the question about man indirectly, not directly from Christology nor directly from man's self-knowledge in general apart from Christ but in consequence of and in analogy to what can be said of Christ. Barth's method is to draw criteria from the creaturely being of the man Jesus and apply them to man in general. Hans Urs von Balthasar put it this way: Christ is not only the ground of being but the ground of what ought to be. He is not so, however, in the sense of a mere ethical demand. What man must become is already fulfilled in Christ. It does not need verification or confirmation to be valid. This leads to the serenity of the kerygma of the later Barth.

The autonomy of Jesus Christ corresponds in the *Church Dogmatics* to God's theonomy, as we have seen, without any shadow of heteronomy. His being and his work are one. In consequence of and in analogy to the autonomy of Jesus Christ, the exercise of man's autonomy must therefore also be thought of as correspondence with his being. Just as man's being is a being in relationship to the justifying grace of God and his freedom is given in and with that grace as a free gift of God, so his autonomy consists in his coming to himself, freely fulfilling the law of the being given him by grace. The ontological framework means that a unity is established between what comes to man from without and what he is within. As Jüngel puts it in his exposition of Barth's doctrine of Baptism, man is posited by God from within, so that the grace of God becomes the inner principle of his being and action.

The radical and exclusive interpretation of this doctrine by the re-application of the an- and enhypostasis doctrine to the being of the Christian, so that his being is defined exclusively in terms of relationship to grace alone, is, however, problematic. It formalises and radicalises the 'Christological constriction' in Barth's theology and makes the consideration of a sound distinction between nature and grace and the contingency of sin and reconciliation with God almost impossible.

The element of heteronomy is not excluded by Barth from man's relationship with God – here a difference is retained between Christology and anthropology – because that relationship begins with a confrontation, a historical encounter between the Word of God in Jesus Christ and man.[12] Man is the sinful being whom God's Word encounters from without. The goal of this encounter is the being of man that he does not have in himself but receives from God in Christ, the true being of man that consists in his correspondence to the movement of God towards him. That is man's being as well as his goal, his *Bestimmung*. At the term of this goal heteronomy is overcome by being absorbed into an inner principle of spontaneous autonomy-obedience:

For the gift and work of the Holy Spirit as the divine power of His Word is that, while Jesus Christ encounters man in it with alien majesty, He does not remain thus, nor is He merely a strange, superior Lord disposing concerning him in majesty from without. On the contrary, even as such, without ceasing to be the Lord or forfeiting His transcendence, but rather in its exercise, He gives and imparts Himself to him, entering into him as his Lord in all His majesty and setting up His throne within him. Thus His control, as that of the owner over his possession, becomes the most truly distinctive feature of this man, the centre and basis of his human existence, the axiom of his freest thinking and utterance, the origin of his freest volition and action, in short the principle of his spontaneous being.[13]

Barth took up and made positive use of the most valuable aspect of Idealism – its affirmation of freedom and subjectivity. He had begun with an affirmation of the freedom and subjectivity of God, as a reaction against its reduction in post-Idealist theology to a pale reflection of the freedom and subjectivity of man. But in the course of his development Barth had gained the insight that this divine subjectivity could not be kept at a distance as the inscrutable will of an arbitrary God. Instead it must be located and accepted in God's self-revelation as the God of man. It must be conceived in an analogy and correspondence in which the freedom of God is the freedom with which he saves and creates man and the freedom with which man responds in thankfulness to God. The eternal love within the Trinity is the same love which is addressed by God to man and in which man responds to God. From this conception of Barth's the way lies open to a conception of God and his relationship with man in terms of freedom (analogy of freedom) or in terms of love (analogy of love).

This is the point at which Barth's achievement is most evident. The broad lines of this theology of autonomy are its rejection of the concept of an arbitrary God in favour of a concept of God that is won from his self-revelation in Christ, and its rejection of the concept of man as an absolute self-determining subject in favour of the concept of the finite man who is created to be the partner of God. This can justly be affirmed to be sound Christian theology and to represent a high point in the creative work of theology in this century. It shows several striking parallels to the conclusions at which Roman Catholic theology finally arrived in affirming a genuine autonomy of man while at the same time distancing itself from the philosophy of the absolute self-determination of the human subject – this despite the starting-point of Catholic theology being far removed both from the Liberal schooling of the early Barth and from the Confessional tradition on which he drew.

Ontology and the problem of Creation

The narrow framework within which Barth affirmed human freedom and rationality left him with too little access to the complexity of its historical and social realisation. This was the substance of Pannenberg's criticism of Barth. Barth's treatment of Creation and nature was also too narrowly conceived, that is purely in function of a relationship to grace and Reconciliation. Thus Creation was emptied of its complexity and richness and treated all too exclusively as a mere outer presupposition of the Covenant, as the bare stage (theatrum) on which a drama is played whose actors and plot belong exclusively to another order. Ultimately this must reflect on Barth's conception of God and his Word. The spiritualising and intellectualising bent of his Confessional tradition, which came so strongly to the fore again at the end of the *Church Dogmatics*, exacts heavy tribute here. To say that Jesus Christ is the fulfilment and transformation of human nature becomes less rather than more convincing when the attempt is made to derive human nature all too exclusively from him. The generosity of the *pro nobis* is diminished by all too radical an insistence on the *extra nos*. Barth's insistence that Jesus Christ is nothing in himself is paralleled by the insistence that we are nothing in ourselves but only in him, and the attempt is made to push this statement to an ontological extreme.

Barth saw too late that the universality of his construction, in which everything is derived from above, from Revelation in Christ, demanded the integration of human existence in the world, of history and of empirical knowledge. The majority of Barth's recent interpreters see the need to go beyond him in this area.[14] Barth's own attempts to include all this complexity were either too minimal (as the concept of the *theatrum gloriae Dei* and the treatment of the Lights of the World in *KD* IV/3 illustrates) or they presupposed a reality and richness of worldly life (as in his treatment of ethics) which he could not expressly mediate with the principle of exclusive derivation from above. The fault does not lie in the assertion that we owe our being and our world exclusively to God, which is the doctrine of Creation, but in the ungenerous and anxious depreciation of God's gifts to us in Creation out of an anxiety that we might claim them for ourselves. Barth could claim that his anxiety was totally justified by the history of modern thought, and especially by the history of Protestant theology in the nineteenth century, but the possibility of sin, about which Barth was significantly ambiguous, is an indication that God has indeed given so much into the hands of man.

For Barth, the ontological and noetic orders had to run parallel. Thus his restrictive theses showed themselves in both areas, on the one hand in his axiomatic restrictions on human knowledge (of which his rejection of all natural theology was the cause and the symptom) and on the other in his ontology, in which he tried to derive all significant statements about human nature and worldly reality from statements about Jesus Christ.

Natural theology and the Lights of the World

As our analysis showed, natural theology was a question with which Barth struggled to the very end of his life. The rejection of natural theology was the converse of his assertion that biblical Revelation in Christ was the unique source of all essential knowledge about God and man. This statement, which had found expression in the first Barmen thesis, forms the framework for his consideration of true words of Revelation and non-revelatory truth (the 'Lights of the World') in *KD* IV/3. Here Barth was evidently struggling with two contrary intentions: the restrictive intention of the Barmen theses and the realisation which he had won in the course of writing the *Church Dogmatics* that the claim to exclusivity also implies the universal scope of the Christian Gospel.

It was the universal scope of Christ's prophetic office that led Barth to affirm the revelatory activity of Christ in taking some (if not all) earthly events and words outside the walls of the Church into the service of his Gospel and using them to reflect his truth. Similarly it was God's universal presence in the world under the title 'Hallowed be thy name' that led Barth in his last lectures on ethics to affirm an objective knowledge of God in the world. In both cases the restrictive intention immediately came into play, in the case of *KD* IV/3 to render problematic and relative every form of human knowledge distinct from Revelation so that it could contribute nothing of importance. Similarly, in the lectures on ethics, Barth hastened to affirm man's (almost) total subjective blindness to natural knowledge of God and his inability to make systematic use of it as a source of knowledge.[15]

It is no wonder, then, that Barth's doctrine on the Lights of the World led to the most contrary interpretations. On the part of the strict Barthians and post-Barthians there reigns confusion, at least in the field of Christian ethics, where it is a question of justifying ethical and political options.[16] Some authors, such as H.-J. Kraus and Christian Link, still take Barth at his word and seek to interpret his doctrine of the 'Lights of the World' in a strictly restrictive sense.[17] However, even where there is no desire to go beyond the limits set by Barth, the possibility may be raised of a material coincidence between an ethical position derived 'from above' (exclusively from a reception of the Word of God) and a non-Christian ethical position.[18] This is the case with Walter Kreck and with Huber and Tödt.

Other authors, however, such as Gestrich, Berkhof and Dekker, interpret the doctrine of the Lights of the World as calling for a development in the direction of a new 'natural theology' that Barth himself did not give. Gestrich points to Pannenberg as a positive example of such development, while Berkhof claims that it is an open question as to how far he actually diverged from Barth's own intentions in calling for a development that he understands to be implicit in Barth's actual practice. In this practice many 'natural' insights and experiences are only subsequently and rather artificially derived from a Christological principle. He claims that Barthians such as Christian Link and Eberhard Jüngel are moving in the same direction as himself. The danger of such an alleged development of Barth's position is immediately evident in Gestrich's proposal, in which the world is set up as a second source of Revelation alongside that made available in the proclamation of Jesus Christ in the Church. Thus the problem of the natural theology of the Enlightenment and its continuation in nineteenth-century Protestant theology re-emerges and Barth's position is reversed, not developed.[19]

If, however, as Barth admits in *KD* IV/3, Creation must be considered, if not apart from at least in distinction to Jesus Christ, and if it may or may not be taken into the service of the Word of God, then the Word of God itself establishes a relative distinction between itself and creaturely reality. To identify the Word of God and Creation is not acceptable to Barth. One must affirm with von Balthasar that it is precisely the *priority* of Revelation that demands the recognition of a relative independence of nature and a relative priority of nature before grace. This is quite compatible with understanding grace as the ground and the goal of nature.[20] A system is thus called for that is more comprehensive than those of Barth or of his Liberal predecessors and recent interpreters. The possibility must be established of integrating statements derived from man's knowledge of himself and his world within the framework established by Revelation without seeking to derive the one exclusively from the other.

The limitations of the analogy of relation

The debate about natural theology thus leads back to the ontological discussion. It can be accepted as one of the essential tasks of the Christian theologian to construct an ontology in order to ensure the consistency of theological statements with one another and to clarify their relationship with the totality of available knowledge and with reality as a whole. Again it is a major achievement on Barth's part to have achieved a high degree of clarity and consistency here. It is only in the light of this achievement that the limitations of his position become evident.

The analogy of relation is the key element in Barth's ontology, which conceives reality exclusively in terms of its relationship to grace. This analogy is posited in and with Creation; however, it is not based (begründet) in Creation but exclusively in the Covenant of Grace. It is at this point that the objection was raised by Hans Urs von Balthasar, Regin Prenter and Emil Brunner that an analogy of relation must imply the inclusion of an analogy of being. It can be shown not only that Barth's intention was to avoid making this concession, but that he did avoid making it. The question, then, is whether Barth's ontology of grace alone is tenable or whether, had he been logical, he *ought* to have conceded an analogy of being within the analogy of faith. On the one hand Härle rejects von Balthasar's reading of an analogy of being implicit in Barth's analogy of relation, but on the other he himself rejects Barth's ontology because he believes, for a variety of reasons, that it is insufficient as an account of reality in general and because as an ontology of grace alone it tends to treat sin and Reconciliation as ontologically necessary rather than contingent. The latter objection is upheld by Konrad Stock.[21]

It was certainly not Barth's real intention to treat sin and Reconciliation as necessary. However, he held obstinately to his rejection of an analogy of being in any form. We are left with an inconsistency in his work. A constructive reinterpretation of Barth must go beyond him here.

The recognition of a relative priority of nature before grace within an absolute priority of grace over nature, as urged by von Balthasar, would have led to a better solution of the relationship between the epistemological and the ontological than either Barth or his opponents in the post-Idealist theologies and philosophies produced. Both try to determine a single point in divine or human subjectivity from which a strict parallel can be established between the means of knowledge and its object. Both construct a deductive form of argument in which rationality and necessity coincide.[22] But the attempt to account for all of reality within such a system fails. Thus Barth's attempt to carry through the analogy of relation in speaking of phenomenal or empirical reality leads to confusion. Helmut Thielicke has shown how Barth's argument for democracy as the only acceptable form of political structure can be reversed precisely by the same argument to which Barth appeals for its support, namely the sole rule of Christ. That argument can be and has equally well been used as a justification of monarchy or dictatorship. Such formal analogies, argues Thielicke, are ambiguous, say everything or nothing, and are inapposite.[23]

Taking up this last point, we may say that they are not capable of making adequate assertions about the nature of the phenomenon about which they speak because they are confined to statements about the relationship between such phenomena and Revelation. Barth's account of inner-worldly knowledge and freedom, despite his intention to consider these in distinction from Revelation, was consistently cramped by the inability to concede them more reality than the relationship to grace expressed in the term *theatrum*, the bare stage on which the drama of Revelation takes place. He was not able to integrate them into a fruitful relationship with the history of Revelation.

For this reason Thielicke prefers the statements of the natural-law philosophy associated with Catholic thought, despite its defects. The reason evidently lies in the ontological recognition of the relatively independent character of worldly phenomena granted to them in Creation. That recognition corresponds with a greater freedom on the epistemological level, so that Thielicke can say that the statements of natural law are at least to some extent withdrawn from the arbitrariness of the thinker and can therefore lead to a greater degree of consensus.[24] To appeal to Barth's 'Parables of the Kingdom' in *KD* IV/3 as a source of theological dialogue with a generally accepted doctrine of human rights, as Wolfgang Huber and Heinz Eduard Tödt do, is possible. But it is only possible if one has already accepted the relatively independent character of statements about human rights, rather than seeking to derive them exclusively from theological statements. The correspondence that is now sought is not an exclusive derivation of the one from the other, either in Barth's sense from above or in that of Liberal theology from below. As Huber and Tödt remark, it is not enough for theology to set up a model of analogy and difference; the peculiar structure of the sphere in question must be respected as well.

Huber and Tödt do not accept traditional Catholic moral theory, but they reject it because they see in it a dualism in which the derivation of moral rights from Christian doctrine is placed side by side with their derivation from reason without clarifying by what method the two might be linked.[25] Jüngel accepts a duality of divine and human law, but only on the basis of the duality of law and Gospel. When he comes to link the two the structure is the analogy of relation. His arguments are in fact strongest where there is an immediate link between the very fact of Revelation and the freedom that he defends, such as the freedom to believe and the freedom to proclaim the Gospel. The arguments become weaker and more disputable where the link with Revelation is less direct (freedom of information in general, freedom to change in general).[26] The analogy of relation is not adequate to the duality involved.

The traditional Catholic natural-law theory has itself long been in a crisis. This is due to the inability of the traditional metaphysical categories on which it relied to integrate the message of Revelation with the scientific categories in which modern science describes and explains the phenomena of human life and culture. On the one hand the compatibility of the traditional metaphysical categories with the message of Revelation itself has been questioned. On the other the inadequacy of terms derived from Aristotelian natural science to translate the modern scientific grasp of reality is evident. Yet the need for terms and relations by means of which the integration of Revelation and empirically perceived reality can be articulated is obvious and both Barthian and Roman Catholic theology need further development in this area.

Emancipation and autonomy

Barth's emancipatory intentions are partly bound into the structure of his theology and remain partly outside it. Much of the evidence that so convincingly shows that Barth is modern and committed to the characteristically modern quest for freedom lies outside his theology – in his biography, in his political and cultural interests.[27] The chief claim to the emancipation of man that we have met in Barth's theology rested on the freeing (Entlastung) of man from the burden laid upon him by religion, Idealism and theosophical speculation. These sought to pander to man's desire to be God. Proclaiming to man his limits and showing them convincingly in Revelation set man free to be a finite creature, a mere man. The apparent restriction revealed itself to be a privilege because it corresponded to the affirmation of man by God. The claim that man is set free in knowing his limits is prolonged in the various expressions of the Calvinist axiom that the finite cannot contain the infinite. This was essentially the principle Barth applied with great rhetorical flourish to the restriction of the category of sacrament to Christ and the consequent definition of the celebration of Baptism as a merely ethical event.

Barth understood his insistence on the primacy of the divine subject from the very beginning as emancipatory. This element carried over into Barth's theology of the Word of God from his early religious socialism, which included an identification of the socialist movement as a provisional manifestation of the Kingdom of God. Three observations may be made here. Firstly, the key to this religious socialism was the affirmation of God as the subject who was active in bringing about his Kingdom. Secondly, Barth's disappointment with the socialist response to the outbreak of the First World War led him to abandon this identification as a hermeneutic principle and to concentrate on the action of God the subject elsewhere, namely in his Word, in Scripture. While he did not abandon his interest in the socialist movement, it now became a subordinate concern and followed from rather than shaped his theology. Thirdly, the autonomy theme in Barth's thought is based in an encounter with God as the subject of his Revelation. Whatever socialist elements are taken up by the mature Barth into his vision of the Kingdom of God must pass, like everything else, through the needle's eye of the ontology of grace and the analogy of relation. In doing so they will form part of man's being and goal (Bestimmung) as determined by God, and man's free acceptance of them will correspond to his nature as graced by God.

It is clear that Barth believed that many elements of modern political thought, such as democracy, equality, justice and free speech, correspond to God's goal for man. But he tried to derive his affirmation of them exclusively from Revelation, not from that consideration of the historical development of society which is constitutive of every modern political theory whether socialist, liberal or conservative. Since we do not see how they can be derived exclusively from Revelation, we are left to observe that Barth had in any case brought them with him, more or less consciously, from his Swiss upbringing, his social and political experience as pastor of Safenwil, and his conflict with National Socialism. He identified them, more or less reflectively, with God's will for man here and now. They became part of the process of negation, reformulation and reaffirmation with which Barth responded to modern thought, whereby those elements that were never the subject of negation were less likely to be reformulated or to call for explicit reaffirmation.[28]

The Church and the world

This point, which was singled out for special attention by Trutz Rendtorff, also calls for a differentiated explanation in terms of Barth's biography and of his theological constructions. Barth's relationship to the Church as institution was first shaped by his upbringing in the Swiss Reformed Church.[29] It was, however, greatly soured by his experiences in the Church conflict with National Socialism from 1933 to 1935. The institution proved itself a great source of weakness, a body ever ready to shirk the grave issues of principle and take refuge in cowardly compromises.[30] Barth on the other hand was driven to the prophetic witness of the Gospel.

Nonetheless Barth did not make the prophetic role of the Church the first principle of his ecclesiology. The constitution of the Church by the Holy Spirit and the building-up (Erbauung, Erhaltung) of the community – the Church's formal and personal aspects – are accorded theological priority. Barth complements this double aspect of the Church with a consideration of her function. The Church is not an end in itself, but exists for the world. It would be attractive to argue with Bäumler that the primacy that Barth gives in practice to this third aspect of the Church is due merely to Barth's natural excitement at discovering an important sphere of investigation and proclamation neglected in previous ecclesiology. This explanation is good but it is not enough. Barth's formal priorities in ecclesiology are undermined by what Schellong aptly called Barth's criticism of the positive character of possessing Christian faith and putting it into practice. Owing to Barth's fear of man's tendency to treat the Word of God as his possession, the subjectivity of God remains in competition with the subjectivity of man – theonomy opposed to an autonomy that might cease to be obedient. As Heinrich Fries remarked, Barth's tendency to reduce the order of Creation to the order of grace shows itself also in his ecclesiology. Barth does too little justice to the specific character and the subjectivity of the Church, to its relatively independent being, out of an anxiety that the glory of God might thereby be diminished.[31]

There is substance in Rendtorff's criticism that the identity of the Church is dissolved in an endless task on the one hand and in the sovereign freedom of the divine subject on the other. What Barth intended is nonetheless not really the dissolution of the Church, much less the reduction of dogmatics to ethics. The counterbalance to this tendency is seen in the final lectures on the ethics of reconciliation, in which ethics is expressed in dogmatic terms: in the request for Baptism, in the (proposed) account of the Lord's Supper, in the explication of ethics as prayer and in terms of the Lord's Prayer.[32] Thus Barth says 'world!' where the theme is Church and 'Church!' where the theme is world! His thinking always expressed itself in dialectically related sets of massive affirmations and negations rather than in finely differentiated utterances. In the second half of KD IV/3, as Wilhelm Dantine documented, Barth's concept of the Christian's 'service to the world' is explicated under the headings of the praise of God, sermons, teaching, evangelisation, mission, theology, prayer, pastoral ministry, giving of personal example, charitable activities, prophetic action and the foundation of community. All in all this is nothing other than the exposition and exercise of the specifically internal Christian and ecclesiastical life.[33]

Autonomy and the sacrament of Baptism

Both the concept of the Church and the relationship between divine and human action are intimately linked in the doctrine of Baptism. Barth's lecture on Baptism in 1943 already contained the basics of his position in *KD* IV/4. Water baptism was treated as a human act, the visible sign of the invisible work of the Holy Spirit. Yet in 1943 Barth still ascribed the power of Baptism to Jesus Christ. In *KD* IV/4 the category of sacrament is reserved to Christ alone and denied to the act of Baptism within the Church.[34]

Barth's reservations about sacrament are due perhaps to many factors – to his upbringing and heritage as well as to his conscientious reading of the New Testament and the powerful influence on him in that regard of his son Marcus's book on Baptism. But one key element is the need to preserve the distinction between God and humanity. This laudable intention takes various forms in the long history of Barth's theology. Characteristic of the development is the slow growth in Barth's acceptance and affirmation of the relatively independent and relatively substantial character of the human subject before God.

In affirming a distinct human sphere of activity so clearly in the Baptism fragment of *KD* IV/4, Barth was making an advance on his previous treatment of creaturely reality. That brought the danger of which Barth had always been supremely aware: the possibility that this human sphere could remain indifferent to grace and treat itself as independent, sufficient to itself, apart from God. It could usurp divine attributes and functions and declare itself absolute. Once it had been affirmed therefore, its radical insufficiency had to be insisted on as had its separation and distance from the sphere and action of God. 'God is in heaven and you are on earth', the principle of the Commentary on Romans, had been modified, not abandoned.

When Barth wished, this was a principle that allowed for a theology of the sacraments. In the earlier parts of the *Church Dogmatics*, he had drawn the line between human and divine activity within the proclamation of the Word and the celebration of the sacraments rather than outside them. He always feared, however, that the affirmation of the sacramental action of Christ in the Church might lead human beings in general and the Church in particular to claim a sacramental character for their every action. In that case, human action would be immune to the threat of God's judgement and lose its contingent and relative character before God. The new anti-sacramental option, however, opened the way for two consequences to be drawn by Trutz Rendtorff: the dissolution of any workable concept of Church and the reduction of dogmatics to ethics. The first was a conclusion that had long been urged by Roman Catholic critics of Barth. The latter can hardly have been Barth's intention. But it must be urged that it was paradoxical of Barth to maintain the absolute centrality of God's Word in Revelation and deny a sacramental character to its day-to-day manifestation and celebration in the life of the Church. Christ's influence and activity in the world cannot be confined to the Church. But where his Revelation is made explicit, as it is in the Church, Christ is at work in a way that corresponds to the historical character of Revelation. Christ's promise to be with the Church, the command to baptise and the meaning of Baptism as incorporation into Christ demand that Baptism be understood within the broad Christian tradition as the sacramental action of Christ himself.

AUTONOMY IN THE *CHURCH DOGMATICS*

Karl Barth's account of the autonomy of humanity in relation to God may not represent the greatest achievement of the *Church Dogmatics*. The weightiest statements in the *Church Dogmatics* are made in other areas – in the methodological insistence on divine Revelation, in the doctrine of Election or in Christology. Yet the treatment of autonomy is central to Barth's Christological anthropology and the latter could lay claim to be one of the chief aims of the work as a whole.

The question of autonomy is important for the *Church Dogmatics* because it represents the chief argument for the Liberal theology that Barth opposed. It presents itself at times in epistemological form as a demand that all statements be reduced to the consciousness of the individual who made them. More radically, that consciousness itself can be represented as the exclusive source of the objects it contains. It can present itself in ethical form as the demand that the individual admit sole responsibility for his own being, knowledge and actions. Belief in God as a transcendent being independent of human will and consciousness has been represented as an abdication of that responsibility.

Against such claims, Barth presented forcefully and cogently the perspective of Christian Revelation. Humanity exists in relationship with God, not in isolation. Concretely, that relationship is established by the call of God, who reveals himself in Jesus Christ. Within the framework of that relationship autonomy can be affirmed. The human being is called to be the free partner of God in prayer, in praise, in witness and in action. Without this positive concept of autonomy, Barth's Christocentric anthropology could not be conceived.

That Christocentric anthropology is developed in Barth's doctrine of Creation. It is here that the limitations of Barth's achievement begin to show. While generously affirming creaturely reality in Christological terms, Barth is reluctant to go beyond paradox in ontological terms for fear of conceding any existence of human beings apart from Christ or any natural knowledge of God. The existence of creaturely reality is affirmed but explicated only in terms of a pure relationship to Christ.

Towards the end of the *Church Dogmatics* Barth affirms a real distinction between the action of God and human action. The human being has a proper sphere of activity. But this is admitted at the cost of allowing nothing of ultimate significance to happen within this sphere. Ultimate is the action of God alone. Barth takes this principle so far as to deny to the concrete expression of Revelation itself within the human sphere its character as divine action. The sacramental character of the proclamation of the Word, affirmed at the beginning of the *Church Dogmatics*, is now denied, together with the sacramental character of Baptism and the Eucharist, as actions of Christ himself here and now.

Nonetheless the movement within Barth's theology from his early dialectical phase is impressive. There is a steady growth in the affirmation of human freedom and autonomy. The limitations with which it is hedged are always in terms of Barth's resistance to a theology that removed God in all but name from its considerations. Indeed for a few

years in the 1960s there were theologians who removed God in name
as well.

The affirmation of the existence, freedom and activity of the God of
Jesus Christ is Barth's first principle. It is his echo of the commandment to love God above all things and like that commandment it includes rather than excludes the existence, freedom and activity of the
human subject, the chosen partner of God and the sister and brother
of Jesus Christ.

Abbreviations

Catholica	*Catholica. Vierteljahresschrift für Kontroverstheologie*, Paderborn and Münster
ET	English translation
KD	Karl Barth, *Die Kirchliche Dogmatik* (*Church Dogmatics*)
RGG	*Die Religion in Geschichte und Gegenwart. Handwörterbuch für Theologie und Religionswissenschaft*, 2nd edn, ed. H. Gunkel *et al.*, Tübingen, Mohr, 1927–31; 3rd edn, ed. Kurt Galling, Tübingen, Mohr, 1957–62
ThExh	Theologische Existenz heute (NS)
ThLZ	*Theologische Literaturzeitung* (Leipzig)
TRE	*Theologische Realenzyklopädie*, ed. G. Krause and G. Müller, Berlin, de Gruyter, 1977–

Notes

Full bibliographical references are given in the bibliography.

INTRODUCTION

1 For the history of the concept of autonomy, see Rosemarie Pohlmann, 'Autonomie', in *Historisches Wörterbuch der Philosophie*, I, 701–19; Günther Rohrmoser, 'Autonomie', in *Handbuch philosophischer Grundbegriffe*, I, 155–70; Hans Blumenberg, 'Autonomie und Theonomie', in *RGG*, 3rd edn, I, 788–92; and Konrad Hilpert, *Ethik und Rationalität*.

2 Martin Heckel, 'Autonomia und Pacis compositio', 144–50, 164–7. To say, as Hilpert does, that the positive notion of autonomy 'goes back to the same cause – the Reformation – and is essentially bound up with it' seems to imply a direct derivation of the one from the other, whereas the relationship, as is clear from Heckel's account, from which Hilpert insufficiently draws, is a negative one and springs from the 'loss of religious unity' (Hilpert, *Ethik und Rationalität*, 102–4).

3 Kant's works will be cited according to the pagination of the original editions. The text used follows the edition of Wilhelm Weischedel. The following abbreviations will be used: *KrV* = *Kritik der reinen Vernunft*; *GMS* = *Grundlegung zur Metaphysik der Sitten*; *KprV* = *Kritik der praktischen Vernunft*; *MS* = *Metaphysik der Sitten*; *Rel.* = *Religion innerhalb der Grenzen der bloßen Vernunft*. (A) indicates the first edition, (B) the second edition as revised by Kant. Here *GMS*, 52. On Kant's conception of autonomy, see Johannes Schwartländer, *Der Mensch ist Person*, 155–6; Hilpert, *Ethik und Rationalität*, 151–91; Ernst Feil, 'Autonomie und Heteronomie nach Kant'; and Gerhard Krüger, *Philosophie und Moral in der kantischen Kritik*.

4 *GMS*, 52, 66–7, 76.

5 Schwartländer, *Der Mensch ist Person*, 160.

6 *GMS*, 87 (tr. Lewis White Beck, 59).

7 *GMS*, 88.

8 Schwartländer, *Der Mensch ist Person*, 146–7, 163. The thesis of Ernst Feil

and the important misinterpretation of Kant which he wishes to correct relate to this point. Feil wishes to prove that the original, political and juridical sense of 'autonomy' remained normative for Kant and expressed itself in the bond between the free will and its determination through the moral law as opposed to an unlimited self-determination of the individual ('Autonomie und Heteronomie nach Kant', 398, 406, 411, 436).

9 *GMS*, 92 (tr. Lewis White Beck, 62).

10 Schwartländer, *Der Mensch ist Person*, 157–8, 163; see *GMS*, 88–96. Feil also draws attention to the restricted use of the term 'heteronomy' in Kant as opposed to its use (after Fichte) for any and every determination through something or someone. Kant does not speak of autonomy or heteronomy in humanity's relation to God ('Autonomie und Heteronomie nach Kant', 423–30).

11 *Rel.* (B), xxi–xxiii, 255; Hilpert, *Ethik und Rationalität*, 179–81. The application of this critical principle to religion (which is not the same as the exclusion of religion) seems to convince Hilpert that Kant dispenses with the relationship to a larger framework that is characteristic of the politico-juridical meaning of autonomy. He does not join discussion with Schwartländer's (and now Feil's) careful analysis of heteronomy in Kant although he makes use of Schwartländer's *Der Mensch ist Person* elsewhere. Instead he defines heteronomy in Kant far more loosely and Kant's arguments for not deriving morality from the perfect will of God are repeated but not discussed (161–3).

12 Schwartländer, *Der Mensch ist Person*, 161–2. The distinction between autarchy and autonomy is one of the best arguments put forward by Schwartländer against the assimilation of Kant's concept of autonomy to the post-Fichtean notions.

13 *MS* Vorrede, vi; *GMS* Vorrede (B), xiii; *Rel.* Vorrede zur zweiten Auflage (B), xxv–xxvi.

14 Schwartländer, *Der Mensch ist Person*, 154–5 (on Kant's typology) and 162.

15 *GMS*, 51–2, 62.

16 *KrV* (B), 561, 568–70.

17 Krüger, *Philosophie und Moral in der kantischen Kritik*, 173.

18 *KprV* (A), 5, 54; Schwartländer, *Der Mensch ist Person*, 148. For all the care which he has given to the presentation of Kant's arguments, Hilpert's attachment to a post-Fichtean notion of autonomy prevents him from seeing this essential perspective.

19 *KprV* (A), 5–7; Schwartländer, *Der Mensch ist Person*, 83; Walter Kasper, 'Autonomie und Theonomie', 29.

20 Kant, 'Beantwortung der Frage: Was ist Aufklärung?', *Kants Gesammelte Schriften*, VIII, 35 (tr. Lewis White Beck, 85).

21 *Ibid.*, 39.

22 Kant, *Opus Posthumum*, *Kants Gesammelte Schriften*, XXI, 106 (my tr.).

23 Kant, 'Erklärung in Beziehung auf Fichtes Wissenschaftslehre', 515–16: 'Also ist die Frage: ob ich den Geist der *Fichte*schen Philosophie für

echten Kritizismus halte, durch ihn selbst beantwortet . . . da hier nicht von einem beurteilten Objekt, sondern dem beurteilenden Subjekt die Rede ist; wo es genug ist, mich von allem Anteil an jener Philosophie loszusagen' (515).

24 Fichte's works are cited according to J. G. Fichte, *Gesamtausgabe* (1977–). References to the older edition, *Sämtliche Werke* (1845–6), are given in parentheses. The following abbreviations will be used: *GA = Gesamtausgabe*; *SW = Sämtliche Werke*; *BWL = Ueber den Begriff der Wissenschaftslehre oder der sogenannten Philosophie, als Einladungsschrift zu seinen Vorlesungen über diese Wissenschaft* (1794); *BG = Ueber die Bestimmung des Gelehrten* (1794); *GWL = Grundlage der gesammten Wissenschaftslehre als Handschrift für seine Zuhörer* (1794–5); *GNR = Grundlage des Naturrechts nach Principien der Wissenschaftslehre* (1796); *Erste E = Versuch einer neuen Darstellung der Wissenschaftslehre* (*Erste Einleitung in die Wissenschaftslehre*) (1797–8); *Zweite E = Zweite Einleitung in die Wissenschaftslehre für Leser, die schon ein philosophisches System haben* (1797–8); *SL = Das System der Sittenlehre nach den Principien der Wissenschaftslehre* (1798); *WG = Ueber das Wesen des Gelehrten und seine Erscheinungen im Gebiete der Freiheit* (1805); *TB = Die Tatsachen des Bewußtseins* (Lectures 1810–1811, published 1817). Here *BWL*, *GA*, I/2, 112, 115 (*SW*, I, 38, 41–2).

25 *GWL*, *GA*, I/2, 259–60, 279 (*SW*, I, 97, 119). Gerold Prauss has shown, on the basis of the computerised index to Kant, that the expression 'Ding an sich' is not the standard form in Kant's writings despite its almost universal use in Kant interpretation but rather the longer and more explicit form 'Ding an sich selbst betrachtet' (*Kant und das Problem der Dinge an sich*, 13–23).

26 Dieter Henrich, *Fichtes ursprüngliche Einsicht*.

27 *Erste E*, no. 5, *GA*, I/4, 191–5 (*SW*, I, 429–35).

28 *Erste E*, *GA*, I/4, 195 (*SW*, I, 434) (tr. Peter Heath and John Lachs, 16).

29 *SL*, *GA*, I/5, 67–8 (*SW*, IV, 56–8).

30 *SL*, *GA*, I/5, 125–6 (*SW*, IV, 130–1).

31 *Ibid.*

32 *SL*, *GA*, I/5, 67 (*SW*, IV, 56).

33 *GNR*, *GA*, I/3, 340–5 (*SW*, III, 30–6); *SL*, *GA*, I/5, 199–203 (*SW*, IV, 218–23); Hilpert, *Ethik und Rationalität*, 227–9. Fichte praises the story of Creation in Genesis for presenting another rational being, God, who could perform this function for the first human pair until they were able to do so for themselves.

34 *BG*, *GA*, I/3, 38 (*SW*, VI, 307).

35 *SL*, *GA*, I/5, 201–2 (*SW*, IV, 221–2).

36 *Zweite E*, *GA*, I/4, 257–8 (*SW*, I, 505) (tr. Peter Heath and John Lachs, 75).

37 *WG* (*SW*, VI, 364–8); *TB* (*SW*, II, 607); Henrich, *Fichtes ursprüngliche Einsicht*, 39, incl. n. 28; Robert Stalder, 'Der neue Gottesgedanke Fichtes', 505.

38 Henrich, *Fichtes ursprüngliche Einsicht*, 17 (my translation).

39 Rohrmoser, 'Autonomie'.

40 At this time the identification between the Churches, Catholic and Protestant, and the anti-revolutionary and anti-democratic policies of the monarchist Restoration was relatively complete. See Kasper, 'Autonomie und Theonomie', 31–2.

41 Rohrmoser, 'Autonomie'.

42 Karl Marx, *Economic and Philosophic Manuscripts of 1844*, tr. Martin Milligan, 144–5.

43 See Kasper, 'Autonomie und Theonomie', 29–31.

44 Wilhelm Dilthey, *Abhandlungen zur Geschichte der Philosophie und Religion, Gesammelte Schriften*, II, esp. 246–8, 257–8, 283, 292.

45 See Pohlmann, 'Autonomie', 716–19.

46 Current works of reference in philosophy usually offer a selection of the various meanings of the term 'autonomy'. Typical is a reference to Kant and to one other area of science such as politics, sociology or biology. Few English-language works of reference include an article on autonomy.

1 AUTONOMY IN THE *CHURCH DOGMATICS*

1 Reiner Strunk, *Politische Ekklesiologie im Zeitalter der Revolution*, 65, 69, 79; Trutz Rendtorff, *Theorie des Christentums*, 93–5.

2 E. W. Mayer, 'Autonomie', *RGG*, 2nd edn, I, 682–3.

3 Eberhard Busch, *Karl Barth. His Life from Letters and Autobiographical Texts*, 1, 9–10, 34–5, 38–54, 81; Karl Barth, *Gesamtausgabe*, V/2, *Karl Barth–Eduard Thurneysen, Briefwechsel*, vol. 1, vi.

4 Karl Barth, 'Nachwort', in *Schleiermacher–Auswahl*, 294, where it is clear that a range of contemporary theological options was discussed and rejected.

5 *Barth–Thurneysen Briefwechsel*, vol. 1, 145, 148–9, in Barth, *Gesamtausgabe*, V/2; Barth, 'Nachwort', in *Schleiermacher–Auswahl*, 294. On the limited extent of Barth's study of Hegel, see Michael Welker, 'Barth und Hegel', 309–13.

6 Karl Barth, *The Humanity of God*, 34–6.

7 For this era, see Heinz Zahrnt, *The Question of God*; and Christof Gestrich, *Neuzeitliches Denken und die Spaltung der dialektischen Theologie*. The most important documents of this era, including Brunner's *Natur und Gnade* and Barth's reply, 'Nein!', have been reissued in '*Dialektische Theologie' in Scheidung und Bewährung 1933–1936*.

8 *KD*, I/1, viii (ET, xiii). See Eberhard Jüngel, 'Von der Dialektik zur Analogie', in *Barth–Studien*, 127–79, esp. 179.

9 *KD*, I/2, no. 23, 'Dogmatics as a Function of the Hearing Church', and no. 24, 'Dogmatics as a Function of the Teaching Church', 890–990 (ET, 797–884).

10 *KD*, I/2, 911–12 (ET, 815–16).

11 *Ibid.*

12 *Ibid.*

13 Paul Tillich, 'Theonomie', in *RGG*, 2nd edn, V, 1128–9.

14 Paul Tillich, 'Kritisches und positives Paradox (Eine Auseinandersetzung mit Karl Barth und Friedrich Gogarten)' and 'Antwort an Karl Barth'. Reprinted in *Anfänge der dialektischen Theologie*, I, 165–74, 189–93.

15 Besides the article in n. 13 above, see Paul Tillich (ed.), *Kairos. Zur Geisteslage und Geisteswendung*, 12–13, 30, 42, 59–60; and Paul Tillich, *Systematic Theology*, I, 83–5; III, 253.

16 *KD*, I/2, 912, 919, 939 (ET, 816, 822, 839). The English translation renders the same word, 'Haltung', in the case of the Bible as 'character' (p. 816) and in relation to the Confessions (p. 822) and to the Church (p. 840) as 'attitude'. Barth uses the same word in all three cases. 'Character' suggests an externally recognisable disposition or feature; 'attitude' in its figurative sense refers to a frame of mind. Barth treats the biblical and ecclesial dimensions of dogmatics primarily in terms of a subjective frame of mind, and only under the confessional aspect of dogmatics does his emphasis dwell on externally defined features.

17 *KD*, I/2, 912 (ET, 816). See Ernst Fuchs, *Hermeneutik*, 3–4: 'Die Frage nach der Maßgeblichkeit der Texte ist [für Barth] die Frage nach der Maßgeblichkeit der *Zeugen*.'

18 *KD*, I/2, 917–19 (ET, 820–2). The English translation has 'autonomous' here, the German original 'auf eigene Füße'.

19 Wolfgang Schlichting, *Biblische Denkform in der Dogmatik*, 62–3. Barth affirms 'Verbal-inspiration' with caution, that is if it is understood as directed toward our own inspiration by the Holy Spirit and coming from a loving attention to every detail of the biblical witness. He distinguishes it from 'Verbalinspiriertheit', literal inspiration in the fundamentalist sense (*KD*, I/2, 575 (ET, 518)).

20 *KD*, I/2, 919 (ET, 822).

21 *KD*, I/2, 922–3 (ET, 824–6).

22 *KD*, I/2, 925–7 (ET, 827–30).

23 *KD*, I/2, 926 (ET, 829).

24 *KD*, I/2, 937 (ET, 838).

25 *KD*, I/2, 939–43 (ET, 839–43).

26 *KD*, I/2, no. 23, no. 24.2.

27 *KD*, I/2, 958 (ET, 857).

28 *KD*, I/2, 959 (ET, 857).

29 *KD*, I/2, 959–62 (ET, 858–60).

30 *KD*, I/2, 961 (ET, 859–60).

31 *KD*, I/2, 960–2 (ET, 859–60).

32 *KD*, I/2, 961 (ET, 860).

33 *Ibid.*

34 *KD*, I/2, 962–3 (ET, 860–1).

35 *KD*, I/2, 963 (ET, 861).

36 *KD*, I/2, 963–5 (ET, 861–6).

37 *KD*, I/2, 971 (ET, 868–9). The English translation speaks merely of a 'tendency to systematisation', missing the suggestive parallel with the Nietzschean 'Will to Power' and the theme of the Titanism of humanity. For this whole question in Barth, see Schlichting, *Biblische Denkform*.

38 *KD*, I/2, 964–5, 968–9 (ET, 862–3, 866).

39 *KD*, I/2, 969–71 (ET, 867–8).

40 *KD*, I/2, 969–70 (ET, 867).

41 *KD*, I/2, 967 (ET, 864).

42 *KD*, I/2, 968 (ET, 865).

43 *KD*, I/2, 970 (ET, 867).

44 *KD*, I/2, 967 (ET, 864).

45 *KD*, I/2, 965 (ET, 863).

46 *KD*, I/2, 971 (ET, 869). See also 989 (ET, 884).

47 Schlichting, *Biblische Denkform*, 135–7, quotes several tributes to this aspect of the *Church Dogmatics*, including this remark by M. Storch.

48 Thus Eberhard Jüngel begins his description of Barth's theology in 'Barth, Karl', in *TRE*, V, 254 (*Barth-Studien*, 28), where he also describes the *Church Dogmatics* as 'systematisch streng komponiert'.

49 See Henri Bouillard, *Karl Barth*, II/2, 207–11. It is this dualism which draws the ire of theologians whose primary orientation is to the development of theoretical structures (see chapter 2). But Barth's own theoretical formulations were distinct from those of the Bible but claimed that they ceded as early as *KD*, I/1, 312–13, 316 (ET, 296–7, 299–300), that his own formulations were distinct from those of the Bible and claimed that they were equivalent to the biblical formulations. In the last resort this was an intentional equivalence to the intention of the biblical formulations (Schlichting, *Biblische Denkform*, 140–3).

50 *KD*, I/2, 973 (ET, 870).

51 *KD*, I/2, 974–81 (ET, 870–7), esp. 981 (ET, 877).

52 *KD*, I/2, 982–3 (ET, 878–9). The Word of God is to be the real subject of dogmatics even to the extent that the dogmatician does not pose his own questions or those of the Church or of his contemporaries but must let the questions along with the answers be dictated to him by the Word of God (*KD*, I/2, 941 (ET, 841), 913 (ET, 817)). This does not mean a simple silencing or censorship of critical and sceptical questions but takes the form of a conviction that these questions are already answered (*KD*, I/2, 916 (ET, 819–20)). The divine subject has already anticipated the protest of humanity within the scope of Revelation and overcome it. It is now a question of rediscovering the human complaint within the bounds of Revelation, where it can no longer be treated with final seriousness. The consequences for dogmatic method are decisive: humanity has no retreat from which to address an independent question to the Word of God, but its autonomy consists in a process of total receptivity in which even its own protest is already articulated for it.

53 *KD*, I/2, 976–7 (ET, 873).

54 *KD*, I/2, 981–2 (ET, 877–8).

55 *KD*, I/2, 989–90 (ET, 884).

56 *KD*, II/2, 193 (ET, 176). For a comprehensive account of Barth's anthropology, see Edgar Herbert Friedmann OSB, *Christologie und Anthropologie*, here esp. 21–4 on anthropology and the doctrine of Election.

57 *KD*, II/2, 194 (ET, 177). The translator missed an important nuance – 'legitimate reality' (not 'ultimate reality').

58 *Ibid.* See also Hans Urs von Balthasar, *Karl Barth*, 247, who writes of man as 'Die Spiegelung der transzendenten Wahl Gottes'.

59 On the similarity and distinction between Christ and other men, see Friedmann, *Christologie und Anthropologie*, 24–8.

60 *KD*, II/2, 194–5 (ET, 177).

61 *KD*, IV/1, 262, 291–300 (ET, 238–9, 264–73).

62 Ulrich Hedinger, 'Der Freiheitsbegriff bei Paul Tillich und Karl Barth', 43. Barth uses the Gethsemane text in *KD*, I/1, 405 (ET, 385); I/2, 171, 855 (ET, 157, 764); II/1, 628 (ET, 558); III/2, 406, 732, (ET, 338, 602); and IV/4, 66 (ET, 60).

63 *KD*, II/2, 195 (ET, 178).

64 *Ibid.*

65 *Ibid.*

66 *KD*, II/2, 196 (ET, 179).

67 *Ibid.* See also Friedmann, *Christologie und Anthropologie*, 27: 'In Jesu menschlichem Wesen aber existieren diese Gegensätze nicht, es charakterisiert sie vielmehr als unsere Sünde, die uns in diesem Menschen vergeben ist.'

68 *KD*, II/2, 197 (ET, 179–80).

69 *KD*, II/2, 197 (ET, 180).

70 *KD*, II/2, 195 (ET, 178).

71 *KD*, III/1, 471–2 (ET, 410).

72 *KD*, II/2, 203 (ET, 185).

73 *KD*, II/2, 68 (ET, 63).

74 *KD*, IV/3, 133 (ET, 119).

75 *KD*, III/2, 113–28 (ET, 96–109).

76 *KD*, III/2, 123–5 (ET, 105–6).

77 *KD*, III/2, 126–7 (ET, 107–8).

78 *KD*, III/2, 127 (ET, 108).

79 *Ibid.* As Stock notes, Barth's criticism of Fichte parallels the philosophical criticism of the Idealist theory of absolute self-consciousness. Barth rejects Fichte's philosophy, however, because of its consequence for the philosophy of religion. He neglects other aspects of Fichte's thought (Konrad Stock, *Anthropologie der Verheißung*, 107, incl. n. 293). In particular the charge of atheism against Fichte is not a nuanced judgement on Barth's part, but results from the crass juxtaposition of the God of Christian Revelation with Fichte's theology, which could at best justify

a charge that Fichte's understanding of God is non-Christian.

80 *KD*, III/2, 128 (ET, 108–9).

81 *KD*, III/2, 113–28 (ET, 96–106) *passim*.

82 *Die protestantische Theologie im 19. Jahrhundert*, 55–7. See also *KD*, III/1, 446–76 (ET, 388–414), esp. 468–73 (*ET*, 407–11). Barth corroborates his argument by reference to that thesis of Dilthey, also taken up by Dietrich Bonhoeffer, *Letters and Papers from Prison*, according to which a humanist rediscovery of Graeco-Roman Stoicism and Epicureanism led to the modern ideal of the autarchy of the rational human being.

83 *KD*, III/2, 276–90 (ET, 231–42), esp. 280, 286 (ET, 236, 240). See also 22–3 (ET, 21), where the line is drawn back to Socrates and Augustine, and forward to Feuerbach and Kierkegaard.

84 *KD*, II/1, 78–9 (ET, 71–3), 150 (ET, 135–6). See also Stock, *Anthropologie der Verheißung*, 131. Barth saw in Nietzsche the culmination of this development.

85 Karl Gerhard Steck, 'Karl Barths Absage an die Neuzeit', in Dieter Schellong and Karl Gerhard Steck, *Karl Barth und die Neuzeit*, 21. Humanity will always want to carry the whole world like an Atlas and never want to be carried itself (*KD*, II/1, 151 (ET, 136)). Humanity's answer to Revelation is a perverse self-assertion (IV/3, 425 (ET, 368) – thesis of no. 70). See also Barth's account of the sin of Judas, which is said to lie in his claim to *decide for himself* what discipleship involves (II/2, 513 (ET, 463)).

86 Barth's account of the sin of Adam and Eve reads like a satire on his theological opponents, not least Bultmann. (Barth expressly stated that in that volume of the *Church Dogmatics* he had engaged in debate with Bultmann *KD*, IV/1, vii (ET, ix)). 'Es ist an der Zeit, daß er [Adam] als nunmehr aufgeklärter Mensch mündig werde . . . von der [durch die Schlange] erfolgten Entmythologisierung Gebrauch mache, von der Gott gehorsamen zur *selbst*gewählten Entscheidung, von seinem Dienst im Garten zu dessen Beherrschung übergehe.' Adam's sin appears in the guise of a 'legitimes Heraustreten aus der Heteronomie in die Autonomie', with an appeal to the 'Erziehung des Menschengeschlechts' (*KD*, IV/1, 482 (ET, 434–5)). Barth's final lectures on ethics published only after his death take up the point again: 'die *Illusion* des sich für souverän, autonom, mündig haltenden und ausgebenden Menschen', who finds that he has let loose a 'Zauberlehrling' (Karl Barth, *Gesamtausgabe*, II/3, *Das christliche Leben. Vorlesungen 1959–1961*, 365.)

87 *KD*, III/2, 133 (ET, 113).

88 *KD*, III/2, 129–43 (ET, 109–21), esp. 131–5 (ET, 111–15). Gestrich points out that existential philosophy, which had at first been the partner of dialectical theology, developed independently and took theological elements into its own system and thus became a rival to that theology (*Neuzeitliches Denken*, 3).

89 *KD*, III/2, 136–7 (ET, 116).

90 *KD*, III/2, 131 (ET, 111).

91 *KD*, III/2, 137–9 (ET, 116–18). There is here an appeal to the same experience of limit-situations (e.g. 135 (ET, 114–15)), especially of the horrors of the Second World War, that had led Bonhoeffer to doubt the efficacy of the limit-situation in raising the human consciousness to God via an existential crisis and had caused him to reject the entire argument to religion from existentialism (Bonhoeffer, *Letters and Papers from Prison*, 122–7, 132).

92 *KD*, III/2, 141 (ET, 119).

93 *KD*, III/2, 143 (ET, 121). Barth therefore uses 'autonomous' both in the sense that he has defined himself and in a sense opposed to that usage.

94 *KD*, III/2, 144 (ET, 122).

95 *KD*, III/2, 144–5, 149 (ET, 122, 125).

96 *KD*, III/2, 145 (ET, 122). See also Stock, *Anthropologie der Verheißung*, 10.

97 *KD*, III/2, 145–6 (ET, 123). Barth concedes the possibility of a further development of the 'autonomous self-understanding' of humanity in the direction of theistic philosophy. In that case humanity's self-understanding would include theonomy. Barth's answer is that such a philosophy cannot conceive of the free God of Christian Revelation (*KD*, III/2, 146–8 (ET, 123–4)). Barth applies the same objection to Brunner's outline of a general philosophy of revelation (*KD*, III/2, 148–57 (ET, 125–32)).

98 *KD*, III/2, 229, 231–4 (ET, 192, 194–6).

99 *KD*, III/2, 234–5 (ET, 197).

100 *KD*, III/2, 270–1 (ET, 214–16).

101 *KD*, III/2, 270–1 (ET, 226–8). The argument leads straight to an excursus on Nietzsche (276–90 (ET, 231–42)) as a warning example of a person without his fellow human beings. On the ladder of relationships and the analogy of relation, see Jüngel, *Barth-Studien*, 212–16.

102 *KD*, III/2, 262–3 (ET, 220).

103 *KD*, III/2, 260–2 (ET, 218–19).

104 *KD*, III/2, 259–61, 268–70 (ET, 217–19, 224–6). Jüngel emphasises that the correspondence here forms the foundation – logical and ontological – for God's activity *ad extra* and therefore for the entire area of anthropology (*Barth-Studien*, 224).

105 Stock, *Anthropologie der Verheißung*, 99–102.

106 For the anthropological area this is documented by Friedmann, *Christologie und Anthropologie*, 269–72; for the ethical by Bouillard, *Karl Barth*, II/2, 255–8. While disputing some of Friedmann's evidence, Stock is in agreement with him on the conclusion (*Anthropologie der Verheißung*, 92, 94, 236). Here von Balthasar's criticism of a 'Christological constriction' in Barth retains its force and it is at this point that most of the recent Protestant criticism or constructive reinterpretation of Barth begins.

107 This theory was developed by Hans Stickelberger, *Ipsa assumptione*

creatur, following on an indication by Jüngel.

108 Friedmann, *Christologie und Anthropologie*, 264.

109 Hermann Volk, 'Die Christologie bei Karl Barth und Emil Brunner', 642.

110 Jüngel, in *TRE*, V, 265–6, presents a diagram of the systematic structure of the doctrine of Reconciliation, which he regards as Barth's masterpiece (also in *Barth-Studien*, 54–5).

111 *KD*, IV/2, 90–1 (ET, 82–3).

112 *KD*, IV/2, 97 (ET, 88).

113 *KD*, IV/2, 98 (ET, 89). See also Friedmann, *Christologie und Anthropologie*, 240, and the entire section 227–45.

114 *KD*, IV/2, 97 (ET, 89). See also Friedmann, *Christologie und Anthropologie*, 234–5. Barth bases the difference between Jesus Christ and us in his unique relationship with God. On account of this relationship with God (in accordance with Barth's ontology of relationship with God) human nature is primarily that of Jesus Christ and secondarily ours.

115 See the opening thesis of no. 57 (*KD*, IV/1, 1 (ET, 3)).

116 *KD*, IV/3, 45–6 (ET, 43).

117 *KD*, IV/3, 122–53 (ET, 110–35), together with the concluding comparison of both sections in IV/3, 171–88 (ET, 151–65). On the distinction between the Lights of the World and the 'true words' spoken *extra muros ecclesiae*, see Aat Dekker, *Homines bonae voluntatis*, 110. Unlike some less perceptive commentators, Dekker sees the distinction clearly and castigates Barth for adopting it.

118 *KD*, IV/3, 1 (ET, 3). Gerhard Gloege sees in the omission of the rest of the first Barmen thesis a moderation of Barth's polemic and the adoption of a more irenical attitude to the world. In fact he takes exception to Barth's alleged mitigation of the doctrine of judgement in favour of the affirmation of the world ('Zur Versöhnungslehre Karl Barths', 164, 177–8). Dekker, however, sees in the adoption of the Barmen thesis and in its explication in *KD*, IV/3 a proof of Barth's consistency (*Homines bonae voluntatis*, 31–2) and in this he can be shown to be correct. The moderation of Barth's polemic is adequately explained by Gloege himself when he observes how 'der "hohe" Ansatz der Versöhnungslehre in der überlegenen Gnadenwahl Gottes das Denken und Reden des urteilenden Dogmatikers temperiert' (164).

119 *KD*, IV/3, 95–100 (ET, 86–90).

120 *KD*, IV/3, 123 (ET, 111).

121 *KD*, IV/3, 123–4 (ET, 111). As Christian Link points out, these true words, exemplified in the New Testament parables, have their truth *extra se*, from outside themselves, and the appropriate understanding of them is not a product of human creative faculties but an event that encounters humankind from without. The world is not already in itself a parable of the Kingdom; it can only become such, through the action of God (*Die Welt als Gleichnis*, 291, 292).

122 *KD*, IV/3, 130 (ET, 116–17). Wilfried Härle points out how Barth arrives

at the affirmation of these 'true words' not by a restriction of his Christological principle in which Revelation in Christ is the unique source of knowledge but by extending it beyond the boundaries of Bible and Church (*Sein und Gnade*, 283).

123 *KD*, IV/3, 124 (ET, 111).

124 *KD*, IV/3, 131-2 (ET, 117-18). Hans Küng, who had at first welcomed this section of *KD*, IV/3 as an extension of the knowledge of God to the witness of Creation, later conceded that Barth had remained faithful to his earlier restrictive views even here (first in 'Karl Barth's Lehre vom Wort Gottes als Frage an die katholische Theologie', later in *Does God Exist?*, 525-7).

125 *KD*, IV/3, 132 (ET, 118).

126 *KD*, IV/3, 124-6, 140, 152-3 (ET, 112-13, 125, 135). Apart from these sketchy examples, Barth is content with a formal discussion of the 'true words'. As Dekker remarks, the material content of these words is not significant since it must in any case coincide with and point to the primary and secondary forms of the Word of God, Jesus Christ and the Scripture with its proclamation (*Homines bonae voluntatis*, 54). Barth had cited Confucius, Feuerbach and Buber in *KD*, III/2, 333-5 (ET, 277-8).

127 *KD*, IV/3, 137-8 (ET, 122-3). See also Dekker, *Homines bonae voluntatis*, 50-1, where Dekker complains that the entire sphere of the relatively profane, which he (not Barth) identifies with human reality as such, is condemned to the status of a marginal phenomenon.

128 *KD*, IV/3, 138-46 (ET, 123-30).

129 *KD*, IV/3, 139 (ET, 124).

130 *KD*, IV/3, 145, 151 (ET, 129, 134). See also Dekker, *Homines bonae voluntatis*, 50-2.

131 *KD*, IV/3, 131 (ET, 117). The point is the sovereignty of Christ. See also Eberhard Jüngel, *Gottes Sein ist im Werden*, 137.

132 *KD*, IV/3, 132-6 (ET, 118-21).

133 *KD*, IV/3, 133 (ET, 119) (my translation). The published version mistranslates 'schwerlich . . . wohl aber' as a parallelism rather than as an antithesis between religion and the Word of God.

134 Bonhoeffer, *Letters and Papers from Prison*, 174-5, 178-81, 188-9, 205-6.

135 *KD*, IV/3, 133 (ET, 119).

136 *KD*, IV/3, 153-4, 157 (ET, 135-6, 139). Link notes: 'Kein zweites Kapitel der Dogmatik ist denn auch mit so sorgfältigen theologischen Abgrenzungen umgeben' (*Die Welt als Gleichnis*, 305).

137 *KD*, IV/3, 153-4 (ET, 136).

138 *KD*, IV/3, 155-6 (ET, 137-8). This is what Küng identifies as Barth's 'tacit correction' (*Does God Exist?*, 525-7).

139 Hendrik Berkhof, 'Barths Lichterlehre im Rahmen der heutigen Theologie, Kirche und Welt', 33. See also Link, *Die Welt als Gleichnis*, 305 n.75).

140 *KD*, IV/3, 154 (ET, 136-7). see also Berkhof, 'Barths Lichterlehre', 34:

'Die Weltgeschichte außerhalb von Christus ist für Barth wohl ein Kreislauf.'

141 *KD*, IV/3, 155 (ET, 137).

142 *KD*, IV/3, 158–62 (ET, 140–3).

143 *KD*, IV/3, 159 (ET, 141).

144 *Ibid.* A contradiction of radical Idealism, as is clear from *KD*, III/2, 2 (ET, 4).

145 *KD*, IV/3. I have corrected the translation ('its creatures').

146 *KD*, IV/3, 160 (ET, 142). See also *KD*, IV/3, 162 (ET, 143).

147 *KD*, IV/3, 159 (ET, 141). Here, as Dekker notes, Barth's intention is to establish that the cosmos is *independent* of humanity (*Homines bonae voluntatis*, 111). Link also observes that the Lights of the World are 'unabhängig von des Menschen Verhältnis und Stellungnahme zur Welt' (*Die Welt als Gleichnis*, 305). Eberhard Jüngel's precise formulation goes as far as is possible in this direction without spilling over into the anthropomorphic and epistemologically untenable language of Barth. Jüngel writes of 'das Wechselspiel von Mensch und Welt, in welchem der Mensch sich kosmomorph und die Welt anthropomorph versteht' (*Entsprechungen*, 155).

148 Balthasar, writing of Barth's book on Anselm, had already noted how the human faculty of inner-worldly knowledge appeared to be reduced in Barth's intention to a mere 'listening' (*Karl Barth*, 173).

149 *KD*, IV/3, 180, 184–7 (ET, 158, 161–4). Barth subjects natural science in particular to severe critical restrictions in order to demolish its claim to be the only valid form of knowledge (*KD*, IV/3, 165–7 (ET, 146–7)).

150 Barth, *Die protestantische Theologie im 19. Jahrhundert*. The seventh chapter is devoted to Kant (237–78, here esp. 250, 272–7). Stock notes how Barth adopts the Kantian restrictions on human knowledge and adds further restrictions of his own, for example on the primacy of the practical reason, as well as omitting any kind of productivity or a priori in human understanding. At the same time Barth avoids a detailed discussion of Kant's epistemology, so that his appeal to Kant remains selective (*Anthropologie der Verheißung*, 107, 172, 178–9, 188–9 with n. 115). The same point is made by Dieter Schellong in Schellong and Steck, *Karl Barth und die Neuzeit*, 97.

151 *KD*, IV/3, 162–71 (ET, 143–50).

152 *KD*, IV/3, 168–71 (ET, 149–50). See also Link, *Die Welt als Gleichnis*, 308.

153 *KD*, IV/3, 167 (ET, 147). For Barth's theology of freedom, see Ulrich Hedinger, *Der Freiheitsbegriff in der Kirchlichen Dogmatik Karl Barths*, and the more specific study of Michael Plathow, *Das Problem des concursus divinus*. Balthasar characterised Barth's concept of freedom as downright Augustinian (*Karl Barth*, 140).

154 *KD*, IV/3, 167 (ET, 147).

155 *Ibid.*

156 *KD*, IV/3, 167 (ET, 148).

157 *KD*, IV/3, 167–8 (ET, 148).

158 *KD*, IV/3, 171–88 (ET, 151–65). It cannot be said that Barth was very successful here. The Karl Barth Conference at the Leuenberg, Switzerland, in the summer of 1977 occupied itself with the question without, in Berkhof's opinion, arriving at any final clarity (Berkhof, 'Barths Lichterlehre', 33).

159 *KD*, IV/3, 173–4 (ET, 153).

160 *KD*, IV/3, 175–88 (ET, 154–65).

161 *KD*, IV/3, 175–9 (ET, 154–7). See also Berkhof, 'Barths Lichterlehre', 34.

162 *KD*, IV/3, 179–82 (ET, 157–60).

163 *KD*, IV/3, 185–8 (ET, 163–5).

164 The objection is raised by Dekker, *Homines bonae voluntatis*, 55–6, 59.

165 *KD*, III/4, 376–8 (ET, 332–3).

166 *KD*, II/1, 200 (ET, 178). See also *KD*, II/1, 205–6 (ET, 183), where Barth reduces such natural theology to human self-knowledge.

167 *Karl Barth. Gesamtausgabe*, II/3, *Das christliche Leben. Vorlesungen 1959–1961*, 196–9, 201, 208–18.

168 Berkhof, 'Barths Lichterlehre', 36.

169 *KD*, IV/4, ix (ET, ix). On Barth's doctrine of Baptism, see Fritz Viering (ed.), *Zu Karl Barths Lehre von der Taufe*; and Eberhard Jüngel, 'Karl Barths Lehre von der Taufe', in *Barth-Studien*, 246–90. For a Catholic response, see Richard Schlüter, *Karl Barths Tauflehre*; Anno Quadt, 'Die Taufe als Antwort des Glaubens'; and Anno Quadt, *Gott und Mensch*, 243–56. In chapter 2 I return to Jüngel's interpretation.

170 *KD*, IV/4, 116 (ET, 106). The distinction between the primary and secondary subject occurs in Barth's treatment of the Church in *KD*, IV/2, 768 (ET, 678), and is applied to Baptism in IV/4, 116 (ET, 105).

171 *KD*, IV/4, 36–7, 116 (ET, 33–4, 106).

172 *KD*, IV/4, 180–214 (ET, 164–95). See also *KD*, IV/4, xi–xiii (ET, x–xii), and the controversy in Viering, *Zu Karl Barths Lehre von der Taufe*.

173 *KD*, IV/4, 6, 155–8 (ET, 5–6, 141–4).

174 *KD*, IV/4, 24–5, 110, 156 (ET, 22–3, 101, 142).

175 *KD*, IV/4, 157 (ET, 143).

176 *KD*, IV/4, 157–8 (ET, 143–4). Schlüter shows that Barth's representation of the Catholic concept of sacrament as a divinised human action is a caricature (*Karl Barths Tauflehre*, 160).

177 *KD*, IV/4, 45 (ET, 41).

178 *Ibid*. On this 'unity in difference', see Schlüter, *Karl Barths Tauflehre*, 270. Jüngel, writing of Barth's doctrine of Baptism, uses the phrase 'Entsprechungs-Unterscheidung' (*Barth-Studien*, 256).

179 Balthasar, *Karl Barth*, 210.

180 *KD*, IV/4, 20 (ET, 19). Schlüter (*Karl Barths Tauflehre*, 99) follows Quadt ('Die Taufe als Antwort des Glaubens', 468) in accepting that the emphasis on human action here is a proof that creaturely reality is adequately respected in Barth's theology. The affirmation of freedom in obedience is,

however, an element in the *Church Dogmatics* from the start and is not quite the same as an adequate account of creaturely reality as a whole.

181 *KD*, IV/4, 20-2 (ET, 19-20). The rejection of sacramental mediation has now been extended to those aspects of the Word of God, such as its presence in Church proclamation, which Barth had called sacramental in the Prolegomena to the *Church Dogmatics*. See also Jüngel, *Barth-Studien*, 275-82; and Quadt, *Gott und Mensch*, 249. Mediation is replaced by the immediate action of God alone (*KD*, IV/4, 35-6 (ET, 32-3)).

182 *KD*, IV/1, 860-5 (ET, 771-4).

183 *KD*, IV/4, 32, 38 (ET, 29, 34, 35).

184 *KD*, IV/3, 619-36, esp. 629-30 (ET, 538-54, esp. 548). See also Jüngel's subtle reconciliation of the earlier teaching with the new emphasis on the internal grace of Christ, in *Barth-Studien*, 271-3.

185 *KD*, IV/4, 6 (ET, 6). The translator, scandalised perhaps, changed the verb into the passive voice: 'The possibility of God consists in the fact that a man . . . is enabled to participate not just passively but actively in God's grace as one who may and will and can be set to work too.'

186 Barth notes that this element in Zwingli's theology was a philosophical one rather than theological, in the belief that he himself had come to a similar position on purely theological and exegetical grounds (*KD*, IV/4, 141 (ET, 128)). But in Schlüter's examination it emerges that Barth's exegesis forcibly imports this distinction into the New Testament and that it originates precisely in the philosophical bias of his tradition (*Karl Barths Tauflehre*, 159, 248).

187 *KD*, IV/4, 15, 219 (ET, 14, 199-200). See also *KD*, IV/4, 151-2, 156 (ET, 138, 142).

188 Stock, *Anthropologie der Verheißung*, 172-4.

189 *KD*, IV/4, 31 (ET, 28).

190 *KD*, IV/4, 39 (ET, 35). Barth suggests that the rejection of infant baptism might enable the Church to be 'nicht unmündig, sondern mündig' (IV/4, xii (ET, xi)). A person's 'Mündigkeit' consists, however, in their immediate exposure to the command of God so that they obey God and none other (IV/4, 170 (ET, 154)).

191 Balthasar, *Karl Barth*, 209.

2 THE AUTONOMY THEME IN BARTH CRITICISM SINCE 1950

1 Bonhoeffer, *Letters and Papers from Prison*, 153, 156-7.

2 Wolfhart Pannenberg (ed.), *Offenbarung als Geschichte*, especially the new preface to the 5th German edn, v-vi. See also James M. Robinson, 'Revelation as Word and as History'; Peter Eicher, 'Geschichte und Wort Gottes', 321-54; and Peter Eicher, *Offenbarung*, 433-9.

3 Professor Pannenberg underlined the above points of agreement and disagreement with Barth in a conversation with me, 27 July 1983.

4 There exists no detailed comparative study of the theologies of Barth and Pannenberg and their interconnections. The dissertation of Bradley

Charles Hanson, 'Hope and Participation in Christ', is essentially a study of Barth's theology which adduces Pannenberg as a corrective to Barth only towards the end of the argument. The contrast with Barth's theology is, however, a feature of introductions to Pannenberg's thought in the English-speaking world.

5 Dietrich Rössler, 'Positionelle und kritische Theologie', 228.

6 Wolfhart Pannenberg, 'Zur Bedeutung des Analogiegedankens bei Karl Barth', 17–24.

7 See especially Wolfhart Pannenberg's unpublished *Habilitationsschrift*, 'Analogie und Offenbarung'; his 'Analogy and Doxology', in *Basic Questions*, II, 181–201; and his frequent review articles on medieval studies. See also the dissertation of Elizabeth Johnson, 'Analogy, Doxology and their Connection with Christology in the Thought of Wolfhart Pannenberg', esp. 281–3, where she points out that the negative moment in analogy is not an equivocation but the negation of a particular limitation which leads to a progression in the analogical operation, and that Pannenberg has never satisfactorily dealt with this point; and her article, 'The Right Way to Speak about God? Pannenberg on Analogy'.

8 Wolfhart Pannenberg, 'Mythos und Wort', 176–7.

9 *Ibid.*, 177–80.

10 *Ibid.*, 185.

11 Wolfhart Pannenberg, 'Wahrheit, Gewißheit und Glaube', in *Grundfragen*, II, 243–5.

12 Wolfhart Pannenberg, *Theology and the Philosophy of Science*, 272–3; and Pannenberg, 'Die Subjektivität Gottes und die Trinitätslehre. Ein Beitrag zur Beziehung zwischen Karl Barth und der Philosophie Hegels', in *Grundfragen*, II, 103.

13 Pannenberg, *Theology and the Philosophy of Science*, 9; Wolfhart Pannenberg (ed.), *Revelation as History*, 134; Pannenberg, *Grundfragen*, II, 244.

14 Pannenberg qualified his earlier statements about the historical evidence for the Resurrection in his reply to the criticisms of Ignace Berten ('Nachwort', in *Geschichte – Offenbarung – Glaube*, 132, 136–7). Pannenberg accepts that the Resurrection is not simply a fact like other facts since the life of the Risen Christ stands in an analogical relationship to our experience of life. With this statement he recognised that he was also modifying his previous position, whereby all talk of eschatological salvation *and of God* was mere metaphor.

15 Wolfhart Pannenberg, *Theology and the Kingdom of God*, 95, 99; Wolfhart Pannenberg, *Reformation zwischen gestern und morgen*, 17; Wolfhart Pannenberg, *Basic Questions*, III, 142.

16 Pannenberg, *Theology and the Philosophy of Science*, 320–1; Wolfhart Pannenberg, 'Wie wahr ist das Reden von Gott?', 39.

17 Pannenberg, *Theology and the Philosophy of Science*, 367.

18 Pannenberg, 'Wie wahr ist das Reden von Gott?', 39. It was this aspect

of Pannenberg's thought that led Eicher to emphasise his 'option for the Enlightenment' and his affirmation of the 'autonomy of the reason' (*Offenbarung*, 426–33).

19 Pannenberg, *Basic Questions*, II, 54.

20 Pannenberg, *Theology and the Philosophy of Science*, 21, 26–7, 125–6, 134, 326. See also Pannenberg, *Basic Questions*, III, 141.

21 Pannenberg, *Theology and the Philosophy of Science*, 129–30, 139, 149.

22 *Ibid.*, 55–6, 335.

23 *Ibid.*, 62–8, 336; Wolfhart Pannenberg, 'Kontingenz und Naturgesetz', 65–7.

24 Pannenberg, *Theology and the Philosophy of Science*, 70, 221–4, 313–15; Pannenberg, 'Wie wahr ist das Reden von Gott?', 37.

25 Pannenberg, *Theology and the Philosophy of Science*, 315, 320, 339–41.

26 *Ibid.*, 343–44; Pannenberg, *Basic Questions*, III, 177.

27 Pannenberg, *Theology and the Philosophy of Science*, 343–4; Pannenberg, 'Wie wahr ist das Reden von Gott?', 41; Pannenberg, *Basic Questions*, III, 96–8.

28 Pannenberg, 'Der Gott der Geschichte', in *Grundfragen*, II, 112–28, here 125–7; and Pannenberg, 'Christologie und Theologie', in *Grundfragen*, II, 129–45, here 144–5.

29 Pannenberg, 'Nachwort', in *Offenbarung als Geschichte*, 5th edn, xiii and n. 13; Pannenberg, *Theology and the Philosophy of Science*, 43.

30 Pannenberg, *Basic Questions*, III, 140, 188; Wolfhart Pannenberg, *Die Prädestinationslehre des Duns Scotus*, 137–8; Pannenberg, 'Kontingenz und Naturgesetz', 34, 37, 73 n. 73.

31 Pannenberg, *Basic Questions*, III, 117, 151–3, 189–90; Pannenberg, *Reformation zwischen gestern und morgen*, 19–20; Wolfhart Pannenberg, *Human Nature, Election and History*, 21.

32 Pannenberg, *Reformation zwischen gestern und morgen*, 17, 21; Pannenberg, *Human Nature, Election and History*, 26–7. Autonomy is thus the immediacy of the individual to God.

33 In an interview (27 July 1983) Professor Pannenberg confirmed this observation of mine.

34 Pannenberg, *Human Nature, Election and History*, 26.

35 Pannenberg, *Theology and the Philosophy of Science*, 433 n. 821.

36 Pannenberg, *Basic Questions*, III, 141.

37 Pannenberg, *Human Nature, Election and History*, 33–4, 72–4, 97.

38 Pannenberg, *Basic Questions*, III, 124–7, 141.

39 Pannenberg, 'Person und Subjekt', in *Grundfragen*, II, 80–95, here 86–8.

40 Pannenberg, *Grundfragen*, II, 84–90.

41 *Ibid.*, 92; Pannenberg, *Basic Questions*, III, 110–11; Pannenberg, *Human Nature, Election and History*, 101.

42 Wolfhart Pannenberg, *What is Man?*, 94; Pannenberg, *Theology and the Philosophy of Science*, 203; Pannenberg, *Human Nature, Election and History*, 104–5.

43 Pannenberg, *Human Nature, Election and History*, 100. On Luther, see *ibid.*, 21. The reference to Calvin occurs only in the German version (16).

44 Pannenberg, *Basic Questions*, III, viii, 92–3, 106–9. The metaphysical objectivity of the concept of God in medieval scholasticism meant that determinism was unavoidable (Pannenberg, *Die Prädestinationslehre des Duns Scotus*, 132).

45 Pannenberg, *Basic Questions*, III, 109–11, 131.

46 *Ibid.*, 114, 172–4, incl. n. 93.

47 Pannenberg, *Grundfragen*, II, 95; Pannenberg, *Basic Questions*, III, 95–6.

48 Pannenberg, *Basic Questions*, II, 231; Pannenberg, *Grundfragen*, II, 95, 106–7; Pannenberg, *Basic Questions*, III, 172–4.

49 Pannenberg, *Basic Questions*, III, 114–15.

50 Pannenberg's epistemology is presented in the thesis of Minus Baskin Jackson, 'An Interpretation of Wolfhart Pannenberg's Theory of Knowledge as Creative Subjectivity'. On Christianity and history, see Pannenberg, *Basic Questions*, II, 113.

51 Johnson traces the development in her dissertation, 'Analogy, Doxology and their Connection with Christology', 272. The question was already posed by Max Seckler in 1968 ('Zur Diskussion um das Offenbarungsverständnis Wolfhart Pannenbergs', 132–4). Pannenberg always maintained *that* God must show his power in history; the question was how and where.

52 Wolfhart Pannenberg, *Jesus – God and Man*. See also Pannenberg's reply to John Cobb, 'A Liberal Logos Christology: The Christology of John Cobb', 135–9; and Pannenberg, *Theology and the Kingdom of God*, 66.

53 Eicher makes a similar criticism of Pannenberg (*Offenbarung*, 560).

54 Pannenberg, *Grundfragen*, II, 104–5; Pannenberg (ed.), 'Nachwort', in *Offenbarung als Geschichte*, 5th edn, xiii; Pannenberg, 'Die Begründung der Ethik bei Ernst Troeltsch', 95.

55 Pannenberg, 'Der Gott der Geschichte', in *Grundfragen*, II, 112–28, here 111 with n. 35, 117–18, 123, 127.

56 Pannenberg, 'Die Subjektivität Gottes und die Trinitätslehre', in *Grundfragen*, II, 96–111; Pannenberg, *Theology and the Kingdom of God*, 70–1: 'The trinitarian idea of God is congruous with historical process, while the notion of a supreme entity speaks of a "divine thing" outside man's history.' Johnson notes that Pannenberg's ideas on futurity and the being of God are controversial and not free from obscurity ('Analogy, Doxology and their Connection with Christology', 248–50, incl. 248 n. 4).

57 This criticism applies to Pannenberg's essay on 'Kontingenz und Naturgesetz'.

58 Barth, *KD*, III/1, 466–76 (ET, 406–14); Barth, *Die protestantische Theologie im 19. Jahrhundert*, 269.

59 Thus Johnson, 'Analogy, Doxology and their Connection with Christology', 262. See also the criticisms of Jüngel, 'Das Dilemma der natürlichen Theologie und die Wahrheit ihres Problems. Überlegungen für ein Gespräch

mit Wolfhart Pannenberg', in *Entsprechungen*, 158–77, esp. 172–3. The Catholic tradition of *analysis fidei* would have much to offer Pannenberg at this point. See also the remarks of Seckler, 'Zur Diskussion um das Offenbarungsverständnis Wolfhart Pannenbergs', 134; and Eicher, *Offenbarung*, 576–7.

60 Pannenberg, *Jesus – God and Man*, 167–8.

61 'Der Rückgang vom Buchstaben der biblischen Schriften auf die durch sie bezeugte Geschichte' ('Nachwort', in *Offenbarung als Geschichte*, 5th edn, xii).

62 Gestrich, *Neuzeitliches Denken*, 319, 385–6.

63 Friedrich Gogarten, *Verhängnis und Hoffnung der Neuzeit*.

64 Hans Blumenberg, *Die Legitimität der Neuzeit*.

65 *Anfänge der dialektischen Theologie*, I, II, ed. Jürgen Moltmann.

66 Jürgen Moltmann, *Theology of Hope*, 50–8, 87, 281.

67 Dorothee Sölle, *Christ the Representative*, 88–91.

68 *Theologie zwischen gestern und morgen*, ed. Wilhelm Dantine and Kurt Lüthi, 7–9.

69 Kurt Lüthi, 'Theologie als Gespräch', in *Theologie zwischen gestern und morgen*, 302, 308–11; Wilfried Joest, 'Barth, Bultmann und die "existenziale Interpretation" ', in *Theologie zwischen gestern und morgen*, 75–8, 85–6.

70 Paul Hessert, 'Barthianische Wurzeln der "Radical-Theology" ', in *Theologie zwischen gestern und morgen*, 246; James M. Robinson, 'Die ersten heterodoxen Barthianer', in *Theologie zwischen gestern und morgen*, 36–7. Hessert based his argument exclusively on the Prolegomena to the *Church Dogmatics*, which was not unfair as it was for some time the only volume available in Germany and in the English-speaking world and therefore the influential one.

71 The importance of the theology of secularisation was emphasised by Lüthi ('Theologie als Gespräch', 307, 319, 325–6, 330) and he deplored Barth's neglect of natural science (305, 323).

72 *Porträt eines Theologen. Stimmt unser Bild von Karl Barth?*, ed. Willi Gegenheimer, esp. 7–8.

73 See Gestrich, *Neuzeitliches Denken*.

74 Rössler, 'Positionelle und kritische Theologie', 215–31. Religious subjectivity had been Pannenberg's charge against Barth.

75 Trutz Rendtorff, 'The Problem of Revelation in the Concept of the Church', in Pannenberg (ed.), *Revelation as History*, 159–81. See also Trutz Rendtorff, 'Historische Bibelwissenschaft und Theologie'.

76 Trutz Rendtorff, 'Radikale Autonomie Gottes. Zum Verständnis der Theologie Karl Barths und ihrer Folgen', in *Theorie des Christentums*, 161–81. The essay was written in 1969, published in 1972, as Rendtorff notes (*Theorie des Christentums*, 201). We return to Rendtorff's Barth interpretation below.

77 Jüngel, 'Karl Barth', *Barth-Studien*, 15–21, esp. 19; and '. . . keine

Menschenlosigkeit Gottes . . . Zur Theologie Karl Barths zwischen Theismus und Atheismus', *Barth-Studien*, 332–47, here 335–6, 346–7.

78 *Ibid.*, 333–4, 344–5. See also Eberhard Jüngel's own analysis and critique of traditional theism in *Gott als Geheimnis der Welt*.

79 Jüngel, '. . . keine Menschenlosigkeit Gottes . . .', 337–9.

80 Jüngel, *Gott als Geheimnis der Welt*, 51; and Eberhard Jüngel, 'Epilogomena 1975', in *Gottes Sein ist im Werden*, 125–6.

81 Steck, 'Karl Barths Absage an die Neuzeit', in Schellong and Steck, *Karl Barth und die Neuzeit*, 7–33, esp. 23, 31.

82 *Ibid.*, 18–19, 21–2. See also *KD*, IV/1, 532–3 (ET, 479).

83 Steck, 'Karl Barths Absage an die Neuzeit', in Schellong and Steck, *Karl Barth und die Neuzeit*, 22–3. Barth's controversy with Harnack is documented in *Anfänge der dialektischen Theologie*, I, 323–45, here 329 (also published in Karl Barth, *Fragen und Antworten, Gesammelte Vorträge*, III, 7–31).

84 Steck, 'Karl Barths Absage an die Neuzeit', in Schellong and Steck, *Karl Barth und die Neuzeit*, 24. Steck's citation of *Die protestantische Theologie im 19. Jahrhundert*, 116–17, is, however, inaccurate. Barth does not say that Luther, Calvin and the theologians of Protestant Orthodoxy were the leaders of the movement of contemporary thought in general, but that they were the leaders of the movement of thought in the *Church* of their day. Nonetheless the quotation from Barth's fifteenth answer to Harnack does support Steck's contention, provided it is not suggested that theology should lead the movement of thought in any other way than by staying strictly within the limits set by the revealed Word of God. See also Barth's remarks in *KD*, I/1, 5 (ET, 7), 9–10 (ET, 11).

85 Steck, 'Karl Barths Absage an die Neuzeit', in Schellong and Steck, *Karl Barth und die Neuzeit*, 9, 11, 17, 25–6, 29, 30–1, 33.

86 Dieter Schellong, 'Karl Barth als Theologe der Neuzeit', in Schellong and Steck, *Karl Barth und die Neuzeit*, 36, 42–3, 53.

87 *Ibid.*, 70. See also Friedrich Wilhelm Marquardt, *Theologie und Sozialismus*; and Shelley Baranowski, 'The Primacy of Theology: Karl Barth and Socialism'.

88 Schellong, 'Karl Barth als Theologe der Neuzeit', in Schellong and Steck, *Karl Barth und die Neuzeit*, 72–3, 81–2.

89 *Ibid.*, 73–4, 80, 83, 85–7.

90 *Ibid.*, 90; see also 91. Schellong speaks here of the truth in Barth's theology needing to be established, of its 'Bewahrheitung'. However, he corrects the false impression that could be given by this statement – that for Barth the Word and action of God could be judged by any criterion outside itself – by pointing out that, for Barth, human action cannot realise the divine reality but can only have the function of pointing towards the divine action.

91 *Ibid.*, 91–3.

92 Adriaan Geense, 'Die Bedingung der Universalität', 10–11, 26.

93 *Ibid.*, 21, 29–32.

94 In the editor's introduction to the journal in which Geense's essay appeared (Gerhard Sauter, 'Zu diesem Heft', 1–3).

95 Gestrich, *Neuzeitliches Denken*, 244–5, 383–4.

96 *Ibid.*, 170–2.

97 *Ibid.*, 7, 233, 256–7, 318–21.

98 *Ibid.*, 248, 251, 258–9, 263. Gestrich maintains that the nihilism of Nietzsche, leading as it did to the existentialist awareness of the radical question of existence, offered the optimal background for Barth's doctrine of God (218).

99 *Ibid.*, 261–3; see also 252.

100 Trutz Rendtorff, 'Christentum ohne Kirche? Zur Überwindung einer falschen Alternative', 140–1; 'Von der Kirchensoziologie zur Soziologie des Christentums. Über die soziologische Funktion der "Säkularisierung" ', 135–7; both in *Theorie des Christentums*.

101 Rendtorff, *Theorie des Christentums*, 162–5.

102 *Ibid.*, 166–7.

103 *Ibid.*, 173.

104 *Ibid.*, 163–4, 171, 174–5, 180.

105 *Ibid.*, 175–8.

106 *Ibid.*, 178. Rendtorff refers to *KD*, IV/3, 946 (ET, 826).

107 *Ibid.*, 175.

108 *Theorie des Christentums*, 182–200, here 188–90, 193–4. Rendtorff illustrates this thesis with reference to current questions in theology, such as praxis, method, anthropology and ecumenism (198).

109 *Ibid.*, 195–7, 199–200.

110 Trutz Rendtorff, 'Der ethische Sinn der Dogmatik. Zur Reformulierung des Verhältnisses von Dogmatik und Ethik bei Karl Barth', in *Die Realisierung der Freiheit*, 119–34, here 121, 124, 126.

111 *Ibid.*, 126.

112 *Ibid.*, 125–7.

113 *Ibid.*, 130–2.

114 Groll's thesis was completed under Rendtorff's direction in the same year as Rendtorff's essay was published (Wilfried Groll, *Ernst Troeltsch und Karl Barth – Kontinuität im Widerspruch*). Groll explains the differences between Troeltsch und Barth as different reactions to a common historical problem.

115 Rendtorff, 'Der ethische Sinn der Dogmatik', 121–3, 127–8.

116 *Ibid.*, 132–4.

117 Trutz Rendtorff, 'Der Freiheitsbegriff als Ortsbestimmung der Theologie'.

118 Rudolf Weth, 'Ort und Funktion der Theologie als Wissenschaft', 32–54.

119 Dietrich Korsch, 'Christologie und Autonomie'; see also the review by Wolf Krötke of *Die Realisierung der Freiheit*.

120 Stock, *Anthropologie der Verheißung*, 108 n. 297. See also Konrad Stock,

'Freiheit als Veränderung', review of *Die Realisierung der Freiheit*.

121 Trutz Rendtorff, 'Karl Barth', in *Klassiker der Theologie*, II, 345.

122 Trutz Rendtorff, 'Der ethische Sinn der Dogmatik', 130, 131, 132; Rendtorff, *Theorie des Christentums*, 181, 199; Trutz Rendtorff, *Gott – ein Wort unserer Sprache*, 24, 37–41 (where Rendtorff makes clear he prefers not to speak of God as a radically transcendent other-worldly being).

123 Falk Wagner, 'Theologische Gleichschaltung. Zur Christologie bei Karl Barth', in *Die Realisierung der Freiheit*, 10–43. Falk Wagner's fundamental position is developed in his article 'Die erschlichene Freiheit', which is an attack on the notion of emancipation in the theology of Liberation.

124 Wagner, 'Theologische Gleichschaltung', 10–11, 12.

125 Korsch, 'Christologie und Autonomie', 164; Krötke, review of *Die Realisierung der Freiheit*, 302.

126 F. W. Graf, 'Die Freiheit der Entsprechung zu Gott. Bemerkungen zum theozentrischen Ansatz der Anthropologie Karl Barths', in *Die Realisierung der Freiheit*, 89–91. See also Korsch, 'Christologie und Autonomie', 154–5.

127 W. Sparn, ' "Extra Internum". Die christologische Revision der Prädestinationslehre in Karl Barths Erwählungslehre', in *Die Realisierung der Freiheit*, 44–75, here 48, 51–2, 74–5.

128 Christophe Freyd, 'Gott als die universale Wahrheit von Mensch und Welt. Die Versöhnungslehre Karl Barths im Lichte der Religionsphilosophie Hegels', 23–4, 87–8.

129 Welker, 'Barth und Hegel', 309–13; Freyd, 'Gott als die universale Wahrheit', 15, quoting Eberhard Busch's biography of Barth, 387.

130 Barth, 'Nachwort', in *Schleiermacher-Auswahl*, 311; Freyd, 'Gott als die universale Wahrheit', 113, 197, 210–14, 253, 255, 313. Freyd shows parallels between Barth and Hegel in relation to the Incarnation (134), the Cross and Resurrection (191), pneumatology (198, 205, 211), Reconciliation (214, 255) and in the assertion of a parallelism between world history and salvation history (270).

131 Freyd, 'Gott als die universale Wahrheit', 206, 209, 213, 225, 279, 296. Freyd criticises Barth (125 n. 222, 217, 251).

132 *Ibid.*, 206–7, 223–6.

133 *Ibid.*, 120 n. 72, 127–9, 204–5, 212.

134 *Ibid.*, 128, 149–50, 152, 178.

135 *Ibid.*, 120, 139, 148, 221, 316–17.

136 *Ibid.*, 162, 187, 288–9.

137 *Ibid.*, 149–52, 258.

138 *Ibid.*, 108–12.

139 *Ibid.*, 130–1, 149–52 (Incarnation); 175, 243, 288 (Resurrection and apocatastasis).

140 *Ibid.*, 114–17, 133–4, 299, 300, 302–3.

141 *Ibid.*, 160, 229–30, 235, 246.

142 *Ibid.*, 270–4.

143 *Ibid.*, 189, 196–7, 205, 303–9.

144 *Ibid.*, 257–8, 261–2. See also chapter 1 above.

145 Christof Gestrich, 'Wie kommt die Theologie zur Wahrheit', 216–19; Gestrich, *Neuzeitliches Denken*, 325–7, with a favourable mention of Pannenberg.

146 Barth, 'Nachwort', in *Schleiermacher-Auswahl*, 307–12, here 311; Gestrich also quotes a similar remark of Barth's in *KD*, III/3, 370–1 (ET, 324) (*Neuzeitliches Denken*, 317).

147 Gestrich, *Neuzeitliches Denken*, 217.

148 *Ibid.*, 218–19.

149 Dieter Becker, 'Menschsein im Dialog'. Recent study of Idealism has discovered elements of a philosophy of relationship (see the introduction above on Fichte). It would, however, be an exaggeration to claim that the Thou played anything but a subordinate role in Idealism before the reaction of Buber and Ebner. They were very conscious of being in opposition to Idealism.

150 See Jürgen Moltmann's critique of Barth in *The Trinity and the Kingdom of God*, 139–44. Here Moltmann accused Barth of holding a 'trinitarian Monarchy', a critique similar to Pannenberg's critique of Barth's concept of God. Moltmann, however, recognised the partnership between God and free humanity in the later volumes of the *Church Dogmatics* (Becker, 'Menschsein im Dialog', 216; Pannenberg, *Grundfragen*, II, 95, 107–8).

151 Becker, 'Menschsein im Dialog', 220–4, 243–8, 250–1. The adoption of anti-Idealist elements enabled Barth to make use of Idealism without being absorbed by it.

152 Eberhard Jüngel, 'Die Möglichkeit theologischer Anthropologie auf dem Grunde der Analogie. Eine Untersuchung zum Analogieverständnis Karl Barths', in *Barth-Studien*, 210–32.

153 *Ibid.*, 229 n. 54; and Eberhard Jüngel, 'Karl Barths Lehre von der Taufe', *Barth-Studien*, 256.

154 Jüngel, *Gott als Geheimnis der Welt*, 385–87. Here it is clear that Jüngel's criticisms of the classical doctrine of analogy are made in the light of Kant's criticism of the same. Kant, however, relied too much on the reduction of analogy to an argument from causality.

155 Eberhard Jüngel, 'Metaphorische Wahrheit', *Entsprechungen*, 150–1. That the tradition of analogy also included the faithful and successful effort to give conceptual expression to Revelation is overlooked by Jüngel here. See also Walter Kasper, 'Christologie und Anthropologie', esp. 215, 217, 219–20.

156 Jüngel, *Barth-Studien*, 211. The theologically conceived analogy of faith predominates in vols. I and II of the *Church Dogmatics*; in vols. III and IV Barth developed the ontological analogy of relation (Härle, *Sein und Gnade*, 205–6).

157 Jüngel, *Barth-Studien*, 228 n. 52.

158 *Ibid.*, 213–16.

159 *Ibid.*, 225–6.

160 Jüngel, '. . . keine Menschenlosigkeit Gottes . . .', in *Barth-Studien*, 339–40, 344–6.

161 Eberhard Jüngel, 'Der Gott entsprechende Mensch', in *Entsprechungen*, 298–9, 316–17; Eberhard Jüngel, 'Freiheitsrechte und Gerechtigkeit', in *Unterwegs zur Sache*, 246–56, here 246, 247, 255–6.

162 *Ibid.*, 247–8, 250–2.

163 *Ibid.*, 252–4.

164 Jüngel, 'Karl Barths Lehre von der Taufe', in *Barth-Studien*, 268.

165 *Ibid.*, 255–6.

166 *Ibid.*, 255–6, 273, 277–8, 281; Jüngel, 'Barth, Karl', in *TRE*, V 265 (*Barth-Studien*, 54). Jüngel therefore hints at what Hendrik Berkhof had established for the question of natural theology, a growing influence of Calvin on the ageing Barth's ethics of Reconciliation, of which the treatment of Baptism is a fragment (Berkhof, 'Barths Lichterlehre', 36).

167 Jüngel, *Barth-Studien*, 257, 262, 273–4, incl. n. 74.

168 *Ibid.*, 272–3.

169 *Ibid.*, 282; Eberhard Jüngel, 'Jesu Wort und Jesus als Wort Gottes', in *Parrhesia*, 82–100, reprinted in Jüngel, *Unterwegs zur Sache*, 126–44, from which I cite.

170 Jüngel, *Unterwegs zur Sache*, 135–7, esp. n. 27.

171 *Ibid.*, 142 n. 45.

172 Stickelberger, *Ipsa assumptione creatur*, 206–7.

173 *Ibid.*, 144–6, esp. n. 120. The quotation is from Hans Urs von Balthasar, *Kosmische Liturgie. Das Weltbild Maximus' des Bekenners*, 254.

174 Härle finds the expression 'ontology of grace' in von Balthasar; this, however, appears to be a misunderstanding, as von Balthasar here means the ontological explication or determination of grace, not an ontology in terms of grace. (The reference is to von Balthasar, *Karl Barth*, 372.)

175 Härle, *Sein und Gnade*, 74, 218–19, 299, 304–5, 309–11.

176 *Ibid.*, 288–94, 311–13.

177 *Ibid.*, 314–27, esp. 325–7.

178 Stock, *Anthropologie der Verheißung*, 92–4, 236, 240.

3 CONCLUSIONS

1 Barth, *The Humanity of God*, 40.

2 *Ibid.*, 41–2.

3 This was Barth's criticism of nineteenth-century Catholicism (*KD*, I/2, 622–37 (ET, 559–72)).

4 See the analysis of Korsch, 'Christologie und Autonomie'.

5 See above, chapter 2; Härle, *Sein und Gnade*, 326; and Becker, 'Menschsein im Dialog', 44.

6 Walter Lindemann, *Karl Barth und die kritische Schriftauslegung*, 87.

7 This corresponds to the tradition of the analysis of faith in Catholic

theology, which affirms an immediacy of the individual believer to God, but one that meets him in the historical mediation of the Word of God rather than setting him apart from and above it.

8 Ilse Bertinetti in her essay, 'Karl Barths Verhältnis zum anthropologischen Materialismus Ludwig Feuerbachs', points out how Barth accepts Feuerbach's projection thesis as the logical conclusion of the theology of his day.

9 Balthasar, *Karl Barth*, 244; Korsch, 'Christologie und Autonomie', 166; Härle, *Sein und Gnade*, 218–19, 299–311.

10 Härle, *Sein und Gnade*, 299 n. 106.

11 *KD*, IV/3, 181–2 (ET, 158).

12 See *KD*, IV/4, 155–8 (ET, 141–4).

13 *KD*, IV/3, 618 (ET, 538).

14 This is true of the Idealist reinterpretation of Barth as it is for Härle, Stock and Pannenberg; it also holds for Berkhof, Dekker, Plathow and Hedinger.

15 Karl Barth, *Gesamtausgabe*, II/3, *Das christliche Leben. Vorlesungen 1959–1961*, 196–201, 208–18.

16 Berkhof, 'Barths Lichterlehre', 41–2.

17 Thus Hans-Joachim Kraus, 'Logos und Sophia', in H. Berkhof and H.-J. Kraus (eds.), *Karl Barths Lichterlehre*.

18 E.g. Walter Kreck, *Grundfragen christlicher Ethik*, 122–3.

19 Gestrich, 'Wie kommt die Theologie zur Wahrheit?'; Berkhof, 'Barths Lichterlehre', 36–40, 47–8; Dekker, *Homines bonae voluntatis*, 54–9.

20 See Balthasar, *Karl Barth*, 390.

21 Härle, *Sein und Gnade*, 214–25. See also Eberhard Mechels, *Analogie bei Erich Przywara und Karl Barth*.

22 See Jüngel, *Barth-Studien*, 228 n. 52.

23 Helmut Thielicke, *Theologische Ethik*, II, 710–21, esp. 717.

24 *Ibid.*

25 Wolfgang Huber and Heinz Eduard Tödt, *Menschenrechte*, 67–8, 71–3, 161–2.

26 Eberhard Jüngel, 'Freiheitsrechte und Gerechtigkeit', in *Unterwegs zur Sache*, 246–56.

27 I am grateful to Professor Jüngel for pointing out to me the significance of Barth's cultural interests for his relationship to the modern era. These do not come to full expression in the *Church Dogmatics*.

28 For Barth's testimony to his anti-ideological understanding of freedom and his pragmatic approach to politics, see the interview 'Liberale Theologie', in his *Letzte Zeugnisse*. '

29 See Barth's self-mocking accounts of his distaste for ritual in Busch, *Karl Barth: His Life from Letters and Autobiographical Texts*, 235.

30 *Ibid.*, 222–55.

31 *KD*, IV/3, 875–8 (ET, 764–7); Christof Bäumler, *Die Lehre von der Kirche in der Theologie Karl Barths*, 27–33; Heinrich Fries, 'Kirche als Ereignis', 88–97, 103.

32 See Jüngel's introduction to Karl Barth, *Gesamtausgabe*, II/3.

33 Wilhelm Dantine, 'Der Welt-Bezug des Glaubens', in *Theologie zwischen gestern und morgen*, 265. See also Dekker's criticism that Barth lays far too much emphasis on the ecclesiastical community (*Homines bonae voluntatis*, 42, 52, 108).

34 A useful survey of the development of Barth's conception of Baptism and of some of the critical responses to it was made by D. C. Porter in his dissertation, 'The Holy Spirit and the Foundation of the Christian Life in the Theology of Karl Barth'.

Bibliography

WORKS BY KARL BARTH

Ad limina apostolorum, Zürich, EVZ, 1967 (ET *Ad limina apostolorum. An Appraisal of Vatican II*, Richmond, Va., John Knox Press, 1968)

Christengemeinde und Bürgergemeinde, Theologische Studien 20, Munich, Kaiser etc., 1946 (ET, 'The Christian Community and the Civil Community', in Karl Barth, *Against the Stream. Shorter Post-war Writings, 1946–1952*, London, SCM, 1954)

Die Christliche Dogmatik im Entwurf, I, Munich, Kaiser, 1927

Fides quaerens intellectum. Anselms Beweis der Existenz Gottes im Zusammenhang seines theologischen Programms, Munich, Kaiser, 1931 (ET, *Anselm. Fides quaerens intellectum. Anselm's Proof of the Existence of God in the Context of his Theological Scheme. Complete with Preface*, Pittsburgh, Pa., Pickwick Press, 1975)

Fragen und Antworten, Gesammelte Vorträge, III, Zollikon-Zürich, Evangelischer Verlag, 1957

Gesamtausgabe, II, *Akademische Werke*, 3, *Das christliche Leben, Die Kirchliche Dogmatik IV/4, Fragmente aus dem Nachlaß, Vorlesungen 1959–1961*, ed. Hans-Anton Drewes und Eberhard Jüngel, Zürich, Theologischer Verlag, 1976 (ET, *The Christian Life*, Edinburgh, T. and T. Clark, 1981)

Gesamtausgabe, V, *Briefe*, 2, *Karl Barth–Eduard Thurneysen, Briefwechsel*, vol. 1, *1913–1921*, ed. Eduard Thurneysen, Zürich, Theologischer Verlag, 1973

Gesamtausgabe, V, *Briefe*, 5, *Karl Barth, Briefe 1961–1968*, Zürich, Theologischer Verlag, 1975

The Humanity of God, London, Fontana, 1967, 33–64 (original *Die Menschlichkeit Gottes*, Theologische Studien 48, Zollikon-Zürich, Evangelischer Verlag, 1956)

Die Kirchliche Dogmatik, 5th edn, 13 part vols., Zollikon-Zürich, Evangelischer

Verlag, 1947–67 (ET, *Church Dogmatics*, 13 part vols., Edinburgh, T. and T. Clark, 1969–80)

Letzte Zeugnisse, Zürich, EVZ, 1969

'Nachwort', in *Schleiermacher-Auswahl*, ed. Heinz Bolli, 2nd edn, Gütersloh, Mohn, 1980 (ET, 'Concluding Unscientific Postscript on Schleiermacher', *Studies in Religion*, Toronto, 7 (1978), 117–36)

'Nein!', reprinted in *'Dialektische Theologie' in Scheidung und Bewährung* (see below) (ET, in K. Barth and E. Brunner, *Natural Theology*, London, Geoffrey Bles, The Centenary Press, 1946)

Die protestantische Theologie im 19. Jahrhundert. Ihre Vorgeschichte und ihre Geschichte, 2nd edn, Zollikon-Zürich, EVZ, 1952 (ET, *Protestant Theology in the Nineteenth Century. Its Background and History*, London, SCM, 1972)

Der Römerbrief, 4th edn, Munich, Kaiser, 1924 (ET, *The Epistle to the Romans*, London, Oxford University Press, 1933)

'Von der Paradoxie des "positiven Paradoxes" (Antworten und Fragen an Paul Tillich)', in *Anfänge der dialektischen Theologie* (see below), 175–89

'Wissenschaftliche Theologie oder Theologie der Offenbarung Gottes? Ein Briefwechsel zwischen Karl Barth und Adolf von Harnack', in *Anfänge der dialektischen Theologie* (see below), 323–47

FESTSCHRIFTEN AND COLLECTIONS

Anfänge der dialektischen Theologie, I, II, ed. Jürgen Moltmann, Theologische Bücherei, Neudrucke und Berichte aus dem 20. Jahrhundert, Systematische Theologie 17/I, II, 4th edn, Munich, Kaiser, 1977

Anspruch der Wirklichkeit und christlicher Glaube. Probleme und Wege theologischer Ethik heute, ed. Helmut Weber and Dietmar Mieth, Düsseldorf, Patmos, 1980

'Dialektische Theologie' in Scheidung und Bewährung 1933–1936. Aufsätze, Gutachten und Erklärungen, ed. Walther Fürst, Theologische Bücherei, Neudrucke und Berichte aus dem 20. Jahrhundert, Systematische Theologie 34, Munich, Kaiser, 1966

Karl Barth and Radical Politics, ed. George Hunsinger, Philadelphia, Westminster Press, 1976

New Frontiers in Theology. Discussions among Continental and American Theologians, III, *Theology as History*, ed. James M. Robinson and John B. Cobb jr., New York, Harper and Row, 1967

Parrhesia. Karl Barth zum achtzigsten Geburtstag, ed. E. Busch, J. Fangmeier and M. Geiger, Zürich, EVZ, 1966

Porträt eines Theologen. Stimmt unser Bild von Karl Barth?, ed. Willi Gegenheimer, Projekte 34, Stuttgart, Radius, 1970

Die Realisierung der Freiheit. Beiträge zur Kritik der Theologie Karl Barths, by

Falk Wagner, Walter Sparn, Friedrich Wilhelm Graf and Trutz Rendtorff, ed. Trutz Rendtorff, Gütersloh, Mohn, 1975

Theologie zwischen gestern und morgen. Interpretationen und Anfragen zum Werk Karl Barths, ed. Wilhelm Dantine and Kurt Lüthi, Munich, Kaiser, 1968

OTHER WORKS

A comprehensive bibliography of secondary literature on Barth up to 1976 was published by Kwiran, Manfred, *Index to Literature on Barth, Bonhoeffer and Bultmann, Theologische Zeitschrift*, Sonderband VII, Basel, Reinhardt, 1977. The Kantonsbibliothek in Aargau, Switzerland, keeps a complete index of literature on Barth, which is duplicated in the Institut für Hermeneutik of the Protestant Theology Faculty at the University of Tübingen.

Balthasar, Hans Urs von, *Karl Barth, Darstellung und Deutung seiner Theologie*, Einsiedeln, Johannes Verlag, 1951/1976 (ET, *The Theology of Karl Barth*, New York, Holt, Rinehart and Winston, 1971)

    Kosmische Liturgie. Das Weltbild Maximus' des Bekenners, Einsiedeln, Johannes Verlag, 1961

Baranowski, Shelley, 'The Primacy of Theology: Karl Barth and Socialism', *Studies in Religion*, Toronto, 10 (1981), 451–63

Bäumler, Christof, *Die Lehre von der Kirche in der Theologie Karl Barths*, ThExh, NS 118, Munich, Kaiser, 1964

Becker, Dieter, 'Menschsein im Dialog, Zum Verhältnis von Martin Bubers dialogischer Anthropologie und Karl Barths christologischem Neuansatz', dissertation, University of Heidelberg, 1982

Berkhof, Hendrik, 'Barths Lichterlehre im Rahmen der heutigen Theologie, Kirche und Welt', in H. Berkhof and H.-J. Kraus, *Karl Barths Lichterlehre*, Theologische Studien 123, Zürich, Theologischer Verlag, 1978, 30–48

Berkouwer, Gerrit C., *The Triumph of Grace in the Theology of Karl Barth*, Grand Rapids, Eerdmans, 1956

Bertinetti, Ilse, 'Karl Barths Verhältnis zum anthropologischen Materialismus Ludwig Feuerbachs', *ThLZ*, 102 (1977), 241–50

Blumenberg, Hans, 'Autonomie und Theonomie', in *RGG*, 3rd edn, I, 788–92. *Die Legitimität der Neuzeit*, Frankfurt, Suhrkamp, 1966

Bonhoeffer, Dietrich, *Letters and Papers from Prison*, revised edn, London, SCM, and New York, Macmillan, 1967 (original, *Widerstand und Ergebung. Briefe und Aufzeichnungen aus der Haft*, ed. Eberhard Bethge, Munich, Kaiser, 1951)

Bouillard, Henri, *Karl Barth*, I, *Genèse et évolution de la théologie dialectique*, II/1, 2, *Parole de Dieu et existence humaine*, Théologie, Etudes publiées sous la direction de la faculté de théologie SJ de Lyon-Fourvière 38, 39, Paris, Aubier, 1957

Busch, Eberhard, *Karl Barth. His Life from Letters and Autobiographical Texts*, Philadelphia, Fortress Press, 1976

'Karl Barth und der römische Katholizismus. Eine Radiosendung in zwei Teilen', *Kirchenblatt für die reformierte Schweiz*, Basel, 131: 17, 21 (1975), 306–10, 321–5

Dantine, Wilhelm, 'Der Welt-Bezug des Glaubens', in *Theologie zwischen gestern und morgen*, ed. Wilhelm Dantine and Kurt Lüthi, Munich, Kaiser, 1968, 261–301

Dekker, Aat, *Homines bonae voluntatis. Das Phänomen der profanen Humanität in Karl Barths Kirchlicher Dogmatik. Ein analytischer Kommentar zu einem Satzteil*, Zürich, EVZ, 1970

Dilthey, Wilhelm, *Abhandlungen zur Geschichte der Philosophie und Religion, Gesammelte Schriften*, II, 5th edn, Stuttgart, Teubner, and Göttingen, Vandenhoeck and Ruprecht, 1957

Eicher, Peter, 'Geschichte und Wort Gottes. Ein Protokoll der Pannenbergdiskussion von 1961–1972', *Catholica*, 32 (1978), 321–54

Offenbarung. Prinzip neuzeitlicher Theologie, Munich, Kösel, 1977

Engert, Joseph, 'Metaphysik und Historismus in Christentum', *Hochland*, 21 (1923–4), 502–17, 638–51

Feil, Ernst, 'Autonomie und Heteronomie nach Kant. Zur Klärung einer signifikanten Fehlinterpretation', *Freiburger Zeitschrift für Philosophie und Theologie*, Freiburg, Switzerland, 29 (1982), 389–441

Review of Hilpert, *Ethik und Rationalität*, Freiburger Zeitschrift für Philosophie und Theologie, 29 (1982), 330–4

Fichte, Johann Gottlieb, *Gesamtausgabe*, ed. Bayerische Akademie der Wissenschaften, Stuttgart Bad Cannstatt, Frommann, 1977–

Sämtliche Werke, ed. I. H. Fichte, Berlin, 1845–6

Science of Knowledge (Wissenschaftslehre) with the First and Second Introductions, ed. and trans. Peter Heath and John Lachs, Century Philosophy Sourcebooks, New York, Appleton-Century-Crofts, 1970

Foley, Grover E., 'The Catholic Critics of Karl Barth in Outline and Analysis', *Scottish Journal of Theology*, 14 (1961), 136–55

Ford, David, *Barth and God's Story. Biblical Narrative and the Theological Method of Karl Barth in the 'Church Dogmatics'*, Studien zur interkulturellen Geschichte des Christentums 27, Frankfurt etc., Lang, 1981

Freyd, Christophe, 'Gott als die universale Wahrheit von Mensch und Welt. Die Versöhnungslehre Karl Barths im Lichte der Religionsphilosophie Hegels', dissertation, University of Hamburg, 1978

Friedmann, Edgar Herbert OSB, *Christologie und Anthropologie. Methode und Bedeutung der Lehre vom Menschen in der Theologie Karl Barths*, Münsterschwarzacher Studien 19, Münsterschwarzach, Vier-Türme, 1972

Fries, Heinrich, 'Kirche als Ereignis. Zu Karl Barths Lehre von der Kirche',

Catholica, 11 (1957), 81–108

Fuchs, Ernst, *Hermeneutik*, 3rd edn, Bad Cannstatt, Müllerschon, 1963

Geense, Adriaan, 'Die Bedingung der Universalität. Über die Rezeption der Theologie Karl Barths, *Verkündigung und Forschung*, Munich, 24 (1979), 4–32

Gestrich, Christof, *Neuzeitliches Denken und die Spaltung der dialektischen Theologie. Zur Frage der natürlichen Theologie*, Beiträge zur historischen Theologie 52, Tübingen, Mohr, 1977

'Wie kommt die Theologie zur Wahrheit? Zu einer offenen Frage im Spätwerk Karl Barths', *Evangelische Kommentare*, Stuttgart, 10 (1977), 216–19

Gloege, Gerhard, 'Zur Versöhnungslehre Karl Barths', *ThLZ*, 85 (1960), 161–86

Gogarten, Friedrich, *Verhängnis und Hoffnung der Neuzeit. Die Säkularisierung als theologisches Problem*, Stuttgart, Vorwerk, 1953

Gollwitzer, Helmut, *Reich Gottes und Sozialismus bei Karl Barth*, ThExh, NS 169, Munich, Kaiser, 1972

Graf, F. W., 'Die Freiheit der Entsprechung zu Gott. Bemerkungen zum theozentrischen Ansatz der Anthropologie Karl Barths', in *Die Realisierung der Freiheit*, ed. Trutz Rendtorff, Gütersloh, Mohn, 1975, 76–118

Groll, Wilfried, *Ernst Troeltsch und Karl Barth – Kontinuität im Widerspruch*, Munich, Kaiser, 1976

Grosche, Robert, 'Die dialektische Theologie und der Katholizismus', *Catholica*, 1 (1932), 1–18

Hamer, Jerome OP, *Karl Barth*, London, Collins, and New York, Alba House, 1962

Hanson, Bradley Charles, 'Hope and Participation in Christ. A Study in the Theology of Barth and Pannenberg', Th.D. dissertation, Princeton Theological Seminary, 1970

Härle, Wilfried, *Sein und Gnade. Die Ontologie in Karl Barths Kirchlicher Dogmatik*, Theologische Bibliothek Töpelmann 27, Berlin etc., de Gruyter, 1975

Heckel, Martin, 'Autonomia und Pacis compositio. Der Augsburger Religionsfriede in der Deutung der Gegenreformation', *Zeitschrift der Savigny-Stiftung für Rechtsgeschichte*, Kanonistische Abteilung 45, 76 (1959), 141–248

Hedinger, Ulrich, *Der Freiheitsbegriff in der Kirchlichen Dogmatik Karl Barths*, Studien zur Dogmengeschichte und systematischen Theologie 15, Zürich and Stuttgart, Zwingli, 1962

'Der Freiheitsbegriff bei Paul Tillich und Karl Barth', *Theologische Zeitschrift*, Basel, 19 (1963), 42–9

Henrich, Dieter, *Fichtes ursprüngliche Einsicht*, Wissenschaft und Gegenwart 34, Frankfurt, Klostermann, 1967

Hessert, Paul, 'Barthianische Wurzeln der "Radical-Theology" ', in *Theologie zwischen gestern und morgen*, ed. Wilhelm Dantine and Kurt Lüthi, Munich, Kaiser, 1968 235–46

Hilpert, Konrad, *Ethik und Rationalität. Untersuchungen zum Autonomieproblem und zu seiner Bedeutung für die theologische Ethik*, Moraltheologische Studien Systematische Abteilung 6, Düsseldorf, Patmos, 1980

Huber, Wolfgang and Tödt, Heinz Eduard, *Menschenrechte. Perspektiven einer menschlichen Welt*, Stuttgart etc., Kreuz, 1977

Jackson, Minus Baskin, 'An Interpretation of Wolfhart Pannenberg's Theory of Knowledge as Creative Subjectivity', dissertation, Union Theological Seminary in Virginia, 1973

Joest, Wilfried, 'Barth, Bultmann und die "existenziale Interpretation" ', in *Theologie zwischen gestern und morgen*, ed. Wilhelm Dantine and Kurt Lüthi, Munich, Kaiser, 1968, 69–87

Johnson, Elizabeth Ann, 'Analogy, Doxology and their Connection with Christology in the Thought of Wolfhart Pannenberg', dissertation, Catholic University, Washington DC, Ann Arbor, Mich., University Microfilms International, 1981

'The Right Way to Speak about God? Pannenberg on Analogy', *Theological Studies*, Baltimore Md., 43 (1982), 673–92

Jüngel, Eberhard, 'Barth, Karl', in *TRE*, V, 251–69 (expanded version in Jüngel, *Barth-Studien*, 22–60)

Barth-Studien, Zürich etc., Benziger, and Gütersloh, Mohn, 1982

Entsprechungen, Gott-Wahrheit-Mensch. Theologische Erörterungen, Beiträge zur evangelischen Theologie, Theologische Abhandlungen 88, Munich, Kaiser, 1980

Gott als Geheimnis der Welt. Zur Begründung der Theologie des Gekreuzigten im Streit zwischen Theismus und Atheismus, Tübingen, Mohr, 1977

Gottes Sein ist im Werden. Verantwortliche Rede vom Sein Gottes bei Karl Barth. Eine Paraphrase, 3rd edn, Tübingen, Mohr, 1976 (ET, *The Doctrine of the Trinity. God's Being is in Becoming*, Monograph Supplements to the Scottish Journal of Theology 4, Edinburgh, Scottish Academic Press, 1976)

Unterwegs zur Sache. Theologische Bemerkungen, Beiträge zur evangelischen Theologie, Theologische Abhandlungen 61, Munich, Kaiser, 1972

Kant, Immanuel, *Werke*, ed. Wilhelm Weischedel, Wiesbaden, Insel, 1956

Kants Gesammelte Schriften, ed. Königlich-Preussische (später die Deutsche) Akademie der Wissenschaften, Berlin, Georg Reimer and de Gruyter, 1900–

'Erklärung in Beziehung auf Fichtes Wissenschaftslehre', published only in *Immanuel Kants Werke*, ed. Ernst Cassirer, Berlin, Bruno Cassirer, 1922–3, VIII, 515–16

Foundations of the Metaphysics of Morals and *What is Enlightenment?*, trans. with an introduction by Lewis White Beck, New York, Bobbs-Merrill, 1959

Kasper, Walter, 'Autonomie und Theonomie. Zur Ortsbestimmung des Christentums in der modernen Welt', in *Anspruch der Wirklichkeit und christlicher Glaube*, ed. Helmut Weber and Dietmar Mieth, Düsseldorf, Patmos, 1980, 17–41

'Christologie und Anthropologie', *Theologische Quartalschrift*, Tübingen, 162 (1982), 202–21

Korsch, Dietrich, 'Christologie und Autonomie. Zu einem Interpretationsversuch der Theologie Karl Barths', *Evangelische Theologie*, Munich, 41 (1981), 142–71

Kraus, Hans-Joachim, 'Logos und Sophia. Biblisch-theologische Grundlegung und Konkretisierung zum Thema 'Das Licht und die Lichter' ', in H. Berkhof and M.-J. Kraus, *Karl Barths Lichterlehre*, Theologische Studien 123, Zürich, Theologischer Verlag, 1978, 4–29

Theologische Religionskritik, Neukirchener Beiträge zur systematischen Theologie 2, Neukirchen-Vluyn, Neukirchener Verlag, 1978

Kreck, Walter, *Grundfragen christlicher Ethik*, Munich, Kaiser, 1975

Krötke, Wolf, Review of Rendtorff, Trutz (ed.), *Die Realisierung der Freiheit*, *ThLZ*, 105 (1980), 300–3

Krüger, Gerhard, *Philosophie und Moral in der kantischen Kritik*, Tübingen, Mohr, 1931

Küng, Hans, *Does God Exist? An Answer for Today*, London, Collins, 1980

Justification. Doctrine of Karl Barth and a Catholic Reflection, New York and Nashville, Nelson Thomas, 1964

'Karl Barths Lehre vom Wort Gottes als Frage an die katholische Theologie', in *Einsicht und Glaube. Festschrift für Gottlieb Söhngen*, ed. J. Ratzinger and H. Fries, Freiburg etc., Herder, 1962, 75–97

Lindemann, Walter, *Karl Barth und die kritische Schriftauslegung. Eine Auseinandersetzung mit der historisch-kritischen Exegese*, Theologische Forschung, Wissenschaftliche Beiträge zur kirchlich-evangelischen Lehre 54, Hamburg, H. Reich, 1973

Link, Christian, *Die Welt als Gleichnis. Studien zum Problem der natürlichen Theologie*, Beiträge zur evangelischen Theologie, Theologische Abhandlungen 73, Munich, Kaiser, 1976

Lüthi, Kurt, 'Theologie als Gespräch' in *Theologie zwischen gestern und morgen*, ed. Wilhelm Dantine and Kurt Lüthi, Munich, Kaiser, 1968, 302–32

Macken, John, SJ, ' "Autonomy" in Catholic Theology', *Milltown Studies*, Dublin, 18 (Autumn 1986), 31–45

Marquardt, Friedrich Wilhelm, *Theologie und Sozialismus. Das Beispiel Karl Barths*, Gesellschaft und Theologie, Abteilung II, Systematische Beiträge 7, Munich, Kaiser, 1972

Marx, Karl, *Economic and Philosophic Manuscripts of 1844*, ed. with an introduction by Dirk J. Struik, trans. Martin Milligan, London, Lawrence and Wishart, 1970

Mayer, E. W., 'Autonomie', in *RGG*, I, 2nd edn, 1927–31, 682–3

Mechels, Eberhard, *Analogie bei Erich Przywara and Karl Barth. Das Verhältnis von Offenbarungstheologie und Metaphysik*, Neukirchen-Vluyn, Neukirchener Verlag, 1974

Moltmann, Jürgen, *Theology of Hope. On the Ground and Implication of a Christian Eschatology*, London, SCM, 1967

The Trinity and the Kingdom of God. The Doctrine of God, London, SCM, 1981

O'Grady, Colm, *The Church in Catholic Theology*, London and New York, Chapman, 1969

The Church in the Theology of Karl Barth, London and New York, Chapman, 1968

Pannenberg, Wolfhart, 'Analogie und Offenbarung. Eine kritische Untersuchung der Geschichte des Analogiebegriffs in der Gotteserkenntnis', *Habilitationsschrift*, University of Heidelberg, 1955

Basic Questions in Theology, I, II, The Library of Philosophy and Theology, London, SCM, 1970, 1971 (original, *Grundfragen systematischer Theologie. Gesammelte Aufsätze*, 3rd edn, Göttingen, Vandenhoeck and Ruprecht, 1979)

Basic Questions in Theology, III, The Library of Philosophy and Theology, London, SCM, 1973 (original of most of this volume, *Gottesgedanke und menschliche Freiheit*, 2nd edn, Göttingen, Vandenhoeck and Ruprecht, 1978; US edn, *The Idea of God and Human Freedom*, Philadelphia, Westminster Press, 1973)

'Die Begründung der Ethik bei Ernst Troeltsch', in Pannenberg, *Ethik und Ekklesiologie. Gesammelte Aufsätze*, Göttingen, Vandenhoeck and Ruprecht, 1977, 70–96

Grundfragen systematischer Theologie. Gesammelte Aufsätze, II, Göttingen, Vandenhoeck and Ruprecht, 1980

Human Nature, Election and History, Philadelphia, Westminster Press, 1977

Jesus – God and Man, Philadelphia, Westminster Press, 1968 (original, *Grundzüge der Christologie*, 5th edn, Gütersloh, Mohn, 1976)

'Kontingenz und Naturgesetz', in A. M. Klaus Müller and Wolfhart

Pannenberg, *Erwägungen zu einer Theologie der Natur*, Gütersloh, Mohn, 1970, 33–80

'A Liberal Logos Christology: The Christology of John Cobb', in *John Cobb's Theology in Process*, ed. David Ray Griddin and Thomas J. J. Altizer, Philadelphia, Westminster Press, 1977, 133–49

'Möglichkeiten und Grenzen der Anwendung des Analogieprinzips in der evangelischen Theologie', *ThLZ*, 85 (1960), 225–8

'Mythos und Wort. Theologische Überlegungen zu K. Jaspers Mythusbegriff', *Zeitschrift für Theologie und Kirche*, Tübingen, 51 (1954), 167–85

'Nachwort', in Ignace Berten, *Geschichte – Offenbarung – Glaube*, Munich, Claudius, 1970, 129–41 (original, *Histoire, révélation et foi. Dialogue avec Wolfhart Pannenberg*, Bruxelles, Editions du CEP, 1969)

Die Prädestinationslehre des Duns Scotus, im Zusammenhang der scholastischen Lehrentwicklung, Forschungen zur Kirchen- und Dogmengeschichte 4, Göttingen, 1954

Reformation zwischen gestern und morgen, lecture given in Munich, 3 November 1968, Aspekte moderner Theologie 7, Gütersloh, Mohn, 1969

Theology and the Kingdom of God, Philadelphia, Westminster Press, 1969

Theology and the Philosophy of Science, Philadelphia, Westminster Press, and London, Darton, Longman and Todd, 1976 (original, *Wissenschaftstheorie und Theologie*, Frankfurt, Suhrkamp, 1977)

What is Man?, Philadelphia, Fortress Press, 1970 (original, *Was ist der Mensch? Die Anthropologie der Gegenwart im Lichte der Theologie*, 5th edn, Göttingen, Vandenhoeck and Ruprecht, 1976)

'Wie wahr ist das Reden von Gott? Die wissenschaftstheoretische Problematik theologischer Aussagen', in *Grundlagen der Theologie – ein Diskurs*, ed. Sigurd M. Daecke *et al.*, Stuttgart, Kohlhammer, 1974, 29–41

'Zur Bedeutung des Analogiegedankens bei Karl Barth. Eine Auseinandersetzung mit Urs von Balthasar', *ThLZ*, 78 (1953), 17–24

Pannenberg, Wolfhart (ed.), *Offenbarung als Geschichte*, ed. Wolfhart Pannenberg with Rolf Rendtorff, Ulrich Wilckens and Trutz Rendtorff, Göttingen, Vandenhoeck and Ruprecht, 1961, 5th edn 1982 (ET, *Revelation as History*, London, Collier and Macmillan, 1968)

Revelation as History, London, Collier and Macmillan, 1968

Plathow, Michael, *Das Problem des concursus divinus. Das Zusammenwirken von göttlichem Schöpferwirken und geschöpflichem Eigenwirken in Karl Barths 'Kirchlicher Dogmatik'*, Forschungen zur systematischen und ökumenischen Theologie 32, Göttingen, Vandenhoeck and Ruprecht, 1976

Pohlmann, Rosemarie, 'Autonomie', in *Historisches Wörterbuch der Philosophie*, ed. Joachim Ritter, Darmstadt, Wissenschaftliche Buchgesellschaft, 1971, I, 701–19

Porter, D. C., 'The Holy Spirit and the Foundation of the Christian Life in the Theology of Karl Barth', M.Th. dissertation, Queen's University, Belfast, 1985

Prauss, Gerold, *Kant und das Problem der Dinge an sich*, Abhandlungen zur Philosophie, Psychologie und Pädagogik 10, Bonn, Bouvier, 1974

Przywara, Erich, 'Religiöse Bewegungen', *Stimmen der Zeit* (Munich) 104 (1923), 445–54

Quadt, Anno, *Gott und Mensch. Zur Theologie Karl Barths in ökumenischer Sicht*, Abhandlungen zur Philosophie, Psychologie, Soziologie der Religion und Ökumenik, NS 34, Munich etc., Schöningh, 1976

'Die Taufe als Antwort des Glaubens. Zur neuen Tauflehre Karl Barths', *Theologische Revue*, Münster, 64 (1968), 468–76.

Rendtorff, Trutz, 'Der ethische Sinn der Dogmatik. Zur Reformulierung des Verhältnisses von Dogmatik und Ethik bei Karl Barth', in *Die Realisierung der Freiheit*, ed. Trutz Rendtorff, Gütersloh, Mohn, 1975, 119–34

'Der Freiheitsbegriff als Ortsbestimmung der Theologie. Karl Barths Freiheitsverständnis im Kontext der europäischen Theologiegeschichte', unpublished lecture delivered at the annual Karl Barth conference at Leuenberg, Switzerland, 14 July 1981

'Historische Bibelwissenschaft und Theologie. Über den Aufbau der Frage, Was ist christlich?', in *Beiträge zur Theorie des neuzeitlichen Christentums. Wolfgang Trillhaas zum 65. Geburtstag*, ed. H. J. Birkner und D. Rössler, Berlin, de Gruyter, 1968, 72–90

Gott – ein Wort unserer Sprache, ThExh, NS 171, Munich, Kaiser, 1972

'Karl Barth', in *Klassiker der Theologie*, II, ed. Heinrich Fries und Georg Kretschmar, Munich, C. H. Beck, 1983, 331–46

'The Problem of Revelation in the Concept of the Church', in *Revelation as History*, ed. W. Pannenberg, London, Collier and Macmillan, 1968, 159–81

Theorie des Christentums. Historisch-theologische Studien zu seiner neuzeitlichen Verfassung, Gütersloh, Mohn, 1972

Robinson, James M., 'Die ersten heterodoxen Barthianer', in *Theologie zwischen gestern und morgen*, ed. Wilhelm Dantine and Kurt Lüthi, Munich, Kaiser, 1968, 13–37

'Revelation as Word and as History', in *New Frontiers in Theology*, III, *Theology as History*, ed. James M. Robinson and John B. Cobb Jr., New York, Harper and Row, 1967, 1–100

Rohrmoser, Günther, 'Autonomie', in *Handbuch philosophischer Grundbegriffe*, ed. Hermann Krings et al. Munich, Kösel, 1973, I, 155–70

Rosato, Philip J., *The Spirit as Lord. The Pneumatology of Karl Barth*, Edinburgh, T. and T. Clark, 1981

Rössler, Dietrich, 'Positionelle und kritische Theologie', *Zeitschrift für Theologie und Kirche*, Tübingen, 67 (1970), 215–31

Sauter, Gerhard, 'Zu diesem Heft', *Verkündiging und Forschung*, Munich, 24 (1979), 1–3

Schellong, Dieter and Steck, Karl Gerhard, *Karl Barth und die Neuzeit*, ThExh, NS 173, Munich, Kaiser, 1973

Schlichting, Wolfgang, *Biblische Denkform in der Dogmatik. Die Vorbildlichkeit des biblischen Denkens für die Methode der 'Kirchlichen Dogmatik' Karl Barths*, Zürich, Theologischer Verlag, 1971

Schlüter, Richard, *Karl Barths Tauflehre. Ein interkonfessionelles Gespräch*, Konfessionskundliche und Kontroverstheologische Studien 33, Paderborn, Bonifatius-Druckerei, 1973

Schwartländer, Johannes, *Der Mensch ist Person. Kants Lehre vom Menschen*, Stuttgart etc., Kohlhammer, 1968

Seckler, Max, 'Zur Diskussion um das Offenbarungsverständnis Wolfhart Pannenbergs', *Münchener Theologische Zeitschrift*, 19 (1968), 132–4

Söhngen, Gottlieb, 'Analogia fidei I, Gottähnlichkeit allein aus Glauben', *Catholica*, 3 (1934), 113–36

'Analogia fidei II, Die Einheit der Glaubenswissenschaft', *Catholica*, 3 (1934), 176–208

Sölle, Dorothee, *Christ the Representative. An Essay in Theology after the 'Death of God'*, Philadelphia, Fortress Press, 1967

Sparn, W., ' "Extra Internum". Die christologische Revision der Prädestinationslehre in Karl Barths Erwählungslehre', in *Die Realisirerung der Freiheit*, ed. Trutz Rendtorff, Gütersloh, Mohn, 1975, 44–75

Stalder, Robert, 'Der neue Gottesgedanke Fichtes. Eine Studie zum "Atheismusstreit" ', *Theologie und Philosophie*, Frankfurt, 54 (1979), 481–541

Stickelberger, Hans, *Ipsa assumptione creatur. Karl Barths Rückgriff auf die klassische Christologie und die Frage nach der Selbständigkeit des Menschen*, Basler u. Berner Studien zur historischen und systematischen Theologie 38, Bern etc., Lang, 1979

Stock, Konrad, *Anthropologie der Verheißung. Karl Barths Lehre vom Menschen als dogmatisches Problem*, Munich, Kaiser, 1980

'Freiheit als Veränderung', review of *Die Realisierung der Freiheit*, *Evangelische Kommentare*, Stuttgart, 10 (1977), 308–9

Strunk, Reiner, *Politische Ekklesiologie im Zeitalter der Revolution*, Gesellschaft und Theologie, Abteilung Systematische Beiträge 5, Munich, Kaiser, and Mainz, Matthias Grünewald, 1971

Thielicke, Helmut, *Theologische Ethik*, Tübingen, Mohr, 1958

Thomas, J. C., 'The Epistemology of Karl Barth', *Heythrop Journal*, 18 (1977), 383–98

Tillich, Paul, 'Antwort an Karl Barth', in *Anfänge der dialektischen Theologie*, ed. Jürgen Moltmann, 4th edn, Munich, Kaiser, 1977, I, 189–93

'Kairos. Ideen zur Geisteslage der Gegenwart', 'Kairos und Logos. Eine Untersuchung zur Metaphysik des Erkennens', in *Kairos. Zur Geisteslage und Geisteswendung*, ed. Paul Tillich, Darmstadt, Otto Reichl, 1926, 1–22, 23–76

'Kritisches und positives Paradox (Eine Auseinandersetzung mit Karl Barth und Friedrich Gogarten)', in *Anfänge der dialektischen Theologie*, ed. Jürgen Moltmann, 4th edn, Munich, Kaiser, 1977, I, 165–74

Systematic Theology, I–III, Chicago, University of Chicago Press, 1951, 1957, 1963

'Theonomie', in *RGG*, V, 2nd edn, 1927–31, 1128–9

Tillich, Paul (ed.), *Kairos. Zur Geisteslage und Geisteswendung*, Darmstadt, Otto Reichl, 1926

Viering, Fritz (ed.), *Zu Karl Barths Lehre von der Taufe. Veröffentlichung des Taufausschusses der Evangelischen Kirche der Union*, Gütersloh, Mohn, 1971

Volk, Hermann, 'Die Christologie bei Karl Barth und Emil Brunner', in *Das Konzil von Chalkedon*, III, ed. A. Grillmeier und H. Bacht, Würzburg, Echter, 1954, 613–73

Die Kreaturauffassung bei Karl Barth. Eine philosophische Untersuchung, Abhandlungen zur Philosophie und Psychologie der Religion, 47/48, Würzburg, Becker, 1938

Wagner, Falk, 'Die erschlichene Freiheit', *Lutherische Monatshefte*, Hamburg, 10 (1971), 343–9

'Theologische Gleichschaltung. Zur Christologie bei Karl Barth', in *Die Realisierung der Freiheit*, ed. Trutz Rendtorff, Gütersloh, Mohn, 1975, 10–43

Welker, Michael, 'Barth und Hegel. Zur Erkenntnis eines methodischen Verfahrens bei Barth', *Evangelische Theologie*, Munich, 43 (1983), 307–28

Weth, Rudolf, 'Ort und Funktion der Theologie als Wissenschaft', in Rudolf Weth, Christof Gestrich and Ernst-Lüder Solte, *Theologie an staatlichen Universitäten?*, Stuttgart etc., Kohlhammer, 1972, 32–54

Zahrnt, Heinz, *The Question of God. Protestant Theology in the Twentieth Century*, London, Collins, and New York, Harcourt, Brace and World, 1969

Zwanger, Helmut, ' "Kritischer müßten mir die Historisch-Kritischen sein!" Hinter Barth zurück?', *Evangelische Theologie*, Munich, 43 (1983), 370–9

Author index

Subject index